From Lenin to Castro, 1917–1959

From Lenin to Castro, 1917–1959

Early Encounters between Moscow and Havana

Mervyn J. Bain

LEXINGTON BOOKS
Lanham • Boulder • New York • Toronto • Plymouth, UK

Published by Lexington Books
A wholly owned subsidiary of The Rowman & Littlefield Publishing Group, Inc.
4501 Forbes Boulevard, Suite 200, Lanham, Maryland 20706
www.rowman.com

10 Thornbury Road, Plymouth PL6 7PP, United Kingdom

British Library Cataloguing in Publication Information Available

Library of Congress Cataloging-in-Publication Data

Bain, Mervyn J., 1973– author.
From Lenin to Castro, 1917–1959 : early encounters between Moscow and Havana / Mervyn J. Bain.
pages ; cm
Includes bibliographical references and index.
ISBN 978-0-7391-8110-2 (cloth : alkaline paper)— ISBN 978-0-7391-8111-9 (electronic)
1. Soviet Union—Foreign relations—Cuba. 2. Cuba—Foreign relations—Soviet Union. I. Title.
DK69.3.C9B34 2013
327.470729109'041—dc23
2013002322
ISBN 978-1-4985-1541-2 (pbk : alk. paper)

∞ The paper used in this publication meets the minimum requirements of American National Standard for Information Sciences Permanence of Paper for Printed Library Materials, ANSI/NISO Z39.48-1992.

Printed in the United States of America

For Rebecca, Sophie, and Jonathan

Contents

Acknowledgments   ix

1 Soviet and Cuban Foreign Policies   1
2 Moscow, Havana, and the World Revolution   29
3 Diplomacy and Statecraft   77
4 Final Thoughts on the "Disappearing" Relationship   121

Index   145
Bibliography   151

Acknowledgments

The research for this book has been conducted in a number of different locations, but primarily Glasgow, Havana, London, Moscow, and New York City. A number of these research trips have been funded by the University of Aberdeen, the British Academy, the Carnegie Trust for the Universities of Scotland, and the Royal Society of Edinburgh. I would like to thank all the people involved in these various organizations for their help, but in particular I would like to thank June Middleton of the University of Aberdeen for all her time, assistance, and patience in helping to prepare these various grant applications. Without this, it would not have been possible to complete this research.

In addition, I also owe a debt of gratitude to Justin Race and Alissa Parra of Lexington Books for their belief in this project and also for answering my numerous questions. Again, without their help and assistance this research would not have resulted in the publication of this book.

I would also like to show my appreciation to Professors E.A. Larin and N. Ivanov of the Latin American Institute of the Russian Academy of Sciences in Moscow for their help. Moreover, I would also like to thank the staff at the Russian State Archive for Social and Political History in Moscow for their assistance while I was in Moscow.

With relation to my research in Cuba I would like to thank the staff at the Russian school in Havana for allowing me access to the contents of their library. However, I owe a particularly large debt to Liliana Fernández Mollinedo of the Centro de Estudios Europeos in Havana whose help, generosity of spirit, and time made my research trip such a success. I would also like to thank her for her friendship. In addition, I also a debt of gratitude to Liliana's husband, Arturo, and daughter, Rachel, for opening the doors of their home to me and making me feel so welcome. I also extend my thanks to the staff at the Centro de Estudios Europeos, José Marti National Library, and Cuban National Archive in Havana for their help during my stay in Cuba.

I would also like to thank Professors Grant Jordan, Trevor Salmon, and Stephen White for their continuing support and advice. Furthermore, I would also like to express my gratitude to Professor John Kirk for his enthusiasm and support which he continues to show not just to my work but also myself.

However, most importantly I would like to thank members of my family but particularly my parents and sister, Karen, and brother-in-law, Steve, for their love and support both in relation to the research and work for this book but also in general. Without this, the completion of this book would not have been possible. In addition, I would also like to thank Jonathan, Rebecca, and Sophie for the enjoyment and sense of fun which they have brought to my whole family. I dedicate this book to them.

Chapter One

Soviet and Cuban Foreign Policies

In January 2009 Raúl Castro made his first visit to Moscow in over 20 years. This trip was symbolic of the relationship that has risen from the ashes of Soviet-Cuban relations between Moscow and Havana from the mid-1990s onward. During his time in the Russian capital the Cuban premier visited the permanent exhibit at the Museum of the Great Patriotic War to the three Cubans who fought for the Red Army during World War II.[1] This not only allowed the Cuban leader to pay his respects to his fellow countrymen, but it is also part of the process which in the twenty-first century has seen both Moscow and Havana make increased reference to the relationship that existed between the countries in the years before the victory of the Cuban Revolution in January 1959. It is this period, but more specifically the era between the Russian and Cuban Revolutions that is the focus of this book.

The academic discipline of International Relations developed as a result of the seismic changes which took place to the international system at the end of the second decade of the twentieth century, with the victory of the Russian Revolution and the aftermath of the horrors of the First World War both being important to this process. Initially International Relations was dominated by the principles of liberalism, which had at its core the ideas of "collective security" that had originated from U.S. President Woodrow Wilson's "14 points" at the Paris Peace Conference in 1919. It was hoped that this would prevent another global war with the creation of the League of Nations being fundamental to this desire. Although this was the case, liberalism was dealt a fatal blow by the events of the 1930s that culminated in the Second World War.[2]

E. H. Carr in *The Twenty Year Crisis* provided one of the most influential critiques of liberalism, and in this work he even suggested that the term "liberalism" should be replaced with "utopianism."[3] Carr's work gave rise to the prominence of realism within International Relations, but this is by no means to suggest that in the 1930s realism was a new theory as it is traceable to Thucydides' writings on the Peloponnesian War. Its core tenet is the belief that sovereign states are the key actors within the international system, but that this system is inherently anarchic. It is thought that states' ultimate goal is their own survival and in order to do this they act to protect their own interests. The outcome is that states attempt to maximize their own power with Hans Morgenthau having famously written, "international politics, like all politics, is a struggle for power."[4] More specifically, John Mearsheimer has written that states attempt to maximize their power at the expense of other states.[5]

Realism would dominate International Relations thinking during the Cold War, but Marxism was also of fundamental importance in the ideological battle between the Soviet Union and United States that would dominate international relations for over 40 years. Marxists believe that class and not nationalism is the most important aspect in international relations with economics being the key to many global problems. As a result, Marxism provided a new model of international relations with the classic billiard ball analogy of realism being replaced by an octopus and its tentacles.[6] Due to the significance of Marxism in Soviet foreign policy it will be examined in more depth in the next section of this chapter.

During the period of this book's focus, liberalism, realism and Marxism were key paradigms of International Relations, but since January 1959 a number of other theories have evolved which can be used retrospectively to analyze the relationship between Moscow and Havana in the era between the Russian and Cuban Revolutions. Related to Marxism was the development in the 1960s of Dependency Theory in Latin America, which tried to explain why a number of countries of the South remained underdeveloped. Dependency theorists believe that it is in the interest of the countries of the North for the countries of the South to remain underdeveloped, with some within these poorer countries acting to protect their privileged position within their respective societies. Dependency has been a key issue throughout Cuban history with Fulgencio Batista in the 1950s often being seen as an example of this "comprador" class who act in this way.[7] The issue of Cuban dependency will be returned to throughout this book, but particularly in the penultimate section of this chapter.

After the victory of the Cuban Revolution the new government in Havana's internal and foreign policies are often perceived to have been dominated by Fidel Castro. This gave rise to the ideas of *Fidel personalismo*, which is the specific Cuban version of the Great Man Theory that concentrates on the emergence of an individual within a country who has been able to dominate a country's political process. Adolf Hitler is often cited as an example of this, with this theory concentrating on the individual's idiosyncrasies rather than the formal decision-making process of the respective countries. In addition to Hitler, Joseph Stalin has also been perceived in this manner and therefore the ideas of the Great Man Theory will also be significant for this book due to his domination of Soviet political life for over 25 years.[8]

In his book *Essence of Decision. Explaining the Cuban Missile Crisis*, Graham Allison examines the Soviet decision-making process in the summer of 1962 to explain the reasons for the Soviet deployment of nuclear missiles to Cuba. Allison offers three different models which provide the answers to this question. In Model I security and stability are key, Model II suggests that a variety of governmental organizations will each have specific reasons for making their decisions, while Model III states that the individual actors within the government will all carefully consider the political situation within the country before making a final decision.[9] Although Allison's book analyzes events after the period of this work, his ideas are still important as they can be used retrospectively to consider the various decisions taken in both Moscow and Havana regarding the two countries' relationship prior to 1959.

In a similar manner neo-liberalism and neo-realism also both evolved after 1959, but again can be used retrospectively to examine Soviet-Cuban relations in the period between the Russian and Cuban Revolutions. Neo-liberalism was developed in the 1970s and has reduced the division between high and low politics and suggests that absolute gains are what most interest states. In comparison, neo-realists believe that relative gains are what concern states.[10] Kenneth Waltz's *Theory of International Politics* is perceived as being key to the development of neo-realism, and in this he has written "self-help is necessarily the principle of action."[11] This would be vital for Soviet interest in Cuba in the years before 1959 and will be returned to at various points throughout this book.

Although by no means a new concept, the ideas of soft power have attracted considerable attention from the academic community.[12] On soft power Joseph Nye has written,

> A country may obtain the outcomes it wants in world politics because other countries—admiring its values, emulating its example, aspiring to its level of prosperity and openness—want to follow it. In this sense, it is also important to set the agenda and attract others in world politics, and not only to force them to change by threatening military force or economic sanctions. This soft power—getting others to want the outcomes that you want—co-opts people rather coerces them.[13]

Much of the academic focus has concentrated on United States' soft power, but during the Cold War the Soviet Union also attempted to increase its own soft power despite the German author Josef Joffe believing this stopped at its "military border."[14] Regarding Soviet soft power Nye has written,

The Soviet Union also spent billions on an active public diplomacy program that included promoting its high culture, broadcasting, disseminating disinformation about the West, and sponsoring antinuclear protests, peace movements, and youth organisations.[15]

This would be vital for Soviet-Cuban relations in the era before January 1959, but particularly in the years from 1945 to 1952.

Toward the end of the twentieth century constructivism evolved as many more traditional theories had failed to explain the end of the Cold War. Constructivism draws ideas from sociology to analyze international relations, with at its center the idea that the actor's knowledge is key in their interpretation and construction of social reality. As a result, culture, history, and the importance of ideas are significant as constructivism examines not just traditional military security but also other issues such as economic disparity, the environment, increase in terrorism, the proliferation of weapons of mass destruction, and social issues, amongst others.[16] However, as with Dependency Theory, Allison's work on the Cuban Missile Crisis, neo-liberalism, and neo-realism constructivism can also be used with hindsight to examine the relationship between Moscow and Havana in the years from 1917 to 1959. Moreover, Grigor Suny has written of the importance of constructivism for not just foreign policy in general, but its long-term importance within Russian foreign policy in particular.[17] The result is that a number of these theories will be significant for this work even if they were developed after 1959.

MOSCOW AND THE WORLD

Throughout Russian history a number of factors have dominated the country's relationship with the outside world resulting in commonalities existing between different eras. Andrei Tsygankov believes that there have been three "schools of thought" competing for prominence within Russian foreign policy from the time of the tsars, with these being the ideas of westernists, statists, and civilizationists. Westernists desired to show Russia as part of the "family of European monarchies" beginning with the modernization process that commenced under Peter the Great. The core belief of civilizationists differs from westernists as they believe Russian values are superior to Western ones and attempts should be made to increase its influence. Tsygankov dates this to the era of Ivan the Terrible.[18] Regarding statists he has written, "Ever since the two-centuries long conquest by the Mongols, Russians have developed a psychological complex of insecurity and a readiness to sacrifice everything for independence and sovereignty."[19] This has been a key concept within Russian foreign policy for a number of centuries with it transcending both tsarist and Soviet times.

In a similar manner, Stephen White has written that the Russian desire for warm-water harbors and the question regarding the country's role in the world have also been highly significant in these two distinct eras. Both Ledonne and Caldwell have also highlighted the Russian wish for warm-water ports, but in contrast to Tsygankov's ideas of civilizationists, Caldwell also states that Russian national security, and thus its foreign policy, has been underpinned by vulnerability along its borders and an inferiority complex due to a perceived backwardness.[20]

Tsarist Russia may not have been a direct colonial competitor to European powers such as France, Portugal, Spain, and the United Kingdom but Ledonne has written, "To reach its periphery was the ultimate goal of Russian foreign policy."[21] Under Ivan the Terrible an expansionist policy was most certainly followed resulting in Russia becoming a Europe-Asian power, but Bartley believes that from the time of Peter the Great, Russia begun to show interest in not just the Pacific but also Latin America.[22] This interest may have been somewhat limited, but Grigor Suny has commented,

> The great paradox of Russia's twentieth century evolution was that a self-proclaimed empire fell in 1917 to be replaced by what became a neo-imperial state that not only refused to see itself as an empire, not only considered itself to be the major anti-imperial power on the globe, but became the unwitting incubator of new states.[23]

Key to this was the fundamental change that took place in Russia's relationship with the West in the aftermath of the Russian Revolution, with the revolution signalling

> a wholesale rejection of an entire way of life and its economic underpinnings increasingly dominant since the seventeenth century, and the substitution of something new and entirely alien in terms of culture and experience. That revolt began with the October Revolution in 1917.[24]

This situation was only further complicated by the Bolsheviks' belief in the world revolution. On this Manuel Caballero has written, "the Russian outburst was not only the Russian Revolution, but the starting point of world revolution. The Bolshevik Party was not only a Russian party, but the embryo of the World Communist Party."[25] This was illustrated by the creation of the Third International, or Comintern, in Moscow in March 1919. At the founding Congress, Vladimir Lenin stated,

> It becomes clear, if we take into account that the course of events since the imperialist war is inevitably facilitating the revolutionary movement of the proletariat, that the international world revolution is beginning and increasing in all countries.[26]

Significantly the Comintern was not part of the apparatus of the new government in Moscow, but was rather the province of the Bolshevik Party. However, the accusation has always existed that this distinction was somewhat academic as not only was the organization's leadership Russian, but the creation at the Second Congress in the summer of 1920 of the twenty-one conditions which local parties had to meet before being granted membership of the Comintern increased Moscow's control over the organization. This only strengthened the idea that the Comintern was merely a vehicle for Lenin's government. On this Lazitch and Drachkovitch have written, "Though officially Soviet Russia remained the avant-garde country of the Communist world revolution, in truth the International Communist movement became the tail of the Russian dog."[27]

Unsurprisingly, the Comintern was highly radical at this time with Rees and Thorpe having written,

> It was believed that revolution, having taken place in Russia, would soon be followed by Communist conquests of power in Western Europe. For Lenin and his followers, it was axiomatic that the revolution could not survive in "backward" Russia alone: the Russian Soviet republic could only survive so long as it was buttressed by a Soviet regime in Germany, in particular.[28]

Moreover, Leon Trotsky is quoted as having said,

> We are putting all our hope on this, that our revolution will solve the European revolution. If the peoples of Europe do not arise and crush imperialism, we shall be crushed— that is beyond doubt.[29]

The result was that the Comintern activities were underpinned by the principles of realism as the Bolsheviks believed that the Russian Revolution could not survive by itself, but if the Comintern engineered another revolution it would help prevent this from happening. The traditional Russian fear of aggression from outside powers was important for this, but it resulted in the Bolsheviks acting in order to try and safeguard their own survival. Regarding the prominence of realism within the Soviet elites' thinking, Grigor Suny has written,

> Lenin, Stalin, and their successors saw the world through a realist lens, calculating how to preserve their power and the system they ruled, how to weaken their opponents, and how to win friends and influence people around the world.[30]

Western Europe may have indeed been the Comintern's primary focus but the Bolsheviks' belief in the world revolution was further shown by the Congress of the Peoples of the East being convened in Baku in September

1920.[31] This was despite the fact that throughout the Soviet era the Developing World was causing ideological problems for the Soviet elite which was in no small part the result of the lack of a working class in this part of the world. This did not mean it was ignored, but what most interested the Kremlin was not the Developing World per se, but rather these countries' relationships with the metropolitan states. This was evident in Lenin's brief writings on Cuba, but also at the Second Congress of the Comintern in 1920 when the Mexican delegate Gómez is reported to have commented about a conversation with Lenin that "he was interested in the masses of people in Mexico, in their relation to the United States, whether there was a strong movement in the United States."[32] More specifically, it was the opportunity which uprisings in the colonies could have for the advancement of revolutions in the metropolitan states that most interested Moscow. Margot Light has written that this would dominate Soviet thinking in this part of the world for a considerable number of years. [33] Significantly, this was still applicable to Cuba due to the nature of Havana's relationship with Washington before January 1959.

By the time of the Third Congress of the Comintern in March 1921 events both within Russia and Europe resulted in a change to the organization's tactics as the original revolutionary fervor had begun to wane. Externally this included the Red Army having been defeated in the Polish War in November 1920 and throughout 1921 Russian isolation began to come to an end with the signing of Treaties of Friendship with Persia, Afghanistan, and Turkey and a commercial agreement with the United Kingdom. Moreover, the possibility of other successful revolutions also appeared to have receded with the defeat of uprisings in Hungary and Bavaria. Internally Russia required rebuilding after the Civil War with this leading to the advent of the New Economic Policy (NEP), which further reduced the original revolutionary ardor.[34] As a result, at this Congress Lenin, using his *Left-Wing Communism: An Infantile Disorder*, argued for a more conciliatory position to be adopted with regards to other reformist organizations as capitalism had entered a period of "temporary stabilization." On this Rees and Thorpe have written

> Lenin urged greater flexibility and a move toward co-operation with the members, although not the leaders, of "reformist" working-class organisations like the established trade unions and Socialist parties. [35]

However, by the time of the Ninth Congress in February 1928 Soviet theorists believed that "temporary stabilization" in capitalism was nearing its end, with this leading to the inevitability of capitalist wars and the subsequent victory of revolutionary socialism. In order to achieve this, further radicalism was required and a "class against class" struggle was called for. The outcome was that former allies from the "temporary stabilization" process, such as

"Left Social Democrats," were now perceived in a much less favorable light.[36]

The reason for this policy change returns to the idea that the activities of the Comintern were really the domain of the Soviet government, with Brownthal having written, "From 1928 onward the Communist International had been nothing more than an instrument of Stalin's internal policy."[37] In the late 1920s the Soviet Union was undergoing yet further upheaval with forced industrialization and collectivization, with this taking place while Stalin was still cementing his place at the pinnacle of the Soviet political elite. Illustrating the close link between the internal Russian situation and the Comintern, McDermott has written that the Soviet leader used these changes in Comintern tactics to "define and defeat his opponents" within the Russian party. However, McDermott has also stated that Stalin believed "that long-term Soviet security interests would be best served by a monolithic, strictly disciplined international Communist movement dedicated to the defence of the USSR."[38] This returns to the ideas that Soviet policy was ultimately underpinned by the principles of realism.

Regarding the radicalism of the "third period" of the Comintern era, Rees and Thorpe have written "Class against class has usually been seen as a disaster."[39] Although this was the case, the "third period" is highly important for this book as it was in this period that the Comintern showed considerable interest in Cuba and events on the island, and as a result this will be returned to in chapter 2.

Highly significant for this belief that the "third period" had been a "disaster" was not just because it had been unsuccessful in heralding a successful revolution or even attracting workers toward the socialist movement, but the advent of fascism in Europe in the 1930s and particularly Nazism in Germany appeared to illustrate its abject failure. As a result, yet another policy change was introduced at the Seventh Congress of the Comintern in the summer of 1935 with the "popular front" strategy being introduced partly as a result of the changing situation in Europe. However, Duncan Hallas has written,

> For Stalin to consolidate his power internationally, it was essential that the Comintern parties be immunized against criticism from the revolutionary left. For the Comintern was now to be swung, by Stalin's agents, to a position well to the right of the social democratic parties, to a position of class collaboration precisely the position taken by the social democrats during and after the First World War and against which the founders of the Comintern had revolted.[40]

Key to this strategy was that local communist parties were to work with other local parties within the political system. Events in Cuba were a good example of the "popular front" strategy when in 1942 two Communist Party of Cuba (PCC) members, Juan Marinello and Carlos Rafael Rodríguez, became Ministers within Batista's government, becoming the first Communist Party members in Latin America to hold such positions. [41]

The "popular front" strategy was highly important for relations between the Soviet Union and Cuba in the period before January 1959, and not solely because of Marinello and Rodríguez holding governmental positions. Moreover, this continued to be the case even after the Comintern had been disbanded in the summer of 1943 before being replaced in October 1947 by the much more European focused Communist International Bureau (Cominform). [42] As a result the ideas of the "popular front" will be returned to throughout chapters 2 and 3.

The Bolsheviks may have put great faith in the Comintern in their desire for world revolution, but from soon after the victory of the Russian Revolution they conducted a form of "dual track" diplomacy as traditional forms of diplomacy were conducted simultaneously with the aforementioned Comintern activities. These two tracks appeared to be contradictory with each other as the Comintern's goal was the overthrow of governments and destruction of the traditional system of international relations that provided the parameters for formal forms of diplomacy. This anomaly only complicated Moscow's relationship with the outside world, but both forms of this "dual track" diplomacy were important for the Kremlin's relationship with Cuba.

The Bolshevik's adherence to the traditional forms of state-to-state diplomacy was evident from soon after their victory in the November 1917 Revolution with their discussions with Germany over the Brest-Litovsk peace treaty. This appeared to be very different from the principles of the world revolution and caused unrest within the Bolshevik party and led Lenin to write the *Theses on the Question of the Immediate Conclusion of a Separate and Annexationist Peace*, in which he compared the situation regarding the peace talks with Germany to those of workers losing a strike, but who significantly had not abandoned their original principles. Moreover, he also wrote,

for victory of socialism in Russia, a certain interval of time, no less than several months, during which the socialist government must have complete free hands for the victory over the bourgeoisie first in its own country and for setting up broad and extensive mass organizational work. [43]

This is key to the foreign policy pursued by the new regime in Russia after November 1917 as many academics have commented that this provided the Bolsheviks with "breathing space" which they required to cement their position in power. [44] What underpins this need was that the most significant consideration taken regarding any foreign policy decision was the survival of the Russian Revolution. On this Pipes has written, "Lenin was prepared to make peace with the Central Powers on any terms as long as they left him a power base." [45] More specifically Light has written, "And his cause after the

Revolution was pre-eminently the survival of the Bolshevik state. It was to ensure this survival that he advanced the idea of peaceful coexistence."[46] In short, the new regime in Russia had acted to safeguard their own survival and thus both forms of their "dual track" diplomacy displayed a strong adherence to the realist paradigm of International Relations theory.

The Bolshevik government's adherence to the practices of formal diplomatic relations led some to question the radicalism of their foreign policy.[47] However, traditional diplomacy continued throughout the 1920s with their participation in the Rapallo Treaty in April 1922 and a number of governments officially recognizing the Soviet government. This included the United Kingdom in February 1924 and Mexico and Uruguay in August 1924 and August 1926, respectively.[48]

Moscow conducting traditional forms of diplomacy, underpinned by realism, did not cease with Lenin's death in January 1924 with it continuing to be significant for the rest of the period which is the focus of the book. In the late 1920s it was significant as further "breathing space" was required while the Soviet Union underwent collectivization and industrialization. Pursuing peaceful coexistence did not mean that the Soviet leadership believed that confrontation with the capitalist world would be avoided, but it gave the Soviet Union the chance to be better prepared for when it commenced. Moreover, it also gave local communist parties the chance to undermine these Western powers as they pursued the radical tactics of the "third period" of the Comintern, with this further benefitting the Soviet Union in its fight against capitalism.

The advent of Nazism in the 1930s may have caused ideological problems for the Comintern, but it increased Moscow's need for peaceful coexistence and collective security against this greater evil. The Soviet Union joined the League of Nations in September 1934, and during the first Soviet speech to this organization Maxim Litvinov, Soviet Commissar of Foreign Affairs, stated,

> throughout the seventeen years of its existence, its efforts for the establishment of the best possible relations with its own neighbours, on the most solid foundations, for rapprochement with all States desiring this, thus making itself a powerful factor for international peace.[49]

Moscow may have shocked the Western powers in August 1939 by the signing of the Nazi-Soviet pact, but this agreement again illustrated both the Kremlin's willingness to conduct traditional diplomacy, and also that the survival of the Revolution was the ultimate consideration in all foreign policy decisions. The Nazi-Soviet pact only increased Western suspicions of the Soviet Union but it most certainly provided Moscow with invaluable time to prepare for war.[50] Again, this returns to the need for "breathing space" which had been so important in Lenin's willingness to sign the Brest-Litovsk peace treaty in 1918, thus illustrating the prominence of realism within the Soviet elites' thinking.

The Nazi-Soviet pact was brought to a sudden and shuddering end when Nazi Germany unleashed Operation Barbarossa against the Soviet Union on 22 June 1941. However, this also brought about rapprochement between the Soviet Union and the Western Powers as they formed a wartime alliance against Hitler's Germany. This was key to the ultimate victory in World War II, and also illustrated the existence of both "peaceful coexistence" with the West and the prominence of realist thinking within the Soviet elite as the Soviet Union's very survival had been placed in jeopardy by Nazi Germany. This was a very different scenario from the immediate aftermath of the Russian Revolution when the same Western powers had tried to crush the fledgling government in Russia. The wartime alliance would also be of fundamental importance for Soviet-Cuban relations in a number of different ways and will therefore be returned to throughout this book.

By 1950 the wartime alliance was confined to history as relations between the Soviet Union and the West quickly sank to new depths. Haslam has argued that the Cold War between Moscow and West began soon after the Russian Revolution, which is undoubtedly correct, but in the aftermath of World War II relations deteriorated rapidly.[51] This was in no small part due to Moscow's control of Eastern Europe in the late 1940s, but the ideological standoff between the Soviet Union and the United States would dominate international relations for 40 years.

Regarding the Cold War, Nigel Gould-Davies has written, "The Cold War was, in essence, a struggle between ideas," with it being a battle for "hearts and minds" with both sides being willing to attack the other's camp in order to achieve this.[52] This is in accordance with Shulman writing that the "central requirement for Soviet foreign policy: to fragment and diminish the power of the Western bloc,"[53] with Gould-Davies believing that culture played a significant part in this process.[54] This returns to the ideas of soft power and would be crucial for Soviet interest in Cuba in the period from 1945 to 1952.

Although this was the case, Light has argued that even in the early 1950s peaceful coexistence remained important for Moscow, particularly for fostering trade, but that a subtle change had occurred in the Kremlin's thinking toward it. The Soviet leadership now believed that the West was forced to participate in this due to the strengthening of socialism, and not as previously for merely trade reasons.[55] Moreover, in the 1950s, but before the 20th Congress of the Communist Party of the Soviet Union (CPSU) that was held in February 1956, Light has written

That the new version of peaceful coexistence was intended to involve more than just the absence of war and expansion of trade relations soon became clear. While international economic links were said to be an objective need of all countries, determined by the international division of labour, political and cultural cooperation was also envisaged.[56]

This would be of fundamental importance for Soviet-Cuban relations, as would the changes implemented in Soviet foreign policy in the aftermath of Stalin's death in March 1953. From this point onward the Soviet Union became much more outward looking, with it desiring an increased presence in the Developing World. These changes coincided with the de-colonization process taking place throughout the Developing World, with Nikita Khrushchev's speech to the Twentieth Party Congress of the CPSU illustrating this change in Soviet foreign policy when he said, "The awakening of the African peoples has begun. The national liberation movement has gained strength in Brazil, Chile and other Latin American countries."[57]

Due to the continuing lack of a working class in the Developing World, the Kremlin believed it could acquire this presence by backing national liberation movements in their fight for independence. Moscow hoped that once these movements were in power they would sever their ties with their former colonial masters, become increasingly left wing and align themselves with the Soviet Union. Often this backing was financial which led Peter Shearman to write that Moscow was trying "to buy influence in the Third World at the expense of the United States and the former colonial powers in Europe."[58] Although this was the case, it was vital for Soviet interest in Cuba after January 1959, but also for some tentative interest which the Kremlin displayed in Cuba in the period between the Twentieth Congress of the CPSU in March 1956 and the victory of the Cuban Revolution, which will be detailed later in this chapter.

HAVANA, WASHINGTON, AND THE WORLD

By December 1898 when Spanish rule over Cuba came to an end, unrest had engulfed the island for over 30 years, but this historic event by no means ushered in a new free era for the Caribbean island. Due to a fear of Cuban independence which would have resulted in political instability, social conflict, and economic upheaval which would have grave knock-on consequences for U.S. owned property, the United States became militarily involved in Cuba in the final few years of Spanish rule. This intervention also had racial undertones due to concerns over a possible "Africanization" of Cuba, but these very same reasons also resulted in many conservative Cubans also preferring U.S. intervention to independence.[59] Regarding the impact of U.S. military involvement, Louis Pérez has succinctly stated, "the

Cuban war for national liberation was transfigured into the "Spanish-American War,"[60] with the result being a denial of Cuban independence.

Washington may have acted militarily in Cuba to prevent the island gaining independence, but this did not mean that the U.S. wanted to officially annex the island or to have continuous military presence throughout it. Rather Washington wanted Cubans to rule themselves, but for the Cuban ruling elite to be dependent on the power and influence of the United States. In short, the U.S. would dominate the island both politically and economically with Samuel Farber writing "The situation essentially represented de facto if not fully de jure colonialism."[61] In 1901 this situation became more formalized with the addition of the Platt Amendment to the Cuban constitution regarding which Pérez has written "It served to transform the substance of Cuban sovereignty into an extension of the United States national system."[62] This is illustrated by the amendment's first article which stated "Cuba shall never enter into any treaty or other compact with any foreign power or powers, which will impair or tend to impair the independence of Cuba."[63]

U.S. influence over Cuba was not just political but also economical with in December 1903 a reciprocity agreement between the two countries becoming law. This provided Cuba with a 20 percent reduction for select exports while a reduction of 25–40 percent on U.S. imports was implemented.[64] This sparked a considerable increase in U.S. investment in the island, but Thomas has noted that this was mostly in the sugar industry which prevented a diversification of the economy taking place, while Pérez has written, "it delivered still another setback to Cuban enterprise and local entrepreneurs."[65]

Pérez has also written that due to the all encompassing nature of the relationship between Cuba and the United States that no part of the island's society was unaffected by U.S. influence. As noted, this not only hindered the development of a local entrepreneurial class, but also saw the arrival of considerable numbers of U.S. tourists, customs, and fashions to the island. In addition, the teaching of the English language increased dramatically in Cuban schools. Moreover, the relationship also had a direct effect on Cuban labor laws as U.S. business did not wish progressive policies to become law as this would have increased their production costs.[66] The lack of such laws would be fundamental for the prevalence of political radicalism on the island from the 1920s onward, which will be analyzed more fully in the next chapter.

Washington may have been able to gain control over Cuba without formal annexation or a continuous military presence throughout the island, but this did not mean that the United States was unwilling to deploy military forces to Cuba to curb unrest. This was most noticeable in 1906 and 1917 when Washington sent troops to Cuba to restore order after protests over the re-elections of Presidents Tomas Estrada Palma and President Mario G.

Monocal, respectively. In 1906 U.S. troops remained for three years while in 1917 they remained in the provinces of Camaguey and Oriente until 1922.[67]

On occasion the United States utilized other means to directly affect events on the island. This was most noticeable in 1920 when Washington sent General Enoch H. Crowder to Havana as the "Special Representative of the President" to resolve the disputed nature of the 1920 Cuban Presidential elections. In a similar manner, thirteen years later the U.S. ambassador, Summer Welles, was directly involved in returning order to Cuba after the general strike of August 1933.[68] The situation in the summer of 1933 had arisen in no small part due to the boom and bust nature of the Cuban economy with this being interlinked with the world sugar price. The Caribbean island may have economically prospered from World War I, but conversely it was also dramatically affected by the Wall Street Crash.[69] The August 1933 strike will be detailed more fully in the next chapter, but this and the "Sergeants Revolt" of September 1933 threw Cuba into chaos. Regarding the role of Welles in resolving the situation, Benjamin has written, "Wholly abandoning the pretence of non-interference, Welles arranged a succession of a provisional President acceptable to Washington."[70] Key to this was the U.S. administration's non-recognition of Ramón Grau San Martín's government, but after Welles's manipulation of the situation and Fulgencio Batista's decision to remove military support for Grau and place it with Carlos Mendieta instead, Washington recognized the government within five days.[71]

Significant for Washington's non-recognition of Grau's government was his decision to unilaterally repeal the Platt Amendment. However, this did not signal a reduction in U.S. influence in Cuba which led Farber to write, "The post-1933 period could be described as a transition for a de facto colonialism to a neocolonial arrangement."[72] Significantly in 1934 a new reciprocity act was signed which involved concessions for 35 U.S. products and 400 Cuban ones. Again, this stifled diversification of the island's economy, but also illustrated the continuing U.S. economic domination of Cuba.[73]

The two countries remained politically intertwined despite Cuba's new liberal constitution of 1940 and, as stated, becoming the first Latin American country to have a communist presence within its government.[74] This close relationship was illustrated by Cuba entering World War II on 9 December 1941, a mere two days after the Japanese attack on Pearl Harbor. Similarly to World War I, Cuba prospered economically from World War II with Batista, who was by this time Cuban President, also winning favor within the United States by aiding the war effort by increasing sugar production and providing training facilities for the U.S. military.[75] This was important because after the April 1952 coup which returned Batista to power, the U.S. quickly recognized his government.

The United States remained the key player in Cuban political life for the remainder of Batista's Presidency, but in March 1958 due to fraudulent Presidential elections and increasing tension on the island, Washington imposed an arms embargo on his government. Pérez believes that this, "move was tantamount to a withdrawal of support."[76] Ultimately this would be crucial for the victory of the Cuban Revolution.

The United States had been the dominant power in Cuba from the time of independence in the late nineteenth century until January 1959 which is crucial for the focus of this book. Pérez has written,

> The restrictions imposed upon the conduct of foreign relations, specifically the denial of treaty authority and debt restrictions, as well as the prohibition against the cession of national territory, were designed to minimize the possibility of Cuban international entanglements.[77]

Although written about the Platt Amendment, the sentiments of this quote could be repeated for Soviet-Cuban relations in the period between the Russian and Cuban Revolutions because Washington's relationship with Moscow cast a long and very dark shadow over it. As a result, U.S.-Soviet relations, and United States foreign policy, are topics which will be returned to throughout this book and therefore a brief analysis of U.S. foreign policy will be provided.

United States military involvement in Cuba in the late 1890s was reflective of the changes which took place in U.S. foreign policy at the end of the nineteenth century and beginning of the twentieth century, with Walter LaFeber having written,

> Fuelled by the industrial revolution of the late nineteenth century, which produced the first telephones, automobiles, and steel complexes as well as the transatlantic marriages, United States foreign policy's focus moved from the North American continent to markets of Europe, Latin America and Asia. This was nothing less than a "new empire" as one influential observer termed it at the time.[78]

Economics was very much at the forefront of this with the United States requiring both markets for their goods and sources of raw materials. However, Washington's belief in an "open door" economic policy resulted in tensions appearing with the traditional colonial powers who wished to preserve trade tariffs in order to safeguard trade with their colonies. This was an issue which would continue for some time, with economics also being significant for the United States entry into World War I in April 1917.[79] The deaths of U.S. citizens at the hands of German U-boats and the Zimmerman letter were also important, but Washington's fear that the money it had loaned the United Kingdom would not be repaid was fundamental in the U.S. entering the war.[80]

The United States may have left the war in a completely different financial position compared to 1914, with Paterson et al. claiming "To Americans, World War I bequeathed an unassailable legacy: the United States became the world's leading economic power."[81] However, the events in Russia in November 1917 also had lasting repercussions for U.S. foreign policy for not just the period of this book, but much of the remainder of the twentieth century. On the immediate challenge which faced President Wilson at the end of World War I as a result of the Russian Revolution, LaFeber has written,

> Wilson moved to control the revolutionary outbreak by demanding that the new nations be governed by American-style democracy, not by Leninist-style communism. In doing so, the President set in motion the U.S. challenge to Russian communism – a challenge which characterised American-Russian relations for nearly the whole of the twentieth century.[82]

The challenge of communism in conjunction with the belief in free trade and democracy were key determinants in Washington's foreign policy for both the period which is the focus of this book and the next 70 years. However, at its core were the principles of realism with the United States continually striving to maximize its own power. As detailed earlier in this chapter, Woodrow Wilson may have been synonymous with the ideas of collective security in the inter-war period, but this did not mean that he abandoned these core tenets of U.S. foreign policy or even the realist paradigm of International Relations. Regarding this LaFeber has written,

> There was idealism here, certainly, but also realism. Indeed, Wilson has become the most influential architect of twentieth century United States foreign policy in part because he so eloquently clothed the bleak skeleton of U.S. self-interest in the attractive garb of idealism.[83]

This was most noticeable in 1920 when Washington dispatched troops to Russia primarily to help Czech troops who had become stranded in the far east of Russia. Paterson et al. also believe that this deployment took place to preserve "open door" trade with Japan, but that it also illustrated Wilson's anti-Bolshevik intentions.[84]

U.S. troops may have been sent to Russia and been deployed to various Latin American countries, including Cuba, but in the 1920s these troop deployments slowed as Washington believed that its power could be achieved not only via military force but also by its economic might. In Latin America this saw U.S. investments increase by over 100 percent in the years from 1924 to 1929, but trade was also conducted with the Soviet Union.[85] This heralded the era of "dollar diplomacy" and with relation to Latin America, the Good Neighbor Policy. However, with regards to the Soviet Union,

Washington still believed that it could undermine the Soviet government with its economic power, and a policy of non-recognition was also implemented due to Washington's perception of the subversive nature of the Bolshevik regime.[86]

The U.S. and world economy may have been thrown into disarray by the Wall Street crash, but it also had important repercussions for U.S.-Soviet relations, because as previously detailed, in November 1933 Washington officially recognized the Soviet regime. The fact that the Soviet regime had survived, not imploded, and appeared likely to remain in place for some time was important for this decision as was the U.S. need to counter China in the far east and a desire for much needed trade to help the U.S. economy recover from the Wall Street crash. However, not everyone in the United States was happy at Franklin Roosevelt's decision to recognize the Soviet government in late 1933 with LaFeber writing that this was particularly the case with many in the U.S. State Department. Writing about Robert Kelly, Head of the U.S. State Department Eastern European Desk, LaFerber has interestingly stated "Kelly warned his superiors that if recognised, the Soviet Union would never keep agreements, but instead ferment revolution – as he argued, they were doing in Cuba."[87] This is a topic which will be examined in detail in chapter 2.

Kelly's reservations about U.S. official recognition of the Soviet Union were reflective of the differences which existed within the United States in the 1930s about the country's foreign policy. A debate endured between isolationalists who wished the United States not to become embroiled in the increasingly tense European situation and internationalists who believed that Washington should have a prominent global presence. For much of the 1930s the isolationalists were to the fore, but this began to change in the late 1930s when Roosevelt became concerned over the increasingly strained nature of relations between Washington and Tokyo, and dramatically came to an end with the Japanese attack on Pearl Harbor on 7 December 1941.[88]

As previously detailed, this heralded the creation of the alliance between Washington, Moscow, and London with old tensions being put to one side due to the greater evil of fascism. Paterson et al. have described this wartime alliance between Washington and Moscow as a "marriage of convenience," but as stated it was highly important for Soviet-Cuban relations. However, even within it the old tensions remained with this becoming evident in discussions regarding the post-war world.[89] Washington wanted a world built on democracy and free trade while London still wished an economic tariff system to protect its colonial trade while Moscow desired control of Eastern Europe.[90]

In a similar manner to the economic effects of World War I, the United States in 1945 was in a completely different position to that which it had been in 1939. On this LaFeber has written,

The United States was beyond question becoming the world's greatest power. British, Russian, Japanese and western European industries and cities were largely reduced to smoking ashes between 1941 and 1945. But untainted U.S. industrial production shot up by 90 percent.[91]

Moreover, Paterson et al. have stated, "The United States emerged from World War II a global power for the first time in its history. American diplomats were self-conscious about their supreme power and attempted to use it to shape an American orientated post-war world."[92] Economically this was evident in the conference at Bretton Woods during July 1944 which created the International Monetary Fund and World Bank.[93] In addition, at this time the United States was the world's sole nuclear power.

However, economics was also closely intertwined with Washington's political aims because as the world descended into the Cold War, United States policy toward the Soviet Union was underpinned by the principle of attempting to contain the spread of Soviet power and socialism. George Kennan's "Long Telegram" of February 1946 is often credited with being the basis for this policy. In this telegram Kennan was not only highly critical of the Soviet system in general but suggested, "To speak of possibility of intervention against USSR today, after elimination of Germany and Japan and after the example of the recent war, is sheerest nonsense."[94] In Europe capitalism had come directly into contact with socialism and fearing the spread of socialism into Western Europe, the Marshall Plan was implemented to try and prevent this. In addition, the $13.2 billion that this plan supplied also aided U.S. industry because U.S. economic prosperity after World War II was threatened by the "sickness" of its best customers: Western Europe. The Marshall Plan aimed to provide the remedy for this "sickness."[95] In addition to the Marshall Plan, the "Truman Doctrine" had also come into existence with this providing economic and military support to Greece and Turkey, again to prevent the spread of socialism.[96]

The dynamics of the embryonic Cold War changed dramatically on 29 August 1949 with the successful testing of the first Soviet atomic bomb.[97] The U.S. response to this was the National Security Council Paper Number 68 (NSC-68) of January 1950 which stated that global tension was likely to continue for a prolonged period of time due to Soviet attempts to expand its power and influence as a result of relentless communist aggression. Crucially it was stated that the U.S. could only counter this challenge with a massive military build-up of its own and increased military spending. LaFeber believes that this led to the nuclear arms race, but the onset of the Korean War in the summer of 1950 was taken as evidence of communism's aggression.[98] NSC-68 was still in accordance with Kennan's ideas of containment, but from 1950 onward military power was at the forefront of these efforts. This would remain the case for both the remainder of the focus of this book, but also for much of the remainder of the Cold War. As detailed, due to the nature of U.S.-Cuban relations prior to January 1959, these events, and Washington's foreign policy in general, would directly affect Moscow's relationship with Havana.

As has been stated, Europe and Asia may have been the primary focus of the Comintern, but the organization did not completely ignore Latin America generally or Cuba specifically. This will be analyzed in much more depth in chapter 2, but it has resulted in a number of academic works having been published on these topics. Caballero in *Latin America and the Comintern 1919–1943* concentrated on Moscow's interest with Latin America as a whole while Daniela Spenser in *The Impossible Triangle: Mexico, Soviet Russia and the United States in the 1920s* focused exclusively on Soviet-Mexican relations in the 1920s. In addition, some Comintern documents that are relevant to Latin America have been published. This includes *Soviet Relations with Latin America 1918–1968* edited by S. Clissold, *Marxism in Latin America from 1909 to the Present: An Anthology* edited by M. Lowry, and *World Communism: A Handbook 1918–1968* edited by W.S. Sworakowski.[99] Moreover, in the 1990s, since the implosion of the Soviet Union, access has been provided to previously prohibited Comintern documents. Erik Ching and Jussi Pakkasvirta have utilized this to write an overview of the documents relevant to Latin America.[100]

Before the Cuban Revolution many within Cuba had shown interest in left-wing politics, giving rise to the publication of a number of books on this. This includes Gary Tennant's *The Hidden Pearl of the Caribbean. Trotskyism in Cuba* which examined pre-1959 Trotskyite groups on the island. Moreover, the Cuban Communist Party (PCC) has also attracted much academic attention, including Boris Goldenberg's article "The Rise and Fall of a Party: The Cuban CP (1925–59)" and Samuel Farber's "The Cuban Communists in the Early Stages of the Cuban Revolution: Revolutionaries or Reformists."[101] The history of the PCC from its creation in the 1920s to 1959 has been charted by K.S. Karol in *Guerrillas in Power* and Robert J. Alexander in *Communism in Latin America* while Louis Pérez and Hugh Thomas have also written about the creation and evolution of the PCC in their histories of Cuba.[102]

In addition, the Soviet Union's pre-1959 relationship with the Developing World in general, and Latin America specifically, has also been the focus of much academic work. This includes *Socialism in the Third World* edited by Helen Desfosses and Jacques Levesque, Luis Aquilar's *Marxism in Latin America*, *The Communist Tide in Latin America: A Selected Treatment* edited by Donald L. Herman, Jan Librach's *The Rise of the Soviet Empire*, Rollie Poppino's *International Communism in Latin America: 1917–1963*, while Timothy Ashby wrote *The Bear in the Back Yard: Moscow's Caribbean Strategy.*[103]

Although this is the case, Christopher Andrew and the former KGB archivist Vasili Mitokhin have written in their book *The World Was Going our Way: The KGB and the Battle for the Third World*,

> For over forty years after the Bolshevik Revolution, Moscow doubted its own ability to challenge American influence in a continent which it regarded as the United States' backyard. By far the most important Soviet intelligence operation in Latin America during the Stalin era was aimed not at subverting any ruling regimes but at assassinating the great Russian heretic Leon Trotsky, who had taken refuge near Mexico City.[104]

Regarding this lack of Soviet interest in Latin America Nicola Miller in *Soviet Relations with Latin America 1959–1987* has written,

> Moscow's early view of Latin America was governed by what became known as the law of "geographical fatalism." Soviet officials saw little hope either of establishing formal political ties or of promoting revolution in countries forced to live within the shadow of the United States and its 1823 Monroe Doctrine.[105]

In *Soviet-Cuban Alliance 1959–1991*, Yury Pavlov, former head of the Latin American Directorate of the USSR Foreign Ministry, was even stronger in his assessment of Soviet interest in Latin America in the early 1950s.

> Latin America . . . did not figure on the list of Soviet foreign policy priorities, as it was believed to be firmly under no-nonsense U.S. control. All Latin American governments were toeing Washington's anti-communist line. This led Joseph Stalin, then in the prime of his glory and power as the despotic ruler of the USSR, to make a statement in February 1951, which became a textbook reference for all students of Latin American affairs. In an interview with *Pravda*, he spoke about "the aggressive core of the United Nations," composed of ten member countries of NATO and "twenty Latin American countries."[106]

Miller's assertion that the Kremlin suffered from "geographical fatalism" prior to January 1959 is important as this has been the traditional academic position regarding Soviet foreign policy toward Latin America as a whole and Cuba specifically. It has been assumed that Moscow perceived the region as being in Washington's "backyard" and that it was the victory of the Cuban Revolution that altered Soviet thinking toward this region of the world. The events in Cuba in 1959 did undoubtedly result in this, but some authors have begun to question the traditional academic position regarding Soviet policy toward Latin America or more specifically Cuba before January 1959.

In the main, Alexandr Fursenko and Timothy Naftali in *The Secret History of the Cuban Missile Crisis: "One Hell of a Gamble"* and Samuel Farber in *The Origins of the Cuban Revolution: Reconsidered* adhere to the general academic trend of Moscow showing little interest in Latin America or Cuba before 1959.[107] However, the authors of both of these books have begun to question this as they have suggested that in the summer of 1958 Fidel Castro's guerrilla movement had made tentative attempts, via a Costa Rican importing company to make contact with the Czech embassy in Mexico City, to acquire weapons from the socialist bloc.[108] Significantly this took place after the agreement between Castro's 26th July Movement and the Cuban Socialist Party (PSP). Fursenko and Naftali link this incident in Mexico City to the alterations that took place in Soviet foreign policy in the aftermath of Stalin's death while Farber has suggested that it was simply a question of the Kremlin attempting to take advantage of any opportunity that arose.[109] This questioning of the traditional academic position is highly important, but both works refer only to this one incident in the period immediately before the victory of the Cuban Revolution.

In the article "Soviet-Cuban Relations, 1956–1960" George Boughton has written specifically about Soviet-Cuban relations prior to January 1959. This is a very important article as it is one of the very few which concentrates solely on Moscow's relationship with Havana in the period before the Cuban Revolution, with its focus being predominantly Soviet media reports in the years immediately prior to the Cuban Revolution.[110] As with the above cited works by Fursenko and Naftali and Farber, Boughton again links Soviet interest to the Soviet foreign policy changes made in the mid-1950s. However, as it was written in the early 1970s, Boughton did not have access to a number of important documents that have only become available since 1991. In addition, it does not analyze diplomatic relations or trade and cultural exchanges.

A similar situation arises with Caballero's *Latin America and the Comintern 1919–1943* as it was written in 1986 resulting in the omission of Comintern documents that have only become available since the disintegration of the Soviet Union in December 1991. Despite this it remains a highly influential work for the study of Comintern policy toward Latin America and Cuba. However, the section on the Caribbean island is only one in his much larger work on the Comintern's interest in Latin America as a whole. [111]

A body of literature on the history of the PCC and the PSP exists and includes the aforementioned works by Alexander, Goldenberg, Karol, and Pérez and also Samuel Farber's "The Cuban Communists in the Early Stages of the Cuban Revolution: Revolutionaries or Reformers?"[112] Again, these are very important but as with Caballero's book they both do not utilize documents that have become available since 1991 and they only examine one specific aspect of Moscow's relationship with Cuba. They do not analyze the bilateral relationship between Moscow and Havana with regards to diplomatic relations, trade, or cultural links.

The issue of not being able to access Comintern documents certainly does not exist with Barry Carr's "Mill Occupations and Soviets: The Mobilisation of Sugar Workers in Cuba 1917–1933," and "From Caribbean backwater to revolutionary opportunity: Cuba's evolving relationship with the Comintern, 1925–34" as he has utilized Comintern documents specific to Cuba to highlight the considerable interest which the organization had in the August 1933 general strike on the island.[113] These articles are highly important in the analysis of Soviet interest toward Cuba within the framework of the Comintern. However, both concentrate on a very specific period within the Comintern era and neither examines the existence of diplomatic, trade, or cultural relations.

This book will analyze the relationship between Moscow and Havana from the time of the Russian Revolution to that of the Cuban Revolution, by examining the interest which the Comintern took in the island, but also the diplomatic, trade, and cultural links which existed in this period. In sum, both aspects on Moscow's "dual track" diplomacy will be analyzed. It will explain the reasons and pressures which underpinned this Soviet interest, which very much questions the traditional perception that prior to January 1959 the Kremlin suffered from "geographical fatalism" with regards to Latin America as a whole, or Cuba specifically. Moreover, it will explain why the Kremlin appeared to take more interest in the Caribbean island than other countries in the region.

Marxist-Leninist ideology will be key for this, as will the Cuban Communist Party and subsequently the Cuban Socialist Party (PSP). The importance of the PSP continued even after the Comintern era, with this partly explaining why in the years from 1945 to 1952 Cuba appeared to partly buck the regional trend of not severing diplomatic relations with Moscow. The significance of the Cuban party will therefore be examined at various stages of this book. Also in these years immediately after World War II the issue of Soviet soft power will be analyzed. Moreover, the international context will also be of great importance for this study. More specifically Cuba's relationship with the United States is of the utmost significance for the interest which the Soviet leadership took in Cuba in the years from 1917 to 1959. This occurred throughout this period with the alliance formed between Washington and Moscow during World War II and the subsequent deterioration in this relationship that heralded the onset of the Cold War being vitally important. In relation to this, Cuban dependency on the United States throughout this era will also be highly important for this study. Particular attention will be given to the influence of the realist and neo-realist paradigms of International Relations theory in Soviet foreign policy. This was vital in general throughout this period and specifically for the interest which the Soviet Union showed in Cuban sugar at various times in this period. As a result, the significance of realism and neo-realism will be returned to throughout this book.

Such an extensive work on this topic has not previously been published, but in order to do this, a number of previously unused Soviet and Cuban sources will be utilized. This will include ones from the Russian State Archive for Social and Political History but also others from the National State Library of Russia and the Russian National Historical Library, all of which are in Moscow. In addition, sources including previously unused ones from the Cuban National Archive, the José Marti National Library, and Cuban Foreign Ministry (MINREX) documents will also be used. Moreover, documents from the Communist Party of the United States of America (CPUSA) Collections at the Tamiment Library at New York University will also be utilized due to the role that the CPUSA played in Cuba in the 1920s and 1930s. This will allow this book to fill the important gap which exists in the scholarly literature on the relationship between Moscow and Havana prior to the victory of the Cuban Revolution in January 1959.

Chapter 2 will detail Comintern interest in Cuba, and in relation to this will also examine the importance of the CPUSA in this. Moreover, it will also analyze the impact which the Russian Revolution had on Cuban political life, which is important for the years 1945 to 1952, when as stated, Cuba appeared to buck the regional trend in not breaking diplomatic relations with Moscow. Chapter 3 will focus on the other aspect of the Kremlin's "dual track" diplomacy by concentrating on diplomatic links between the two countries. In addition to this, it will also examine cultural and trade links that existed between the Soviet Union and Cuba in the period between the Russian and Cuban Revolutions. The evolution of Soviet foreign policy and the changing nature of United States policy toward the Soviet Union and also Cuba, which have been outlined in this chapter, will also be important in explaining the relationship in this period. A number of conclusions will be given, including that in the years between the Russian and Cuban Revolutions, Moscow did not suffer from "geographical fatalism" with regards to the Caribbean island as it took a considerable interest in it.

NOTES

1. "65 Aniversario de la Gran Victoria," *Edicion de la Embajada de la federación de Rusia en Cuba*, Numero 4, (2010): 28.

2. Chris Brown, *Understanding International Relations*, (New York: Palgrave, 2001).

3. E.H. Carr, *The Twenty Years Crisis 1919–1939: An Introduction to the Study of International Relations*, (London: Palgrave, 2001).

4. Hans Morgenthau, *Politics Among Nations*, (New York: Knopf, 1955), 25.

5. John Mearsheimer, *The Tragedy of Great Power Politics*, (New York: W.W. Norton & Company, 2010), 14.

6. Karl Marx, *The Communist Manifesto*, (Harmondsworth: Penguin Books, 1982). Andrew Gamble, *Timewalkers: The Prehistory of Global Colonisation*, (Cambridge, Mass: Harvard University Press, 1999).

7. Andre Gunder Frank, *Latin America: Underdevelopment or Revolution: Essays on the Development and Underdevelopment and the Immediate Enemy*, (New York: Monthly Review Press, 1969). Michael Erisman, *Cuba's Foreign Relations in a Post-Soviet World*, (Gainesville: University Press of Florida, 2000), 43–45.

8. Erisman, *Cuba's Foreign Relations*, 2000, 30–33. Daniel L. Byman & Kenneth M. Pollack, "Let Us Now Praise Great Men. Bringing the Statesmen Back In," *International Security*, Vol 25, No. 4 (Spring 2001): 107–146.

9. Graham T. Allison, *Essence of a Decision. Explaining the Cuban Missile Crisis*, (Boston: Little, Brown & Company, 1971).

10. M.J. Smith, "Liberalism and International Reform" in *Traditions of International Ethics*, ed. T. Nardin and D. Mapel (Cambridge: Cambridge University Press, 1992), pp. 201–224. J.L. Richardson, "Contending Liberalism: Past and Present," *European Journal of International Relations*, 3:1 (1997): 5–33.

11. Kenneth Waltz, *Theory of International Politics*, (New York: Random House, 1979), 111.

12. Soft power is not a new concept, as writing in 1939 E.H. Carr stated that three categories of international power existed: military, economic, and power over opinion. Carr, *The Twenty Years Crisis*, 2001, 108.

13. Joseph S. Nye, Jr, *Soft Power. The Means to Success in World Politics*, (New York: PublicAffairs, 2004), 6.

14. Quoted in Nye, *Soft Power,* 2004, 11.

15. Nye, *Soft Power,* 2004, 73.

16. Emanuel Alder, "Constructivism," in *Handbook of International Relations*, ed. Walter Carlneas, Beth Simmons, & Thomas Risse (Thousand Oaks, Cal: Sage, 2003), 95–118. M. Hollis & S. Smith, *Explaining and Understanding International Relations*, (New York: Oxford University Press, 1990). 196–216. Alan Collins, *Contemporary Security Studies*, (New York: Oxford University Press, 2007).

17. Ronald Grigor Suny, "Living in the Hood: Russia, Empire, and Old and New Neighbours," in *Russian Foreign Policy in the Twenty-first Century and the Shadow of the Past*, ed. Robert Legvold, (New York: Colombia University Press, 2007), 35.

18. Andrei P. Tsygankov, *Russia's Foreign Policy. Change and Continuity in National Identity*, (Lanham: Rowman and Littlefield Publishers, 2006), 1–29.

19. Tsygankov, *Russia's Foreign Policy*, 2006, 6.

20. Stephen White, *Gorbachev and After*, (Cambridge: Cambridge University Press, 1991). 179–180. John P. Ledonne, *The Russian Empire and the World 1700–1917. The Geopolitics of Expansion and Containment*, (Oxford: Oxford University Press, 1997), 347. Laurence T Caldwell "Russian Concepts of National Security" in Legvold, *Russian Foreign Policy,* 2007, 280–283.

21. Ledonne, *The Russian Empire*, 1997, 1.

22. Russell H. Bartley, *Imperial Russia and the Struggle for Latin American Independence 1808–1828*, (Austin: The University of Texas, 1978), 16–23.

23. Grigor Suny, "Living in the Hood," 2007, 41.

24. Jonathan Haslan, *Russia's Cold War. From the October Revolution to the Fall of the Wall*, (New Haven: Yale University Press, 2011), 1.

25. Manuel Caballero, *Latin America and the Comintern 1919–1943*, (Cambridge: Cambridge University Press, 1986), 7.

26. Quoted in Alfred E. Senn, *Readings in Russian Political and Diplomatic History, Volume II, The Soviet Period*, (Homewood, Illinois: The Dorsey Press, 1966), 43–44.

27. Branko Lazitch & Milorad M. Drachkovitch, *Lenin and the Comintern. Volume 1*, (Stanford University: Hoover Institution Press, 1972), 529–530.

28. Tim Rees & Andrew Thorpe, "Introduction" in *International Communism and the Communist International 1919–43,* ed. Tim Rees and Andrew Thorpe, (Manchester: Manchester University Press, 1998), 3.

29. Lazitch & Drachkovitch, *Lenin and the Comintern*, 20.

30. Grigor Suny, "Living in the Hood" 2007, 57.

31. John Riddel, *To See the Dawn. Baku, 1920: First Congress of the People of the East*, (New York: Pathfinder Press, 1993).

32. Quoted in S. Clissold, *Soviet Relations with Latin America 1918–1968* (London: Oxford University Press, 1970), 2.

33. Margot Light, *The Soviet Theory of International Relations*, (New York: St Martin's Press, 1988), 80–81.

34. Lazitch & Drachkovitch, *Lenin and the Comintern*. 1972, 532.

35. Rees & Thorpe, "Introduction," 1998, 3.

36. Duncan Hallas, *The Comintern. A History of the Third International*, (Chicago: Haymarket Book, 1985), 130–134.

37. Julius Brownthal, *History of the International 1914–1943*, (Camden, New Jersey: Nelson, 1963), 528.

38. Kevin McDermott, "Stalin and the Comintern during the 'Third Period', 1928–1933" *European History Quarterly*, Volume 25, (1995): 418.

39. Rees & Thorpe, "Introduction," 1998, 5. McDermott also states this. McDermott, 'Stalin and the Comintern," 1995, 409.

40. Hallas, *The Comintern*, 1985, 145. Kevin McDermott and Jeremy Agnew have spoken of a "triple interaction" of reasons which underpinned this change in Comintern tactics. These were "national factors, internal dynamics in the Comintern leadership and the shifting requirements of Soviet diplomacy." Kevin McDermott & Jeremy Agnew, *The Comintern. A History of International Communism from Lenin to Stalin*, (Basingstoke: Macmillan Press, 1996), 120.

41. Julia E. Sweig, *Inside the Cuban Revolution. Fidel Castro and the Urban Underground*, (Harvard University Press, Cambridge, Massachusetts, 2002), 126.

42. Fernando Claudin, *The Communist Movement from Comintern to Cominform*, (New York: Monthly Review Press, 1975).

43. Vladimir Lenin, "Theses on the Question of the Immediate Conclusion of a Separate and Annexationist Peace," in *A Documentary History of Communism, Volume 2 Communism and the World*, ed. Robert V. Daniels, (Hanover: University Press of New England, 1984), 22–23.

44. R. Pipes, *The Russian Revolution 1899–1919*, (London: Fontana Press, 1990), 602. Michael T. Florinsky, "Soviet Foreign Policy. The Paradox of Soviet Foreign Relations." *The Slavonic and East European Review*, Volume 12, Number 36 (April 1934), 536. Light, *Soviet Theory*, 1988, 28.

45. Pipes, *The Russian Revolution*, 1990, 603.

46. Light, *Soviet Theory*, 1988, 28.

47. For example please see: Piero Melograni, *Lenin and the Myth of World Revolution. Ideology and Reasons of State, 1917–1920*, (Atlantic Highlands, NJ: Humanities Press International, 1989).

48. *Diplomaticheskii slovar ' A-U, Tom 1*, (Moscow: Izdatelstvo Nauka, 1984), 314–325.

49. Maxim Litvinov, "Speech to Assembly of League of Nations," in *The Communist International 1919–1943 Documents, Volume 2*, ed. Jane Degras, (London: Frank Cass & Co Ltd, 1971), 94.

50. John Lewis Gaddis, *We Now Know. Rethinking Cold War History*, (Oxford: Oxford University Press, 1998), 10–11. Martin McCauley, *Origins of the Cold War, 1941–1949*, (Harlow: Pearson Longman, 2008), 106.

51. Haslan, *Russia's Cold War*, 2011, 1. Joseph Nye has written of the three different "schools of thought" for the causes of the outbreak of the Cold War. These are traditionalists who blame Stalin and the Soviet Union, revisionists who think that the United States was responsible, and postrevisionists who believe that it was a systemic problem. Joseph S. Nye, Jr. & David A. Welch, *Understanding Global Conflict and Cooperation. An Introduction to Theory and History*, (Boston: Longman, 2011), 134–136.

52. Nigel Gould-Davies, "The Logic of Soviet Cultural Diplomacy," *Diplomatic History*, Vol 27, No.2, (April 2003):195.

53. Marshall D. Shulman, *Stalin's Foreign Policy Reappraised*, (Boulder: Westview Press, 1985), 10.

54. Gould-Davies, "The Logic of Soviet Cultural Diplomacy," 2003, 195.

55. Light, *Soviet Theory*, 1988, 35 & 37.

56. Light, *Soviet Theory*, 1988, 41. Shulman, amongst others also makes this point, but also that Soviet foreign policy in the years from 1946 to 1952 can be split into two distinct periods, 1946 to 1948 and 1948 to 1952. Shulman, *Stalin's Foreign Policy Reappraised*, 1985, 257–259.

57. *Pravda*, February 15, 1956, 7.

58. Peter Shearman, *The Soviet Union and Cuba*. (London: Routledge & Kegan Paul, 1987), 5.

59. Hugh Thomas, *Cuba or the Pursuit of Freedom*. (London: Eyre & Spottiswoode, 1971), 418. Louis A. Pérez, *Cuba Between Reform and Revolution*, (New York: Oxford University Press, 2006), 136–141, Walter LaFeber, *The American Age. United States Foreign Policy at Home and Abroad since 1750*, (New York: W.W. Norton & Company, 1989), 189–190. Louis A. Pérez, *Cuba and the United States: Ties of Singular Intimacy*, (Athens, Ga: University of Georgia Press, 2003), 83–91. Jules R. Benjamin, *The United States and the Origins of the Cuban Revolution. An Empire of Liberty in an Age of National Liberation*, (Princeton: Princeton University Press, 1990), 62. Richard Gott, *Cuba. A new history*, (New Haven: Yale University Press, 2004), 93–101. In addition, LaFeber has also written that Washington did not want to let "unpredictable races into the Union," LaFeber, *The American Age*, 1989, 197.

60. Pérez, *Cuba Between Reform*, 2006, 137–138.

61. Samuel Farber, *The Origins of the Cuban Revolution Reconsidered*, (Chapel Hill: The University of North Carolina Press, 2006), 71. Benjamin has called this "semi-sovereignty." Benjamin, *The United States and the Origins of the Cuban Revolution*, 1990, 71. Gott has named it a "pseudo democracy." Gott, *Cuba*, 2004. 113. Soviet authors have described Cuba as an "anglo-American protectorate," and a "monopoly of the United States." E.A. Larin, *Kuba kontsa XVIII--pervoĭ treti XIX veka*, (Moscow, Nauka, 1989), 17. A.D. Bekarevich & V.A. Borodaev, *Velikii Oktiabr i kubinskaia revoliutsiia*, (Moscow, Nauka, 1987) , 17.

62. Pérez, *Cuba Between Reform and Revolution*, 2006, 143.

63. Quoted in Pérez, *Ties of Singular Intimacy*, 2003, 109.

64. Thomas, *Cuba*, 1971, 469.

65. Pérez, *Between Reform and Revolution*, 2006, 152. Thomas, *Cuba*, 1971, 469. In addition, Cuban-U.S. trade increased from $27m in 1898 to $300m in 1917. The reciprocity act of 1903 was highly important for this increase. LaFeber, *The American Age*, 1989, 197.

66. For the full effects of the relationship on Cuban society please see Pérez, *Ties of Singular Intimacy*, 2003, 113–148.

67. Pérez, *Between Reform and Revolution*, 2006, 169, Thomas, *Cuba*, 1971, 474–478.

68. Pérez, *Between Reform and Revolution*, 2006, 171–173, Thomas, *Cuba*, 1971, pp. 615–625. Gott, *Cuba*, 2004, 135–141.

69. For the impact of World War I on Cuba. Thomas, *Cuba*, 1971, 531–532 & 537–538. Regarding the impact of the Wall Street Crash please see Pérez, *Ties of Singular Intimacy*, 2003, 180–193.

70. Benjamin, *The United States and the Origins of the Cuban Revolution*, 1990, 87.

71. Pérez, *Ties of Singular Intimacy*, 2003, pp. 193–199. Benjamin, *The United States and the Origins of the Cuban Revolution*, 1990, pp. 87–89. Thomas, *Cuba*, 1971, 615–625. On this Thomas has written, "The reluctance of the United States to recognize the government caused its downfall – an act which cast long shadows over events in the 1950s a generation later." Thomas, *Cuba*, 1971, 635.

72. LaFeber, *The American Age*, 1989, 72.

73. Pérez, *Between Reform and Revolution*, 2006, 213.

74. Gott, *Cuba*, 2004, p.140. Sweig, *Inside the Cuban Revolution*, 2002, 126.

75. Benjamin, *The United States and the Origins of the Cuban Revolution*, 1990, 100–102.

76. Pérez, *Between Reform and Revolution*, 2006, 235.

77. Pérez, *Between Reform and Revolution*, 2006, 143.

78. Walter LaFeber "The U.S. Rise to World Power, 1776–1945" in *United States Foreign Policy*, ed. Michael Cox and Doug Stokes, (Oxford: Oxford University Press, 2008), 51.

79. Thomas G. Paterson, J. Gary Clifford, & Kenneth J. Hagan, *American Foreign Policy. A History since 1900*, (Lexington: DC Heath & Company, 1983), 263, 310–314. LaFeber, *The American Age*, 1989, 394–395.

80. William R. Keylor, *The Twentieth Century World and Beyond*, (Oxford: Oxford University Press, 2006), 60–64. Paterson et al, *American Foreign Policy*, 1983, 251. LaFeber, *The American Age*, 1989, 279–280.

81. Paterson et al, *American Foreign Policy*, 1983, p.295. LaFeber, *The American Age*, 1989, 272.

82. LaFeber "The U.S. Rise," 2008, 53.

83. LaFeber, *The American Age*, 1989, 284.

84. Paterson et al, *American Foreign Policy*, 1983, 291.

85. LaFeber *The American Age*, 1989, 340 & 329–331. Paterson et al, *American Foreign Policy*, 1983, 319.

86. LaFeber, *The American Age*, 1989, 301.

87. LaFeber, *The American Age*, 1989, 361–362.

88. LaFeber, *The American Age*, 1989, 363–370.

89. Paterson et al, *American Foreign Policy*, 1983, 389.

90. For the various discussions which took place between the Allied side during World War II please see William R. Keylor, *The Twentieth Century World and Beyond*, (Oxford: Oxford University Press, 2006), 172–178.

91. LaFeber "The U.S. Rise," 2008, 57.

92. Paterson el al, *American Foreign Policy*, 1983, 435.

93. Keylor, *The Twentieth Century World*, 2006, 245–246.

94. "The Charge in the Soviet Union (Kennan) to the Secretary of State," http://www.gwu.edu/~nsarchiv/coldwar/documents/episode-1/kennan.htm (accessed 14 April 2012). LaFeber, *The American Age*, 1989, pp. 449–452, Paterson et al., *American Foreign Policy*, 1983, 451–452.

95. Keylor, *The Twentieth Century World*, 2006, 243–244. Paterson et al, *American Foreign Policy*, 1983, 437. Regarding this LaFeber has written, "Marshall warned that American prosperity depended on European recovery." LaFeber, *The American Age*, 1989, 456.

96. Keylor, *The Twentieth Century World*, 2006, 41 & 251.

97. Haslan, *Russia's Cold War*, 2011, 110.

98. LaFeber, *The American Age*, 1989, 479–482 & 505. Paterson et al, *American Foreign Policy*, 1983, 457.

99. Caballero, *Latin America and the Comintern*, 1986. Daniela Spenser, *The Impossible Triangle: Mexico, Soviet Russia and the United States in the 1920s*, (Durham: Duke University Press, 1999). Clissold, *Soviet Relations with Latin America*, 1970. M. Lowry, *Marxism in Latin America from 1909 to the Present: An Anthology* (Humanities Press, Atlantic Highlands, NJ, 1950). W.S. Sworakowski, *World Communism: A Handbook 1918–1968* (Stanford, Ca: Hoover Institution Press, 1973).

100. Erik Ching and Jussi Pakkasvirta, "Latin American Materials in the Comintern Archive ," *Latin American Research Review*, Volume 35, Num 1, (2000): 138 – 149.

101. Gary Tennant *The Hidden Pearl of the Caribbean. Trotskyism in Cuba*, Revolutionary History, Volume 7, No 3 (London: Porcupine Press, 2000). Boris Goldenberg, "The Rise and Fall of a Party: The Cuban CP (1925–59)." Samuel Farber, "The Cuban Communists in the Early Stages of the Cuban Revolution: Revolutionaries or Reformists," *Latin American Research Review*, Vol 18, No 1, (1983): 59–83.

102. K.S. Karol, *Guerrillas in Power*, (London: Jonathan Cape Ltd, 1971), 55–186. Robert J. Alexander, *Communism in Latin America*, (New Brunswick: Rutgers University Press, 1957), 270–294. Pérez, *Cuba Between Reform and Revolution*, 2006, 183–233. Thomas, *Cuba*, 1971, 574–580. The Cuban Communist Party (PCC) changed its name to the Cuban Socialist Party (PSP) in January 1944. Sworakowski, *World Communism*, 1973, 101.

103. Helen Desfosses & Jacques Levesque, *Socialism in the Third World* (New York: Praeger Publishers, 1978). Luis Aquilar, *Marxism in Latin America* (Philadelphia: Temple University Press, 1978). Donald L. Herman, *The Communist Tide in Latin America: A Selected Treatment* (The University of Texas at Austin, 1973). Jan Librach, *The Rise of the Soviet Empire* (New York: Praeger, 1964). Rollie Poppino's *International Communism in Latin America 1917 –1963* (London: The Free Press of Glencoe, 1964). Timothy Ashby, *The Bear in the Back Yard. Moscow's Caribbean Strategy* (Lexington: Lexington Books, 1987).

104. Christopher Andrew & Vasili Mitrokhin, *The World Was Going Our Way. The KGB and the Battle for the Third World*, (New York: Basic Book, 2005), 27.

105. Nicola Miller, *Soviet Relations with Latin America 1959–1987*, (Cambridge: Cambridge University Press, 1989), 5–6.

106. Yuri Pavlov, *Soviet-Cuban Alliance 1959–1991* (New Brunswick: Transaction Publishers), 2.

107. Alexandr Fursenko & Timothy Naftali, *The Secret History of the Cuban Missile Crisis: "One Hell of a Gamble."* (London: John Murray, 1997), 12. Farber, *The Origins of the Cuban Revolution*, 2006, 144.

108. Farber, *The Origins of the Cuban Revolution*, 2006, 145 & 156. Fursenko & Naftali, *The Secret History of the Cuban Missile Crisis*, 1997, 12.

109. Farber, *The Origins of the Cuban Revolution*, 2006, 145 & 156. Fursenko & Naftali, *The Secret History of the Cuban Missile Crisis*, 1997, 12.

110. George J. Boughton "Soviet-Cuban Relations, 1956–1960," *Journal of Interamerican Studies and World Affairs*, Vol 16, No 4 (November 1974): 436–453.

111. Caballero, *Latin America and the Comintern*, 1986.

112. Farber, "The Cuban Communists in the Early Stages of the Cuban Revolution", 1983, 59–83.

113. Barry Carr, "Mill Occupations and Soviets: The Mobilisation of Sugar Workers in Cuba 1917–1933,"*Journal of Latin American Studies*, 28, (1996): 129–158. Barry Carr, "From Caribbean backwater to revolutionary opportunity: Cuba's evolving relationship with the Comintern, 1925–34" in *International Communism and the Communist International 1919–43*, ed. Tim Rees and Andrew Thorpe (Manchester: Manchester University Press, 1998), 234–251.

Chapter Two

Moscow, Havana, and the World Revolution

As detailed in the previous chapter, the victory of the Russian Revolution in November 1917 sent a seismic shock through the international system with many people taking great interest, tinted with considerable trepidation, in the events unfolding in Russia. On 8 November 1917 the Cuban newspaper *The Havana Post* stated,

> Soldiers and Workers Commission having overthrown Kerensky's Provisional Government announce programme of immediate peace, handing over large landed estates to peasantry; vesting authority in Council of Soldiers and Workmen's delegation. [1]

This quote perfectly illustrates the basis of much of this trepidation: the Bolsheviks' desire for "breathing space" that was to be created by removing Russia from World War I and their political ideology. However, interest was also apparent with the appearance of a number of left-wing groups around the world, with Latin America being no different as a number of such groups emerged throughout the region. It was the impact of the Russian Revolution, and also migration from Europe which was fundamental to their emergence. [2] This process was repeated in Cuba and left-wing politics on the island and Moscow's interest in it will be the main focus of this chapter.

Again as outlined in chapter 1, the Third International, or Comintern, was created in Moscow in March 1919 in the attempt to spark other revolutions. The first congress was dominated by Russian delegates and it could have been thought that Latin America would have been of little significance or interest for the organization due to geographical distance and the influence of the United States in the region. However, as a result of the existence of left-wing groups, Karen Brutents, Head of the International Department of the Central Committee of the Communist Party of the Soviet Union (CPSU) in the 1980s, wrote that Moscow did show interest in Latin America. This was despite the fact that none of the Bolshevik leaders had travelled to Latin America although Leon Trotsky had lived in the New World when he spent the years of the First World War in New York City, or that none had written extensively on the region.[3]

The Comintern's interest in Latin America was illustrated by the fact that the important Comintern agent Michael Borodin was sent to Mexico in 1919.[4] Moreover, at the Second Congress in August 1920, Latin America was represented by the aforementioned Mexican delegate Gómez and M.N. Roy.[5]

Latin America's standing within the Comintern can also be illustrated by the positions which the region's countries held in the various forums of this organization, with its structure closely resembling that of the Bolshevik party. As a result, the Central Bureau and the Presidium were the most important bodies within the organization. At the Third Congress held in the summer of 1921, Roy and an Argentinean delegate (name unknown) were both given consultative voting rights for the Comintern's Central Bureau. In December 1922 the Fourth Congress convened with the candidate member to the Central Bureau for South America being Stirner.[6] Again at the Fifth Congress in the summer of 1924, South America had one candidate member of the Central Bureau in the form of O. Pérez Solis, but the Brazilian Astrojildo and Stirner gained full membership to the newly created International Control Committee, with the Argentine V. Kodovela becoming a candidate member of the organization's Presidium. This was the first time that Latin America had such representation in the most important body of the Comintern.[7]

This, and Brutent's comments, would suggest that Latin America was of considerable importance for the Comintern leadership, but Caballero has written, "In the plan for fostering world revolution proposed by the Third International from its foundation in 1919, Latin America occupied the last place."[8] However, in 1925 a Latin American Secretariat was created within the Comintern, which in 1928 was enlarged to include a Caribbean Bureau and a South American Bureau.[9] In addition, the Sixth Congress of the Comintern held from 17 July to 1 September 1928 was highly significant for the region as in his opening speech to the Congress the organization's leader Grigory Zinoviev stated that Latin America had been "discovered."[10] This was important, and in conjunction with Joseph Stalin in 1927 talking about the Argentine economy and the creation of the Latin American Secretariat in 1925, it appeared that the region was increasing in significance for the Comintern and the Soviet leadership.

As detailed in chapter 1, the goal of the Comintern was to engineer another revolution. If this materialized, the result would be to help secure

Soviet security as the Soviet government would no longer be the sole socialist regime in the world. In short, this returns to the central tenets of the realist paradigm of International Relations. The increased interest in Latin America was in correspondence with this, but also Soviet policies toward the Developing World countries in general. That is that the Kremlin's real interest was not in this part of the world per se, but rather in the effects of any revolutionary activity in the less developed countries for the metropolitan states. Light's writings on this were also outlined in the previous chapter, but this principle was still applicable for Latin America because any revolutionary successes would have repercussions for the United States due to its investment in the region.

The idea of increased Soviet attention in Latin America is given more credence as Latin American representation in various Comintern bodies also increased at the Sixth Congress. Significantly the region gained full membership to the Central Bureau in the form of Mexico with R. Carrillo, Argentina with R. Ghioldi, Brazil with A. Ledo, Uruguay with E. Gómez, and Chile with Fermun-Araea. Furthermore, D. Reacko representing Colombia and Ecuador and significantly Cuba with López became candidate members. This will be detailed more fully in the next section of this chapter. In addition, Roco replaced Kodovela as the South American representative in the Presidium with Kodovela gaining membership to the International Committee. [11]

The year of 1928 was highly important for Latin American communist parties as not only had their representation in various Comintern forums increased, but in April 1928 the First Congress of the Latin American communist parties was held in the Uruguayan capital Montevideo, attended by 15 parties including the Cuban Communist Party (PCC). Moreover, a Soviet trading company, Yuzantong, had been created in Buenos Aires, which may partly explain the "hike" in trade which took place between the Soviet Union and Argentina in the late 1920s which will be detailed in chapter 3, and also Stalin's comments about the Argentine economy. However, the accusation has always existed that this trading company was really being used as a cover for more clandestine Soviet behavior, but even if the real purpose of this company was more clandestine activity it still illustrated increased Soviet interest in the region. In addition to this, the newspaper *El Trabajador Latinoamericano* began to be published, which Caballero believes was partly funded by money sent from Moscow. In June 1929 the Second Congress of Latin American Communist Parties was held in Buenos Aires, further illustrating the increased activities of left-wing parties in Latin America. [12]

As a result, a number of authors including Munck believe that the Comintern showed their most interest in the region during the "third period" of the organization's history. This was introduced at its Sixth Congress in the summer of 1928 and called for a "class against class" struggle. Eric Ching certainly believes this to be the case as he has written about Comintern activity in El Salvador in 1932.[13] This increased attention was underpinned by the ideas regarding Moscow's interest in the Developing World that were outlined in chapter 1. What drove this were the effects that unrest in colonial countries could have for the metropolitan states. The countries of Latin America may have gained their independence in the nineteenth century, but this was still applicable to the region due to the influence and power, not least economic, that the United States had in the continent.

As detailed above, the Latin American communist parties were extremely loyal to Moscow and the Comintern with the PCC being no different. However, in the years between the Russian and Cuban Revolutions, which is the focus of this book, Moscow's interest in left-wing activity on the island can be split into two distinct periods. The first was from the creation of the Third International in March 1919 until the Seventh Congress of the Comintern in August 1935 when the ideas of the "popular front" were introduced. The second period was from this point until January 1959 and the victory of the Cuban Revolution. The tactics followed by the Comintern in these two different periods may have been very different from one another and the Third International was disbanded in the summer of 1943, but Moscow showed considerable interest in Cuba during both.

THE PERIOD TO THE SEVENTH CONGRESS

Cuba appears to follow a similar path to those of the communist parties in the rest of Latin America, with the PCC being formed in August 1925 before gaining membership to, and representation in, various Comintern forums as has been detailed. Although this is the case, Carr has written that the PCC was "established relatively late," but Cabellero has stated

> the Communist Party of Cuba had the extraordinary opportunity (so far only experienced by the Chilean Communists) of being perceived not as an "international" movement but rather as an "off-spring" of the revolutionary traditions of Cuba.[14]

This revolutionary heritage was not just to the nineteenth century and the wars of independence, but also to the early twentieth century as a result of the appearance of forms of labor organization that had concentrated mainly on the sugar industry. With regards this Carr has written, "Yet collective worker action and strikes appeared in 1908–1912 and as early as 1902 in the Cruces and Cienfuegos area of Santa Clara province."[15] Moreover, Goldenberg has written of the Socialist Workers' Party being created as early as 1905 with it subsequently gaining membership of the Second International.[16] Further strike action amongst mill workers took place in late 1917 regarding the issues of union recognition and an eight-hour working day. Carr believes that these strikes failed due to a combination of reasons including the intervention of the U.S. military, but also that the strike action did not spread from Santa Clara and Camaguey provinces and that the mill workers did not gain support from the field workers.[17]

Further strike action occurred amongst mill workers in September 1924, but other social forces had started to come to prominence from the start of the 1920s onward with Pérez having written of the increase in nationalism at this time. This was evident in 1922 with the creation of both the Asociación de Buen Gobierno in Havana and also the Junta Cubana de Renovación in 1923.[18] Regarding this organization Pérez has written that it

> called for protection of national industry and commerce, agrarian reform, a new trade treaty with the United States, educational reform, expansion of health services, women's rights, and end to U.S. intermeddling in Cuban internal affairs.[19]

Also in 1923 Goldenberg has written that Carlos Baliño, a co-founder of the Socialist Workers Party and a contemporary of Cuban national hero José Marti, was fundamental to the creation of Agrupacion Comunista de la Habana which made contact with the Communist Party of Mexico.[20] Moreover, Thomas has written of other similar groups being formed in various parts of the island including in Manzanillo and Oriente provinces.[21]

As can be seen, Caballero was most certainly correct in his assertion that by the time of the creation of the PCC in August 1925 Cuba had a history of labor organization and movement. This was important for the fledgling PCC as was the contact made by Agrupacion Comunista de la Habana with the Mexican Communist Party, as an emissary, Enrique Flores Magón, was dispatched to Cuba to help in the creation of the party which was formed by the amalgamation of Agrupacion Comunista de la Habana and self-styled communists among university students.[22] Significantly on its creation the PCC "formally accepted the leadership of the Comintern in Moscow."[23] Carr has detailed the composition of the early PCC which mirrored other Latin American communist parties due to the importance of migrants in it. This did not only include Spanish migrants, but also Jewish and Chinese immigrants.[24] In addition to this, regarding the early PCC, Carr has written, "Cuban communism attracted a small but often outstanding group of individuals. Students, intellectuals, skilled workers and artisans." Unsurprisingly he highlights Julio Antonio Mella.[25]

Although this is the case, both Carr and Thomas have written of the somewhat inauspicious beginnings of the PCC with Carr detailing that due to the immigrant composition of the party its original pronouncements were written in Yiddish before being translated into Spanish.[26] In addition, Thomas has written "Flores Magón explained what a 'cell' was and how to organise 'nucleos' inside unions, clubs, sporting groups and so on."[27]

The PCC also faced other issues at this time including the death of Carlos Baliño in early 1926, a strong reaction against its creation by the Machado government with this leading to Mella's exile in 1926, and the irregular frequency of meetings of the party's Central Committee.[28] Contary to Goldenberg, Carr has written that the PCC had poor links to other communist parties in Latin America, especially with the Mexican Communist Party, and that "a product of infrequent communications which led to an almost total ignorance in Moscow of Cuban conditions."[29]

However, in the Comintern archive in the Russian State Archive for Social and Political History in Moscow, a letter exists which is dated 6 December 1919 written by Marselo Salinas who proclaimed to be the Secretary of the Communist Section of Cuba. In this letter Salinas asked for membership of the Comintern. In addition, this letter also had the heading of the Communist Party of the United States (CPUSA) on it.[30] No answer to this request exists, but a document entitled "Report on the Cuban Section of Cuba" dated 21 January 1920 sent from Madrid does. The author's name is absent from the report, but it states,

> When the steamer from Mexico to Spain stopped for a short time at Havana, Cuba, I went ashore and sought out Comrade Marselo Salinas, whose name and address had been given to me by a comrade in Mexico. Salinas was a member of the Industrial Workers of the World (I.W.W) and although he now calls himself an anarchist he is thoroughly in sympathy with the communist principles of the Third International. I think that conditions in Cuba were very like those in Mexico, and that it was the word "socialist" that had gotten into bad grace rather than the facts.
>
> At any rate there was no real Socialist Party in Cuba. There were some middle-class reformers who referred to their organisation as socialist, but nothing more.
>
> That is virtually all that I know about the movement in Cuba. I have heard that the Cuban unions are very radical in that they have negotiated very well-organised general strikes. Comrade Salinas was to send me a report on the whole economic, political situation in Cuba, but, up to present, it has not arrived.[31]

In light of this report, Salinas's request for membership to the Comintern was obviously not granted, but the existence of both his letter and this anonymous report are highly significant. Salinas's request illustrated the interest in left-wing politics and the Russian Revolution in Cuba, but also the island's links to the CPUSA. In addition, the author of the report dated 21 January 1920 may have only been in Havana for a matter of hours, but these documents unequivocally prove that Moscow had information, although severely limited, about Cuba even before the PCC had been created.

Another Comintern file on Cuba for 1924 contains a report on the anarchist movement within the island and also a copy of the newspaper *El Sembrado. Periódico Quincerial Ideas, Critica y Combate* dated 19 July 1924.[32] In addition, two letters exist from 1923 entitled "Federation of Students. Commission of Foreign Relations, University of Havana" which detailed student protests against the Venezuelan and Peruvian governments that had taken place in the Cuban capital. Very interesting is the fact that they were signed by P. de Entenza, director of Commission of Foreign Relations, and Mella.[33] This partly questions Carr's assertion that Moscow had little knowledge of Cuba, but significantly two years prior to the creation of the PCC, one of its founders was in correspondence with Moscow.

In addition, the PCC sent a letter to the Comintern dated 10 August 1925 detailing the conditions in Cuba.[34] Due to its date this must have been sent in the infancy of the PCC. A further report on the Cuban situation was sent to Moscow on 7 October 1925 written by Francisco Pérez Escudero.[35] Moreover, in a document entitled "Report on Cuba" sent in 1926 the report also states,

> In August 1925 at the time of the anti-fascist league organisation, Comrade Flores Magón, envoy of the Mexican Communist Party, helped with the formation of the Cuban Communist Party. At the congress from 16 to 18 August, the communist group accepted the 21 points for membership to the Third International and also the organisation statutes, directives and tactics, and demands for unity for this section of the Comintern.[36]

These documents are highly significant as not only do they illustrate the role of Flores Magón in the creation of the PCC, but also the party's loyalty to the Comintern from its inception.[37] In addition, the frequency of the reports may have been sporadic, but those which were sent were reasonably detailed in their content regarding the internal Cuban situation. The Comintern most certainly had information on Cuba from not only the time of the PCC's creation in August 1925, but from even before this.

Furthermore, Mella sent another report to the Comintern in 1926 entitled "Información para la Prensa Obrea y Revolución" that outlined both the general situation in Cuba and also reported that student and workers protests were taking place. The report began by stating, "A regime of terror underpinned by Yanqui imperialism exists in Cuba, with its victims being the proletariat." Mella continued in this dispatch with a concise history of Cuba from 1898.[38] In addition, Moscow also received in 1926 a "Report on Cuba" that not only described the island as being "semi-colonial" and that problems existed in the payment of public sector workers, but also described the composition of Cuba's society. It detailed this as 48 percent agricultural, 21 percent industrial, 16 percent in transport, 12 percent in domestic labor, and 3 percent intellectual. Moreover, it also stated that in 1923 Cuba had bought $181,717,272 worth of manufactured goods from the United States. [39]

This trend continued with another report sent by the Cuban party to the Comintern headquarters in the Soviet capital in 1926 that contained information on both the first Conference of the PCC held in May 1926 and also a transcript of Mella's trial. Interestingly this was written on PCC headed notepaper which also contained the hammer and sickle. [40] In conjunction with this a report entitled "Save the Lives of Vivo and Ordoqui" was also sent during 1926 which detailed the repression which the communist party and labor movement were facing from the Machado government. This report stated,

> The Machado government in Cuba has recently put into jail hundreds of strik-
> ers on the sugar plantations controlled by Wall Street, including of the Nation-
> al Confederation of Labour of Cuba and the Communist Party, two of them
> Jorge A. Vivo and Joaquin Ordoqui having been taken from their cells in the
> Principle Castle during the middle of the night, their whereabouts being un-
> known and in view of the systematic murder of other workers by the brutal
> Machado regime, we fear their death. [41]

This document's final dramatic statement did not come to fruition as neither Vivo nor Ordoqui were killed with Ordoqui subsequently becoming both the editor of the PCC's newspaper *Hoy* and also a significant member of the party illustrated by his participation in the discussions with Batista in the autumn of 1938 that resulted in the PCC gaining legal status. This will be discussed in the next section of this chapter, but it meant that Moscow had knowledge of this prominent leader of the Cuban Party from the mid-1920s.

These documents in the Russian State Archive for Social and Political History in Moscow prove that the Comintern was receiving information about Cuba and the situation on the island from soon after the creation of the Third International and even before the creation of the PCC. The frequency of these reports may have been sporadic, but their existence is important and challenges the idea of "an almost total ignorance in Moscow of Cuban conditions." [42] It appeared that Moscow did have information on Cuba, some of which was quite detailed, but that the real issue was the infrequency of information being received by the Comintern. Moreover, they also illustrate the importance of outside help, in the form of Flores Magón, in the birth of the PCC. [43] In addition, it also gives more credence to the idea detailed by Carr, Goldenberg, Poppino, and Caballero that Moscow was sending "agents" not just to Latin America, but also Cuba with Fabio Grobart being particularly significant. [44]

This would make it appear that Cuba was becoming more important for the Comintern, because as stated in the previous section of this chapter the Cuban delegate López became a candidate member of the Central Bureau of the Comintern at the Sixth Congress of the Comintern held in the summer of 1928.[45] This was an important appointment for the PCC as the party had not existed at the time of the Fifth Congress in the summer of 1924, meaning that at the first opportunity the PCC had gained representation to a significant Comintern forum. The fact the Comintern had "discovered" Latin America at the Sixth Congress may have aided this appointment, but it did not reduce the significance of this appointment for the PCC.[46]

This would correspond with Poppino's assertion that the staging of the Latin American Communist labor conference held in Montevideo in May 1929, which the PCC had attended, marked an increase in significance of Latin America for the Soviet leadership. With regards to this he has written

> The Montevideo conference was the first large-scale Communist meeting in Latin America and was generally interpreted by the Communists of this region as evidence that the leadership in Moscow had finally recognized their potential.[47]

The importance of Latin America and Cuba specifically increasing for the Comintern is given further credence by other documents in the Comintern archive in the Russian State Archive for Social and Political History as a significant change occurred in them in 1928. As detailed, documents on Cuba in the years from 1919 to 1928 exist in this archive, but they took the form of information being received infrequently by Moscow. The flow of information all appeared to be in one direction, from west to east, but this changed in 1928 as two documents exist which were sent from the Secretariat of the Comintern in Moscow to the PCC. The first letter, which stretches to seven pages and is dated 5 January 1928, begins by stating

> Dear Comrades, on the strength of documents in the possession of the Communist International and of information supplied by the delegates of the PCC concerning the political activity of the Cuban party during the last year, the Communist International confirms the correctness of the general policy lines laid down in its resolution in January which was borne out by facts. For this reason it confirms once more its contents and asks the Party to apply it to the full. The Communist International is also of the opinion that the changes which have taken place since in the political and economic situation of the country make it necessary to lay more stress on certain points in the present activity and the future tasks of the PCC.[48]

This is a highly important letter, and also contains instructions on how the PCC should proceed in the current situation in Cuba. It continues

> In order to accelerate the revolutionary process, it is essential for the Communist Party to take an active part in the struggle, and in the course of action, to unmask the national leaders, showing up their weak points and their incapacity

to lead the struggle to an end, which it has succeeded to get away the masses
from their influence and to become its sole leader. [49]

Toward the end of the letter highly significantly it is stated, "It goes without
saying that the task will not be accomplished peacefully simply by through
the ballot-box— it will be accomplished by revolutionary methods."[50] The
letter concludes by saying that it is a "splendid opportunity of intensifying its
political activity."[51] Interestingly the second letter was sent eight days later
on 13 January 1928 and called for the PCC to utilize the trade unions more
and it should also increase its role in the National Confederation of Cuba
(CNOC).[52]

These two letters sent in early 1928 are highly important for a number of
different reasons. Significantly they prove that the flow of information between Moscow and Cuba was not all in one direction as the earlier sporadic
correspondence that had been sent from Cuba to Moscow. Furthermore, they
also illustrate that the Comintern was both "dictating" tactics to the PCC and
also that the organization did have knowledge of the Cuban situation due to
the specific content of these instructions. Moreover, they also highlight the
fact that in the period between the Russian and Cuban Revolutions the radical part of the Kremlin's "dual track" diplomacy had shown interest in Cuba,
because if this had not been the case, these letters simply would not have
been sent. The nature of these letters would correspond with the aforementioned reports of the Comintern dispatching agents to Cuba, which increased
in the late 1920s and early 1930s. [53]

This increased attention was underpinned by the same general principles
of Comintern interest in Latin America that were detailed in the previous
section of the chapter: that is that the appearance of a successful revolution
would help safeguard Soviet security as the regime in Moscow would no
longer be the sole socialist regime in the world. The upshot of this was that
realism was highly significant. Furthermore, it is also in accordance with the
Kremlin's policies toward the Developing World in general due to the adverse effects for the metropolitan states of successful revolutionary behavi-
our in the less developed countries.

This was still applicable to Cuba because any revolutionary success on
the island would have negative repercussions for the United States due to the
nature of Cuban-U.S. relations. Furthermore, Havana's relationship with
Washington and the geographical location of the island further increased the
importance of Cuba for the Comintern and Moscow. At this time the U.S.
administration was still pursuing a policy of nonrecognition toward the
Bolshevik regime with, as detailed in chapter 1, the increase in U.S.-Soviet
trade in the late 1920s being underpinned by Washington's belief that this
would undermine the Soviet government. This only heightened the traditional Russian fear of insecurity which was highlighted in the opening chapter of

this book with both Tsygankov's ideas on the role of statists in Soviet foreign policy and also Grigor Suny's belief that this increased the prominence of constructivism within Moscow's foreign policy being detailed. In addition, Grigor Suny has also written

> Lenin, Stalin, and their successors saw the world through a realist lens, calculating how to preserve their power and the system they ruled, how to weaken their opponents, and how to win friends and influence people around the world.[54]

Moreover, McDermott has stated that after 1928, Stalin believed "that long-term Soviet security interests would be best served by a monolithic, strictly disciplined international Communist movement dedicated to the defence of the USSR."[55] This was crucial for Soviet attention in Cuba, because any revolutionary success on the island, which would negatively impact on the United States due to Cuban dependency on the U.S., could be used to counterbalance Washington's continued aggressive policies toward the Kremlin. Therefore it would help safeguard Soviet security. The outcome was that due to the Kremlin's prevalence of realist thinking, Cuba's geographical location, its relationship with Washington, and the nature of Cuban-U.S. relations Moscow's attention in the Caribbean island commenced from soon after the Russian Revolution. This is certainly contrary to the traditional perception that prior to January 1959 the Kremlin suffered from "geographical fatalism."

The timing of these letters is also highly significant as they appear to be part of the "discovery" of Latin America in general by the Comintern in the late 1920s. In addition, the timing is also important as the instructions sent to the PCC were highly radical and illustrate the ultra left position of the "third period" of the Comintern which would become official policy at the Sixth Congress in the summer of 1928. The letters may have been sent at the start of 1928, but by this time the "temporary stabilization" period of capitalism was coming to an end to be replaced by the "class against class" ideas of the "third period" that were detailed in chapter 1.[56] The instructions sent from the Comintern to the PCC that were contained in these letters, including the fact that it was revolutionary struggle and not electoral means that would produce their goals, perfectly illustrate the ideas of the "third period" of the Comintern. This is not only important for its own reasons, but again as outlined in the previous chapter it was in this "third period" that the Comintern showed its most interest in Cuba. In addition, as detailed, the importance of Cuba for this organization was only increased due to the island's location and its relationship with the United States, because revolutionary activity could be used to counteract Washington's prolonged aggressive policies toward the Kremlin which included the continued nonrecognition of the Soviet regime.

Caballero certainly believes that the Comintern focused its most attention on Cuba in the "third period" of this organization because writing about the era after the Sixth Congress of the Comintern in 1928 he wrote, "is the strong accent put on Brazil and Cuba (and to a lesser extent, Peru,) as perhaps the leading areas of Latin America revolution in the near future."[57] The economic situation on the island in the late 1920s was highly significant for this, with Pérez having detailed how recession came to Cuba even before the Wall Street Crash.[58]

However, even before this Cuban economic dependence on U.S. capital was vital for Moscow's interest in the island at this time. Pérez has detailed the U.S. economic domination of the island and has written,

> Low wages and weak labor organisations, persisting legacies of the colonial system, offered additional inducements to North American investment. These were not preferred conditions for foreign investors—they were requisite ones, and as such they formed part of the economic environment which the United States was committed to creating and maintaining. It was not sufficient to have preferential access to local markets and local resources. It was necessary also as a corollary condition to depress wages, prevent strikes, and discourage labour organizing.[59]

The effect of this was to heighten labor unrest and make it ever more extreme, which despite U.S. efforts was apparent in the number of strikes and appearance of left-wing groups. This gave Cuba the appearance as a "hot bed" of radicalism with this only increasing the attention which the Comintern focused on the island as the chance of revolutionary success appeared to be greater in Cuba than elsewhere in the region. The upshot was that an unforeseen consequence of the U.S. economic domination of Cuba was to increase Moscow's attention in the island, only heightening the significance of Havana's relationship with Washington for Soviet interest in Cuba.

Documents in the Comintern archive in the Russia State Archive for Social and Political History illustrate both this Soviet interest in Cuba, and also its continuation due to the correspondence between the PCC and the Comintern that took place from the time of these important letters of early 1928 onward. However, on first appearance it would appear that the post-1928 correspondence had returned to its previous format of information being sent from the Caribbean to Moscow. A number of documents exist which were sent by the "Liga juvenil comunista de Cuba," including a letter entitled "Informo" dated 5 September 1930 which was signed by this organization's general secretary, Angel Acosta. In this Acosta details the economic and political situation within the island and accuses Machado of defending the interests of Wall Street.[60] The brutality of the Machado regime was again highlighted in another document sent from the PCC to the Comintern which reported the death of Jose Wong. It begins by stating

> And again! A new bourgeois and fascist government has instigated a practical and brutal reign of terror against the working class of Cuba. The assassination of Comrade Jose Wong Ha Au Mentado is one more crime on the list perpetrated by the Machado regimes. [61]

This correspondence is important as it once again shows that this organization was in possession of information about the Caribbean island. Direct correspondence sent from the Comintern to Cuba may not exist in the archives after 1928 but this did not mean that the Third International was losing interest in Cuba, as the attention which the Comintern was giving to the island was conducted via the CPUSA and the Caribbean Bureau of the Comintern. [62] It appeared that Moscow was still "dictating" tactics to the PCC with this becoming apparent in December 1930 with a letter sent from the Central Committee of the CPUSA to the Central Committee of the PCC. A transcript of this exists in the Comintern archive in the Russia State Archive for Social and Political History, with it also being sent to the Executive Committee of the Comintern and the Caribbean Bureau. Moreover, it was also published in the U.S. periodical *The Communist* in January 1931. [63] In this it states that the PCC faces a number of challenges including a lack of bolshevization of the party and trained cadres, but also instability in its leadership. The CPUSA absolves the PCC of part of the blame for these shortfalls as it also states that the government repression which the Cuban party faced had also been significant. [64] However, it continued that the PCC needed to change its tactics when it states,

> The struggle for the legality of the trade unions must be brought to the foreground . . . The struggle for free speech must likewise be developed, but to call upon the masses to struggle for free speech in the abstract at a moment when the masses are starving will leave them cold and not start them into action. The raising of demands only for these democratic rights without making them merely a part of the struggle for bread has the effect of blurring the differences between the Communists and the Nationalists. It is our task to most sharply emphasize these differences. [65]

This is highly significant as it illustrates both that it was thought that the PCC desired to alter its policies, but also that great interest was being taken in the events in Cuba. Toward the end of the letter it is stated,

> The Communist Party of Cuba must broaden its ranks in order to be able to carry through the tremendous tasks now facing it. It must build its nuclei among the workers in the shops. All remnants of the old theories of manoeuvring with the masses and leading them from the top must be liquidated, and

instead the entire Party itself must become a mass organisation. The attraction into the Party of trade union officials and other individuals strategically situated is not in itself wrong. Only this must never be considered as a substitute for recruitment of the rank and file in ever greater numbers. The situation is most favourable, both for the recruitment of large numbers of energetic and devoted revolutionary workers into the Party and for rebuilding the revolutionary trade unions on a much broader mass basis. [66]

Due to the loyalty of the CPUSA to the Comintern, the American party was being used as a "vehicle" by this organization to transmit policies to the PCC. This in itself is significant, but so too is the fact that it appears that Moscow believed a revolutionary opportunity existed in Cuba. However, it is apparent that it was thought that the PCC desired to alter its policies. This continued in the summer of 1931 when the article "Our Present Tasks in Cuba" was published in *The Communist*. The article stated,

> The Caribbean buru of the Communist International has formulated a series of practical directives to the Central Committee of the Communist Party of Cuba suggesting concrete measures for the carrying out of the Party's immediate tasks. [67]
> These included the mobilization of the masses, organisation of unemployed, closer links with the trade unions and a strengthening of the party. [68]

Goldenberg has written of these Comintern criticisms of the PCC at this time with the lack of bolshevization of the party being particularly important. Central to this was the leadership of the PCC with Goldenberg having written that they

> were certainly revolutionaries, but just as certainly they were not Bolsheviks. Rather they were Communists of the heart, idealists, individuals, radical democrats, nationalists and anti-imperialists, regarding themselves as the most radical participants in the movement against Machado. [69]

The issue of nationalism was highly significant as Goldenberg and Carr both believe that this was a key motivating factor for the leadership of the PCC and even superseded their loyalty to Moscow. [70] This was also apparent when the PCC "ignored" the advice of the Comintern and did consider making overtures to caudillos about possible armed uprisings in 1930. [71] However, the PCC did mobilize a general strike in March 1930 with 200,000 workers participating in it which severely hit Havana and the neighboring port of Manzanillo. [72]

Carr also believes that other problems existed, predominantly that the PCC was too concentrated on Havana to the detriment of the rest of the island and that a time lag occurred between events and the information that the Comintern was receiving regarding Cuba; this was a problem which the

Comintern faced throughout its existence and was by no means unique to its dealings with Cuba.[73] However, in the year after the general strike of March 1930 policy changes did begin to take place with Goldenberg having even suggested a "purge" within the PCC occurred. Significantly he believes that they were underpinned by the directives from Moscow which had been communicated via the Caribbean Bureau.[74] The PCC focused more on agrarian issues and particularly workers within the sugar industry, but also the island's Negro community were all part of these policy changes.[75] On this Carr has written,

> Intensifying the drive to organise the most proletarianised segments of Cuban society was certainly consistent with the strategy of the Comintern's third period and the effort to penetrate the sugar sector is definitely one example of Comintern directives shaping the direction of the Cuban Communists' strategy.[76]

In addition, the PCC had become more prominent within the CNOC, but despite these policy changes, problems within the PCC appeared to continue to exist. In May 1933 the Cuban party sent a letter to the CPUSA asking for help from their U.S. counterparts and the Caribbean Bureau over a "renegade" part of the party under Sandalio Junco. A copy of this letter exists in the Comintern archive in the Russian State Archive for Social and Political History.[77] This not only illustrates that the PCC was continuing to experience internal problems, but significantly also that the Comintern had knowledge of them.

This letter's significance is further increased because 1933 marked the "high point" of Comintern activity in Cuba. In particular the general strike of August 1933 was key to this because although the PCC had not called for this strike to commence it became central to the unfolding events which brought the Cuban capital to a virtual standstill and would eventually lead to the end of the Machado government. Carr has described this situation as "the most substantial revolutionary opportunity seen in Latin America before the 1950s."[78] On 3 August 1933 the PCC issued a manifesto which concentrated on economic demands including the payment of all unpaid wages and an eight-hour working day. In addition, it even called for the creation of "soviets." Although this was the case, five days later, after an offer from Machado to meet the PCC dominated CNOC, the PCC called for the workers to return to work. On this Thomas has written that "the Communists had in fact decided that the danger of U.S. intervention was such that any recourse, even a temporary alliance with Machado, was licit in order to try and avoid it."[79] This fear was only heightened by the role of the U.S. Ambassador Summer Welles in the unfolding situation, which was outlined in chapter 1. However, regarding this decision both Carr and Goldenberg have stated that it was a mistake and resulted in public support falling for the PCC. Both blame the Comintern and its directives for this mistake with Carr even writing that envoys of the Caribbean Bureau were present at the meetings where these issues were discussed. It did, however, give the Cuban party legal status.[80]

Carr has argued that the importance of the call for the creation of "soviets," that continued throughout the island until October 1933, may have been overplayed and they were in reality "self-defence groups." He believes that this was particularly the case in the countryside, with Realengo 18 in the east of the island being highly radical, but that they may have also resulted from the PCC's recently acquired ability to act free of government repression.[81]

What is certainly beyond question is that many believed that the events of the summer of 1933, with the PCC being highly significant in them, were genuinely revolutionary. Writing in 1934 the Russian born journalist M.J. Olgin, who by this time was a prominent member of the CPUSA, wrote

> The revolutionary movement in India, Arabia and a number of other colonies, the victories of the Chinese Soviets, the revolution in Cuba, the revolution in Spain, the revolutionary uprising in Austria, the growing revolutionary movement in France and the U.S. are a few of the many upheavals marking the Third Period.[82]

His ideas may be slightly tempered by Olgin's close association with the CPUSA, but this most certainly cannot be said about Robert Kelly who in the early 1930s was the Head of the U.S. State Department Eastern European Desk. As quoted in chapter 1, LaFeber has interestingly stated "Kelly warned his superiors that if recognised, the Soviet Union would never keep agreements, but instead ferment revolution – as he argued, they were doing in Cuba."[83] Moreover, Carr has written,

> The Comintern did realise the significance for the prospects of an anti-imperialist revolution of events in Cuba—and the unique conjecture of the anti-Machado insurrection and the worker-peasant insurgency of August–December 1933—…was the most substantial Comintern presence seen in Latin America.[84]

The general principles that underpinned the Comintern were important for this; it was not the Developing World countries that most interested this organization, but rather the effects of revolutionary activity in these countries for the metropolitan states. This was only heightened due to the prolonged U.S. aggression toward the Soviet Union, illustrated by Washington's continued nonrecognition of the Soviet regime. The result of this was that revolutionary activity on an island in such a geographical location could provide a counterbalance to these U.S. policies. Moreover, Cuban economic dependence on the United States had both increased labor unrest despite attempts to prevent this and also brought recession to the island which had culminated in the Wall Street Crash. This labor radicalism had heightened Soviet attention in Cuba as it appeared that the opportunity of revolutionary success on the island was greater than elsewhere in the region. This had been an unforeseen consequence of Cuban economic dependence on the United States, but illustrated the importance of Cuban-U.S. relations for Soviet attention in the island.

Although this was the case, this revolutionary opportunity in Cuba quickly passed with the PCC once again facing repression from the government. A report from the PCC sent to the Comintern on 4 November 1933 details that this repression, which also included the events of Mella's funeral on 29 September 1933, had resulted in 120 deaths and 215 detentions.[85] As stated, Carr and Goldenberg believe the Cuban party made mistakes, with many of these being blamed on incorrect Comintern directives, particularly due to the radicalism of the "third period" which prevented the PCC from attempting to form alliances with reformists who were not communist.[86] This was symptomatic of the "third period" in general which, as detailed in chapter 1, Rees and Thorpe have described as "class against class has usually been seen as a disaster."[87] The Cuban situation in 1933 appeared to be no different from this. Moreover, the Comintern on a global scale throughout its history did not produce a successful revolution's outcome resulting in the Cuban episode by no means being unique but rather being in accordance with this general trend. In addition, other issues, but chiefly the importance of nationalism within the PCC, further reduced the likelihood of the Comintern's directives producing revolutionary success in Cuba.

However, this does not diminish the importance of the Comintern giving considerable attention to Cuba and the PCC at this time which is evident both from an examination of the organization's documents and also by the number of Comintern agents that were sent to Cuba in the late 1920s and early 1930s. Moreover, the Soviet Union also sent greetings to the Second Congress of the PCC in April 1934.[88] In addition, support remained for the Soviet Union and the Comintern in Cuba, illustrated by a proclamation from PCC in November 1934 for a demonstration on calle 7 in Havana on the anniversary of the Russian Revolution. The proclamation began by stating

> Stand up for the banner of the Socialist International, against the preparation for war and for the defence of the Soviet Union.
> Stop the move of German fascism and back the fighting spirit of the world leader of anti-fascism E. Thaelman.[89]

Although this was the case, the flow of information between Cuba and the Soviet Union had been sporadic, but particular attention was given to the events of the summer of 1933 when via the CPUSA and Caribbean Bureau, the Comintern played an important part in the PCC decision making process. This interest was driven by the underlying principles of the Comintern that were detailed in chapter 1; chiefly that if this organization engineered another successful revolution it would help secure the safety of the Russian Revolution. In short, the fundamentals of realism were underpinning this belief. Moreover, due to the traditional Russian fear of aggression from outside powers the ideas of statists and constructivism within Soviet foreign policy were also important. Interest in Cuba was only intensified due to the island's relationship with the United States, because any revolutionary success would have serious repercussions for the U.S. due to its financial investments in the island. Labor radicalism on the island only increased the chances of this occurring with this resulting from unforeseen consequences of the nature of Cuban economic dependence on the United States. Moreover, this further heightened Soviet attention in the island as revolutionary activity could be used to counteract prolonged U.S. aggression toward the Kremlin, including nonrecognition of the Soviet regime until November 1933. In addition, this interest began even before the creation of the PCC in August 1925, but increased due to the unfolding situation in Cuba in the late 1920s and early 1930s. In sum, the radical aspect of Moscow's "dual track" diplomacy had shown considerable interest in Cuba in the period from the creation of the Third International in March 1919 to the Seventh Congress of the organization in the summer of 1935. This was certainly contrary to the perception that prior to January 1959 the Kremlin had suffered from "geographical fatalism" with regards to Cuba specifically or Latin America in general.

THE PERIOD OF THE "POPULAR FRONT"

The revolutionary opportunity in Cuba in the early 1930s and in particular around the events of the summer of 1933 may have quickly receded, but it did not signal an end to the Comintern's interest in the Caribbean island. As stated in chapter 1, the tactics of the Comintern underwent fundamental change in the summer of 1935 as during its Seventh Congress the radicalism of the "third period" was replaced by the more cautious "popular front" strategy. Key to this was the advent of Nazism in Europe and Stalin's desire to defeat his internal opponents which required that local communist parties moved politically to the right. Central to this policy change was that communist parties were to work with local parties within the political system. This would be vital for Moscow's continuing relationship with the PCC in the period until the break in bilateral diplomatic relations in April 1952.

However, in a precursor of this congress, a meeting of Latin American communist leaders took place in Moscow in late 1934 to discuss the political situation in the region with importantly the Comintern leader Dimitri Manuilsky playing a prominent role in the meeting. Blas Roca, General Secretary of the PCC, represented the Cuban party, with the outcome of this meeting being detailed by the Peruvian Eudocio Ravines in the book *La Gran Estafa*. In this Ravines wrote,

> The great decisions of the Comintern for Latin America were insurrection in Brazil, a popular front in Chile, exaltation of nationalism in Mexico, and the formation of a mass party, a party of "our people" on the island of Cuba.[90]

This meeting in the Soviet capital in late 1934, the decisions made at it, and Manuilsky's involvement in them were crucial as it highlighted not just the Third International's continuing attention in Latin America in general, but Cuba specifically. Regarding this Garcia and Alonso have written, "Cuba was the laboratory where the tactics of Manuilsky's insurrection and the Popular Front of Dimitrov would be tested at the same time."[91]

Blas Roca returned to Moscow in 1935 when he again represented the PCC at the Seventh Congress of the Comintern. At this congress Roca became a candidate member of the Central Bureau of the organization, illustrating both his and the PCC's standing within the Comintern.[92] Roca has spoken of the problems in the international system at this time, chiefly the emergence of fascism, and the reforms which the Comintern implemented as a result of them.[93] In addition, Roca also addressed the congress and began his speech by stating,

> The Cuban delegation to the Seventh Congress expresses its full agreement with the line contained in the report of Comrade Dimitroff, and with the draft resolution under discussion by the Congress. The speech of Comrade Dimitroff not only has developed brilliantly a broad and bold tactic in the application of the broadest anti-fascist united front in the capitalist countries, but it also contains most valuable suggestions and teaching for the achievement of the most important tasks in the struggle against imperialism in colonial and semi-colonial countries.[94]

Due to the Comintern remaining the center of the world revolution and the PCC's loyalty to the organization, the sentiments of Roca's speech are not surprising.

In his speech Roca continued to detail how the Cuban party was adhering to these tactics, including attempts to create a united front with the Cuban Revolutionary Party. This may have ended in failure, but the PCC was influential in the creation of a Pro-Amnesty Committee to protest against the imprisonment of political prisoners. This committee comprised representation from amongst others "the Agrarian Party, the women Autenticas, the Cuban Revolutionary Party, Young Cuba, APRA (American People's Revolutionary Association), National Confederation of Labor, the Communist Party, and other organisations."[95] Significantly Roca stated that "the most important success" was due to the announcement of elections to be held in December 1935 and that,

> We have addressed all the anti-imperialist parties, proposing to them the adoption of a joint tactic in regard to the elections, with a proposal to participate on the basis of the formation of a united single candidate, but pointing out that if in a meeting of these parties active sabotage of the elections was agreed upon the formation of a front for common action, we are prepared to support such an attitude with all our forces.[96]

The PCC may have still have been illegal at this time, but their desire to create a coalition of this type was highly significant as it highlighted the Cuban party's loyalty to the Third International and adherence to the organization's new tactics of the "popular front."[97]

This was further highlighted by Roca's concluding comments of his speech when he said,

> Our Party will be able to fulfil the tasks raised by the Congress, to organize the anti-imperialist popular front, to carry forward the revolution, with the help and guidance of the Communist International, in light of the teachings of our dear leader, the great chief of the world revolution, Comrade Stalin.[98]

The revolutionary opportunity of the summer of 1933 may have receded, but the PCC was continuing to show its loyalty to the Comintern, with this organization also remaining interested in the Caribbean island. This is also apparent with an examination of the Comintern archives in the Russian State Archive for Social and Political History for the period from 1936 until 1940 as 39 documents on Cuba exist.[99] The flow of information was once again in a west to east direction from the Caribbean to Moscow with the documents predominantly outlining the situation on the island. This included correspondence from Blas Roca in 1937 and November 1938 on the Cuban political situation.[100] This, however, does not detract from the fact that the Comintern continued to have information on Cuba in the period after both the fundamental change in its tactics which were instigated at the Seventh Congress of the organization in the summer of 1935 and also Moscow's need for peaceful coexistence and collective security in its fight against fascism.

As outlined in chapter 1, this had resulted in the Soviet Union joining the League of Nations in September 1934. Although this was the case, dislike and distrust between Moscow and Washington remained, which in combination with the realist thinking that was prevalent in both the Comintern leadership and especially within the Kremlin, resulted in any revolutionary activity on Cuba providing a potential counterbalance to U.S. policy toward the Soviet Union.

In addition, interestingly in 1939 two documents exist in the archive of the Commissar for Foreign Affairs in the Russian State Archive for Social and Political History. The first is of a text entitled "Independent Cuba" written by Vyacheslav Molotov, Soviet Commissar of Foreign Affairs, on 2 November 1939 that was sent to the PCC newspaper *Noticias de Hoy*. In this not only was Molotov highly critical of the role of the United States in Cuba, and referred to the situation as "imperialism," but also that Moscow was in contact with Cubans living in Washington and the USA regarding Cuba. In addition, Molotov also referred to the Cuban newspaper *Diario de la Marina* as "fascist." What appears highly significant was that this was written in the months following both the Nazi-Soviet Pact which had been signed on 23 August 1939 and the onset of World War II. The impact of both on the PCC will be returned to later in this chapter. However, it seems that Molotov believed that Cuba would become more important for the Soviet Union due to the disruption in global trade due to the effects of World War II, but also that the Soviet Union had analyzed the Cuban response to the Nazi-Soviet pact as he wrote that he had produced a document entitled "What opinion of the Cuban Government" for the Supreme Soviet.[101]

This document is extremely important for a number of different reasons. Significantly it is not in the Comintern archive, but instead in the archive of the Commissariat of Foreign Affairs. This is highly significant as it shows that it was not just the Comintern that was interested in Cuba in this period, but rather members of the Soviet ruling elite with the Commissar of Foreign Affairs having knowledge of the Cuban island three years before the creation of diplomatic relations between Moscow and Havana. In relation to this, not only had he been able to produce a document for the Supreme Soviet on Cuba, but it was significant that this document had even been written. In a similar manner to Comintern interest in Cuba being underpinned by the effects that revolutionary success could have for the United States due to its investments in the region, the real focus of Soviet interest in the Cuban reaction to the Nazi-Soviet pact could be for the effects of the response on the island for the United States due to these same investments and possible disruption to trade. The existence of this analysis is highly significant as it illustrated the importance which the Soviet Union attached to Cuba and its relationship with the United States because if this had not been the case this analysis simply would not have taken place. Moreover, it appears that Molotov believed that Cuba may become more important for the Soviet Union due to the disruption in global trade that would result from World War II. This did take place once diplomatic relations had been created between the two countries in April 1942 and will be examined in chapter 3.

The other document dated 10 November 1939 re-publishes the one of eight days earlier, but was sent to the CPUSA.[102] This is important as it not only gives credence to the "real" purpose of the analysis of the Cuban response to the Nazi-Soviet pact being the reaction in the United States, but also that the CPUSA and people within the United States remained important in correspondence between Moscow and Cuba.

However, these two documents are important for other reasons as significantly Molotov was in contact with the PCC. Other avenues of correspondence with Cuba would not have been open to Molotov due to the lack of diplomatic relations in 1939, but they highlight the importance of the PCC and Cuba for the Soviet elite. In this manner, by 1939 the PCC enjoyed legal status and it also had a considerable membership. As a result, it would appear that the Cuban party illustrated the "successes" of the "popular front" strategy of the Comintern, increasing Moscow's attention in the Caribbean island. This would become increasingly important in the 1940s, but was in accordance with the central goals of the Third International; these were to try and cultivate another revolution and with regards to the Developing World the effects that revolutionary activity could have for the metropolitan states.

This attention was despite the Soviet Union having lost some of its "pariah" status in the international arena in the mid to late 1930s, highlighted by its recognition by Washington and its membership in the League of Nations. Although this was the case, tension between Moscow and Washington remained not least because of the fundamental difference between their respective political models and the signing of the Nazi-Soviet pact. The result was that any revolutionary success in Cuba could have negative consequences for the United States due to the nature of Cuban-U.S. relations at this time. The Platt Amendment may have been repealed in 1933, but Washington continued to dominate the island because in 1934 a new reciprocity act was signed with LeFeber having written, "The post-1933 period could be described as a transition for a de facto colonialism to a neocolonial arrangement."[103]

Moreover, these documents' very existence highlights the attention which the Soviet ruling elite gave to Cuba at this time. This is contrary to the idea that Moscow suffered from "geographical fatalism" with regards to Cuba and Latin America prior to the Cuban Revolution. In addition, these documents also illustrated that as in the period up to the Seventh Congress of the Comintern much of Moscow's information on Cuba was acquired via the United States and the CPUSA.

As a result various correspondences between the PCC and the CPUSA continued to take place at this time. This included Blas Roca writing to the Central Committee of the CPUSA on 6 February 1935 asking for a loan of 3,000 pesos.[104] In July of the same year the Small Commission of the CPUSA agreed to keep campaigning for the release of the Cuban Welcoming Committee who had been arrested on the island.[105] Solidarity between the two parties was highlighted in the resolution of the Central Committee of the CPUSA to the Seventh Congress of the Comintern which stated its desire, "to combat American imperialism and to render the utmost assistance to the national liberation movements especially in China, in the Caribbean and South America."[106] In addition to this illustrating the parties solidarity, it also showed that the CPUSA, and therefore the Comintern due to the American party's loyalty to the organization, perceived the United States as an imperial power and the PCC as part of a national liberation movement. This returns to the principal reason underpinning Soviet interest in Cuba: the effect of revolutionary activity on the island for the United States.

After discussions between Batista, Blas Roca, and Joaquín Ordoqui, the PCC had by the autumn of 1938 acquired legal status with the paper *Hoy* also being freely published from May 1938 onward. Batista's desire to win free elections was significant in this with Thomas having written that Batista's move to the left at this time had resulted in both a number of "benevolent laws" being passed and also from mid-1937 the Partido Union Revolucionaria (PUR) being allowed to exist. Thomas describes this as "essentially a front party" for the PCC with Juan Marinello being highly prominent in it.[107] Moreover, Thomas believes that Batista had,

> by mid-1938 alienated most of the respectable representatives of Cuban public life and all the old middle-class and professional groups; but he had popular support, he was admired and even, in a way, loved by the masses; the middle-class parties knew it and were paralysed by their own weakness from doing anything about it.[108]

Goldenberg has portrayed Batista as having more Machiavellian motives when he wrote that Batista had "turned to the Communists, fully confident that he could use them for his own purposes."[109]

Whatever Batista's motives were, an unforeseen consequence of the PCC gaining legal status was Soviet attention in Cuba as it appeared to prove the "successes" of the "popular front" tactics of the Comintern. These "successes" became more apparent at the party's Third Congress held in Santa Clara in January 1939. This was attended by 347 delegates with the PCC claiming to have some 23,300 members.[110] Undoubtedly the party's legal status aided these figures, but fraternal delegates in the form of Cavillo from Mexico, Morris from Canada, and Silva from Venezuela attended the congress. Significantly the CPUSA was represented by Wiliam Z. Foster and Alexander Trachtenberg.[111] The CPUSA presence is highly significant due to its continued close ties with the Comintern. In addition, the staging of the congress would only further illustrate the correctness of the "popular front" strategy, with the importance which Moscow attached to the PCC at this time being further highlighted by Molotov's correspondence with the Cuban party in November 1939 which was detailed earlier in this chapter.

In addition, the PCC gaining legal status also led to the Comintern journal *World News and Views* to state, "Batista...no longer represents the centre of reaction...the people who are working for the overthrow of Batista are no longer acting in the interests of the Cuban people."[112] This highlights the continued attention which the Comintern gave to Cuba and the correctness of the PCC's alliance with Batista, as it illustrated the "success" of the "popular front" strategy.

The further standing of the PCC within the Comintern was highlighted at the organization's Eighth Congress in June 1941. At this the Central Bureau fell in size to 37 full members and 24 candidate members. The difficulty of travel to the Soviet capital due to the Second World War may party explain this, but significantly Blas Roca became a candidate member of the Central Bureau.[113]

Soviet interest in Cuba had been an unforeseen consequence of the PCC gaining legal status, but the party's dalliance with Batista had other repercussions. This meant that the PCC could participate in the November 1939 elections for the Constituent Assembly, with Blas Roca writing that the parties of the left had won 344,051 votes which represented a "decisive majority" over the right.[114] In addition to this, relations with Batista also prevented the PCC from facing many of the ideological problems which the signing of the Nazi-Soviet pact in August 1939 had for other Latin American communist parties.[115] Garcia and Alonso have written that the PCC followed a neutral line while Blas Roca has described the actions of Chamberlain and Daladier as "anti-popular and anti-Soviet."[116] However, Goldenberg has written,

> The sudden switch in the international Communist line resulting from the 1939 Hitler-Stalin pact,..., had a much less adverse impact on the Cuban party than on many other Communist parties. Prior to the pact, the Comintern line had called for an international united front against fascism; but with the signing of the Soviet-Nazi accord and the start of the war, Communists everywhere were called upon to oppose involvement in an "imperialistic" conflict.
>
> This the Cuban Communists could do without compromising their collaboration with Batista, who—at least until the middle of 1941—had no inclination to let Cuba become embroiled in a faraway European conflict.[117]

This situation changed dramatically with the Nazi invasion of the Soviet Union in June 1941 and the United States entering World War II in December 1941. This also had a huge impact on the relationship between Moscow and Havana and the diplomatic effects will be examined in the next chapter, but it also fundamentally altered the role of communist parties in Latin America as a whole. Benjamin has written that, "they turned out to be some of the most effective anti-fascist organizers at the grass-roots level."[118] This was partly due to their links with the working class and that "their work was not inhibited by the popular Latin prejudices against North American Protestantism, liberalism and intervention."[119] The PCC was no different from this general trend within the region, but Benjamin believes that the PCC also gained in other ways. He has written,

> Once the Soviet Union and the United States became partners in the struggle against totalitarianism in 1941, Batista could place United Nations' rhetoric and Allied solidarity in the service of defending his important alliance with the Cuban Communists. Now that Soviet foreign policy coincided with U.S. wartime goals, the PSP became one of the most vociferous and effective supporters of close cooperation between the United States and Cuba. Under these circumstances, Batista was able to ignore U.S. complaints about the growing strength of the party.[120]

This highlights the significance of World War II for the relationship between the Soviet Union and Cuba in general with the PCC playing an important role within Cuban society during the wartime years. This only increased in 1942 when Juan Marinello and Carlos Rafael Rodríguez were appointed to Batista's cabinet. On accepting these positions they became the first Communist Party members in Latin America to hold such positions. This was truly historic and came only two years after Cuba's "progressive" constitution of 1940 with Alexander writing that Juan Marinello had told him in an interview "that the Communists were principally responsible for the fact that the 1940 Constitution was one of the most advanced, in terms of labor and social provisions, of any in the hemisphere."[121] Alexander does suggest that other parties, most notably the Auténticos, were also significant in this, but this is not to discount the influence of the PCC in the new Cuban constitution. Sweig believes Marinello and Rodríguez appointments marked "the height of Communist political participation in Cuban political policy."[122] In addition, regarding the PCC, Karol has written it was "the most important Communist Party in Latin America."[123] This sentiment was repeated by Alexander when he wrote, "Cuba, the 'Pearl of the Antilles,' has been the scene of operations of one of the most important and powerful of the Latin American Communist Parties."[124]

This was important as it meant that the PCC was in line with the ideas of the "popular front" strategy which the Kremlin pursued at this time. As a result, Soviet interest in Cuba is not surprising as the PCC was enjoying more "success," both in terms of its membership and political participation, than other Latin American communist parties at this time. Moreover, as detailed, Garcia and Alonso have described that the Comintern perceived Cuba as being a "laboratory" from the time of the meeting of the Latin American Communist parties in late 1934 in Moscow.[125] It appeared that this "laboratory" was producing positive results. In addition to this, these historic PCC appointments achieved on an island in Cuba's geographical location would have made it somewhat strange if Moscow, as the capital of the world revolution, had ignored them.

The Second World War had a number of consequences for the relations between Moscow and Havana, while also fundamentally changing the role of the PCC within Cuban society, but it had been these, and the alliance between Moscow and Washington, that had given the PCC the opportunity to gain access to Batista's government. This was somewhat ironic, but it did illustrate the "successes" of the "popular front" of the Comintern. However, the standing of the PCC within the island was further improved by the dissolution of the Comintern in May 1943.[126]

On this Poppino has written,

> The attitude and the prestige of the Latin American Communist parties were further enhanced by actions such as the formal dissolution of the Communist International (Cominitern), which led Latin Americans to believe that the Soviet Union no longer encouraged world revolution, and by the propaganda efforts of the Soviet Union and its major allies to portray Soviet communism as a variant of democracy. The Soviet Union came to be regarded as a distant, powerful, and friendly giant among nations disposed to cooperate with free nations everywhere for the betterment of mankind. By extension, the Latin American Communists were viewed as primarily nationalists, basically democratic, and seeking, like members of other parties, to increase their influence by peaceful, constitutional means.[127]

Although this was the case, suspicion of Latin American Communist parties remained, with the PCC being no different. However, in 1944 in an attempt to defuse this suspicion the PCC, in line with other communist parties in Latin America, changed its name to the Partido Socialista Popular (PSP). On this Alexander has written,

> Juan Marinello , . . explained this change in name as a manoeuvre to limit the effectivness of the campaign being waged by "reactionaries" against the Communists on the basis of the "Comunista" part of their title. He went on to say that the change in name was a very successful move and gained the Party just what it wanted, a big increase in strength.[128]

This did appear to be the case because the PSP did very well in the 1944 Presidential elections. In addition, at the end of the World War II some estimates have the party's estimated membership as high as 50,000.[129] Furthermore, in terms of votes cast the PSP reached its "all-time high-water mark" in the parliamentary elections of June 1946 when it polled 176,000 votes or 10 percent of the entire ballot.[130] This would also appear to be in accordance with Alexander having written, "The Latin American Communists were at their zenith of their power and influence during 1945 and 1946."[131]

However, it is contrary to the ideas of Bethell and Roxborough who have detailed "a marked shift to the right"[132] taking place politically in the region in the immediate aftermath of World War II. Specifically with regards to Cuba, reports of intimidation against PSP members exist and in January 1945 these intimidations even extended to Soviet couriers entering Cuba.[133]

Ironically, in the period immediately after the end of World War II relations between the PSP and Moscow appeared to be at their lowest ebb for some time. Key to this was the Cuban party's relationship with the CPUSA. Prior to this, as detailed, this relationship had been crucial for the PCC due to both the solidarity between the two parties, but also as the Comintern had used the American party as a "vehicle" through which to communicate with the PCC. However, in the mid-1940s this close relationship caused tension to appear between the Moscow and the PSP.

In 1945 the influence of "Browderism" within the CPUSA came to a sudden end. Earl Browder, the leader of the American party, had mistakenly concluded from the events of the Tehran conference in December 1943 when Stalin, Winston Churchill, and Franklin D. Roosevelt had met that peaceful compromise would continue after the end of hostilities. As a result, he proposed that the CPUSA should be renamed and that its members should work within the two party U.S. political system.[134] These ideas incurred the wrath of the Kremlin and were denounced in an article by the French communist Jacques Duclos whose critique of Browder's policies was scathing. In this article Duclos wrote,

> However, while justly stressing the importance of the Teheran Conference for victory in the war against fascist Germany, Earl Browder drew from the Conference decisions erroneous conclusions in no ways flowing from a Marxist analysis of the situation. Earl Browder made himself the protagonist of a false concept of the ways of social evolution in general, and in the first place, the social evolution of the United States.[135]

Crucially for the PSP Duclos cited the Cuban party as being one which had followed Browder's ideas when he wrote, "the Communist Parties of several South American countries (Cuba, Colombia) regarded the position of the American Communists as correct and in general followed the same path."[136]

Although this was the case, Blas Roca has stated in an interview that "in the decade of the 1940s Browderism did not have great repercussions, although some people thought it had, but it had no practical effect; simply the Party continued on the principles of Marxist-Leninism."[137] However, he makes no direct reference to the PSP, refers instead to the parties in Venezuela, Colombia, Panama, and Chile, and interestingly states that it was the effects of the Marshall Plan that had the most effect on Cuba.[138] As this interview was conducted in 1984 an element of revisionism may be apparent, but it would appear that Blas Roca was being to an extent disingenuous.

With regards to the activities of the PSP within Cuba, Roca seems to be correct as the party continued to perform well in Presidential elections, had a large membership, and played a significant role in Cuban political life. This is significant and will be examined, but "Browderism" most certainly did affect its relationship with Moscow. No documents on Cuba in the archive for the Commissariat of Foreign Affairs exist at this time. However, this did not mean that the Kremlin had lost interest in Cuba as illustrated by the creation of the Institute of Cuban-Soviet Cultural Exchange in Havana in the summer of 1945, but relations with the PSP had soured. This institute and its effect on Soviet-Cuban relations will be examined in depth in the next chapter, but significantly it took until December 1946 for a prominent member of the PSP to participate in its activities.[139] This appeared surprising as it could have been thought that due to the institute's importance for the Kremlin's interest in Cuba and the PSP's loyalty to the Soviet Union, members of the Cuban party would have been involved in its activities from its creation. With this not being the case it highlights the tension that existed between Moscow and the PSP over the issue of "Browderism." This is only heightened due to the inclusion of the PSP in Duclos's article which had purged Browder and brought his influence within the CPUSA to an end.

The Kremlin may have been unhappy at the PSP's close association with "Browderism" in the CPUSA, but its size and "successes" meant that it could not simply ignore the Cuban party especially as these events had taken place on an island in such a geographical location. The Comintern may have been disbanded in 1943, but the principles of the "popular front" strategy appeared to remain important, because in the 1948 Presidential election the PSP won some 140,000 votes or about 7.5 percent of the entire ballot. [140] The more "success" the PSP continued to have within the Cuban political system the more that the Kremlin would have believed that a revolutionary opportunity existed on the island. This was evident by the creation and backing that Moscow provided for the aforementioned Institute of Cuban-Soviet Cultural Exchange.

Crucial to this was the fact that the wartime alliance between Moscow and Washington had come to a sudden and abrupt end and the subsequent onset of the Cold War. As detailed in chapter 1, the United States, after George Kennan's "Long Telegram" of February 1946, concentrated on containing communism which was evident with the advent of the Marshall Plan in Europe. This may have prevented the spread of communism into Western Europe, but it also heightened Soviet anxiety regarding its security with this being a return to the age-old Russian concern of facing hostile outside powers. At this time Europe may have remained the center of geopolitical issues, but it was at this very moment that Soviet interest in Cuba increased. The island's location and relationship with the United States were key to this, because any communist success in Cuba could have repercussions for U.S. investments on the island and undermine U.S. capital in general. In short, this could counteract events in Europe. This would appear to be in line with Mearsheimer's ideas on realism that states act to maximize their power at the expense of others, and Grigor Suny's belief that the Soviet leadership displayed realist thinking from soon after November 1917, which were both detailed in chapter 1. In addition, it is also in accordance with Moscow's policies toward the Developing World in general that were also outlined in the previous chapter.

However, this certainly questions the idea that prior to January 1959 the Kremlin suffered from "geographical fatalism" with regards to Cuba specifically or Latin America in general, as it very much appeared that Moscow was trying to exert its influence on a global scale. Moreover, this was taking place while Stalin was still leader of the Soviet Union, which is important as it has traditionally been thought that this only commenced after the changes that were implemented in Soviet foreign policy in the aftermath of his death in March 1953.

The PSP's "rehabilitation" into the Soviet fold was also aided by Blas Roca's pamphlet *Al Combate* that was published in February 1946 in which he "pointed to the Party's 'error' in the recent past, which it blamed on the nefarious influence of the now deposed Earl Browder."[141] Tension may have existed, but simply due to the nature of Cuban-U.S. relations, the geographical location of the island, and the "success" of the PSP meant that the Soviet Union could not ignore it, with this acting as a possible counterbalance to U.S. policies in Europe.

The situation is further complicated by Cuba's internal political situation at this time. It may have been moving ever more to the right with the onset of the Cold War, illustrated by the PSP's removal from the Confederation of Cuban Workers (CTC) and cases of intimidation against PSP members and volunteers existing, which included in April 1947 the PSP radio station *Mil Diez* being taken over by force by the Ministry of Communication.[142] Moreover, a number of Soviet citizens were arrested on the island in June 1949, which will be detailed more fully in chapter 3.[143] In addition to the move to the right the Cuban political system also became increasingly violent and corrupt at this time. However, as this took place it meant that the PSP retained significance within the island's political situation due to the continued perception of PSP members as being honest and hardworking. Thomas has written that in an effort to curb the political corruption some parties considered forming alliances with the PSP.[144] Furthermore, Pérez-Stable has written, "PSP effectiveness within the political process strengthened constitutional democracy as the emergent logic of Cuban Politics."[145]

The result was that the PSP provided legitimacy for the Cuban political system which would have disappeared if the party had been outlawed, making an already tense political situation worse. Both Ramón Grau's and Carlos Prio Socarras's governments were unwilling to do this as the PSP remained legal until after Batista's return to power in 1952. The PSP continued to have influence in the Cuban political system as late as 1952 when at the time of Batista's coup the party had nine seats in the lower house of the Cuban parliament. This led Pérez to write, "the party remained an effective political contender."[146] In sum, in the late 1940s and early 1950s the PSP performed an important role within the Cuban political system. However, this also highlighted the "successes" of the "popular front" strategy which in turn increased Moscow's interest in the PSP and Cuba. This also impacted considerably on the bilateral diplomatic relationship between the Soviet Union and Cuba and will be examined in the next chapter.

In addition to this, it also resulted in Cuba appearing to buck the regional trend of politics moving ever more to the right at this time. Government harassment of the PSP and its members may have taken place, but it played a significant part in Cuban politics and remained legal for a much longer period than communist parties elsewhere in Latin America. The PSP continued to have legal status after the onset of the Cold War and subsequent events such as the Berlin airlift and start of the Korean War. Cuban economic dependence on the United States remained at this time, but this treatment of the PSP would suggest a degree of political independence from Washington existed. This has not traditionally thought to have been the case.

Soviet attention in Cuba is further evident due to the existence of documents that exist on Cuba in the archive of the Commissariat of Foreign Affairs. After a gap of ten years this archive has documents on Cuba with a report on the PSP dated 25 November 1950 prepared by V. Grigorian, Chairman of the International Department of the Central Committee, for Molotov. This report is a detailed history of the Cuban Communist Party since its creation in 1925, the reasons for its name change, and the leaders of the party and their positions within it. Moreover, it also states that as of 1 January 1950 the PSP had 40,000 "active" members and 100,000 "nonactive" members. It also details that *Noticias de Hoy* had a readership of 20,000 and that in July 1950 the Party organized protests against the U.S. intervention in Korea. Interestingly it also reports that an anti-communist front had been created in Cuba at the same time. However, it states that despite facing government repression, "The Peoples' Socialist Party of Cuba appears to be one of the strongest and most influential communist parties in Latin America. They show effective assistance to the other Latin American communist parties."[147]

The content of this report appears to be providing basic information for Molotov about the Cuban party and the situation on the island suggesting that he did not possess a great knowledge of either. However, due to the aforementioned report "What opinion of the Cuban Government" that the Soviet Commissar for Foreign Affairs had prepared for the Supreme Soviet in August 1939, it seems that this report of November 1950 was merely providing Molotov with up-to-date information on the situation in 1950 as the history of the Party constitutes only a small part of the report's overall content. Moreover, the very fact that the report exists is highly significant as it highlights both the Soviet Union's interest in Cuba and also that the tension of "Browderism," which significantly is not mentioned in the report, had receded. However, the membership of the party is referred to, which is important as it illustrated the "success" of Soviet policies due to the PSP's loyalty to Moscow. Significantly one week later on 2 December 1950 this report was forwarded to Georgy Malenkov, Anastas Mikoyan, Leventi Beria, Lazar Kaganovich, Nikolai Bulganin, Nikita Khrushchev, and Stalin himself. The outcome was that the pinnacle of the Soviet ruling elite was receiving information regarding Cuba and the PSP, illustrating Moscow's interest in both.

In addition to this, Grigorian prepared a shorter report for Stalin that is also dated 25 November 1950. The report focused on Juan Marinello having been in Moscow as part of the delegation of Latin American communist parties and how he had become "familiarised with Soviet life" while in the Soviet capital. It was forwarded to Malenkov, Molotov, Beria, Mikoyan, Kaganovich, Bulganin, and Khrushchev.[148] Due to the principles of the Great Man Theory detailed in chapter 1, it is crucial that this report was written for Stalin, because due to his domination of the Soviet political system at this time it further highlights the attention which Cuba was receiving from the Kremlin in the early 1950s. If this had not been the case, this report for Stalin would simply not have been written.

In addition, it corresponds with what Marinello said in an interview about his trip to Moscow in 1949, when he stated that he saw the horrors of the aftermath of World War II, but also the advances made in the Soviet Union. Moreover, he also stated that he had not had the opportunity to meet Stalin, making the report which the Soviet leader received about Marinello less surprising.[149] The result was that Stalin was merely acquiring information on the leader of the PSP, but the existence of the report illustrates both his and thus the Soviet Union's interest in the PSP and Cuba.

On 10 January 1951 Grigorian sent another report to Stalin detailing the situation regarding the PSP newspaper, *The Final Hour*. It was also forwarded to Malenkov, Molotov, Mikoyan, Beria, Kaganovich, Bulganin, and Khrushchev.[150] Moreover, on 11 February 1951 Molotov received a request for 300 tons of cotton paper for this newspaper. On the following day not only did the Soviet Commissar for Foreign Affairs agree to this request, but he increased the shipment to 500 tons.[151] The existence of these documents is highly significant as they further highlight the Soviet interest in Cuba and the PSP. Moreover, it also illustrates that Moscow continued to be willing to fund communist newspapers in Latin America in the 1950s as it had done in the 1920s with *El Trabajador Latinoamericano*, which was detailed earlier in this chapter. In addition, the documents prove that the very top of the Soviet elite were receiving information about both Cuba and the PSP.

The outcome was that as long as the PSP continued to play an important role within the Cuban political system the Kremlin believed that there was a revolutionary opportunity on the island with this underpinning its attention on Cuba. The PSP may have felt the wrath of Moscow in 1945 over the events that brought "Browderism" to an end within the CPUSA, but the Cuban party's "successes" also meant the Soviet Union could not ignore the Caribbean island. Events far removed from the Caribbean were also important because as a result of Cuba's geographical location and relationship with the United States, any revolutionary activity on the island could have negative repercussions for U.S. capital and therefore counteract U.S. policies elsewhere which Moscow perceived as being anti-Soviet. This included Europe, but also after 1950 the Korean peninsular due to the onset of the Korean War. The Kremlin very much displayed realist thinking, and significantly the documents that exist in the archive of the Commissariat of Foreign Relations on Cuba are after a ten year gap dated 1950 giving credence to the fact that geopolitical considerations were significant in Soviet interest in the Caribbean island. Moreover, prior to January 1959 the Soviet leadership most certainly did not suffer from "geographical fatalism" with regards to Cuba. This is contrary to traditional thinking regarding Soviet policies toward Cuba specifically and Latin America in general at this time.

The last document that refers to Cuba that exists in the archive of the Commissar for Foreign Affairs in the Russian State Archive for Social and Political History is dated 2 April 1952 and details the break in diplomatic relations between the Soviet Union and Cuba that took place in April 1952, a matter of weeks after Batista returned to power in Havana. This will be examined more fully in chapter 3, but it is not surprising that with the end of bilateral diplomatic relations that no documents would exist in this archive on Cuba from this point onward. However, many of the documents that do exist, and have been cited above, are not related to the Cuban government, but rather the PSP and before it the PCC. Therefore, the lack of such documentation after April 1952 is symbolic of an apparent downturn in the Kremlin's interest in the Caribbean island resulting from the potential for revolutionary success on the island appearing to have receded with Batista's return to power. Significantly Batista's attitude to the PSP had changed considerably from the 1940s and earlier as not only were members of the Cuban party not in his government of the 1950s as they had been previously, but the party was also outlawed. In short, by breaking relations with the Soviet Union and outlawing the PSP, Batista illustrated to Washington his pro-U.S. credentials, which in the increasingly tense geopolitical situation of the 1950s was highly important. However, this also put Cuba in line with the rest of Latin America and the political move to the right which had taken place. In addition, the United States hegemonic power in the region, and dislike for communism, was illustrated in the summer of 1954 with the removal of the progressive government of Jacob Arbenz in Guatemala.[152] It very much appeared that in the early to mid-1950s the opportunity of revolutionary success was at its lowest ebb in Latin America and Cuba for some time. This was somewhat ironic as this coincided with Stalin's death in March 1953 and the changes in Soviet foreign policy that were detailed in chapter 1 that resulted in Moscow attempting to acquire a much greater global presence.

Even after April 1952 the PSP followed the policies of the "popular front" that it had pursued since the summer of 1935 and the Seventh Congress of the Comintern. This organization may have been disbanded in 1943, but these policies had brought the Cuban party its "successes" of the 1930s and 1940s. Its belief in these policies was further illustrated when they famously described Fidel Castro's attack on the Moncada barracks of July 1953 as "putchism." In addition, even as late as 1957 Gott has written, "Marinello still dreamed of a popular front that would organize strikes and demonstrations, and participate in elections, and the Party remained hostile to groups supporting a strategy of armed insurrection." [153]

As the 1950s progressed, this left the PSP somewhat peripheral to the political events on the island, but Alexander has described the party adapting a form of "dual Communism" of simultaneously having both a clandestine and legal organization with this aiding its survival in the changed political landscape of post 1952 Cuba.[154] However, during 1957 their policies toward Castro's movement began to change, with this accelerating in 1958. On this, Karol has pointedly written, "Only in 1958 did the Party accordingly take the weighty step of making direct contact with the Sierra, long after all the other opposition forces had done so."[155] This culminated in the "unity pact" between Castro's 26 July Movement and the PSP signed on 20 July 1958. Thomas has argued that the repression which the PSP faced from Batista's government at this time was also significant in their decision to align themselves with Castro's movement.[156]

As outlined in the previous chapter, Fursenko and Naftali, Farber, and Boughton have all written that the "unity pact" in conjunction with the changes in Soviet foreign policy implemented in the aftermath of Stalin's death were crucial to the tentative interest which the Kremlin took in Castro's movement before January 1959.[157] Prior to this, Soviet interest in the revolutionary opportunity on the island did appear to have lessened after the break in bilateral diplomatic relations in March 1952.

Despite this the PSP had remained loyal to the Kremlin throughout this period and attention on Cuba within the Soviet Union also continued. These were highlighted by the PSP's presence, in the form of Blas Roca, at the 19th and 20th Congresses of the Communist Party of the Soviet Union (CPSU) held in Moscow in October 1952 and February 1956, respectively.[158] Interestingly, Marinello has spoken of his visit to Moscow in 1953 during which he and Blas Roca attended celebrations in the Soviet capital for the 100th anniversary of the birth of José Marti. He has said that it was attended by a number of important people and that "the Soviet Union was represented by Ilya Ehrenburg, then President of the Writers' Union."[159]

In addition to this, Soviet attention in Cuba in the 1950s also comprised limited levels of trade and Soviet press reports of events on the island. These will be examined in the next chapter, but are indicative of Soviet attention in Cuba in the period from the end of bilateral relations in April 1952 to the victory of the Cuban Revolution in January 1959. Thus some interest in and knowledge of the island remained in the Soviet Union, but this was by no means to suggest that it had been to the level or acquired in such a "systematic" manner as had been the case before April 1952. This is understandable due to both the end of bilateral relations and the lack of an organization such as the Comintern which had been so important in the earlier relationship between the PCC and Moscow.

THE SOVIET INFLUENCE IN CUBA

In his speech to the First Congress of the PCC on 17 December 1975 Fidel Castro said

> We owe a debt of great gratitude to the glorious Party of the Soviet Union and its heroic people who will never be removed from our hearts. In their solidarity with Cuba, a country situated thousands of miles in distance from the Soviet Union, they carry out the internationalism of Marx, Engels and Lenin and the immortal October Revolution that shows with its invincible strength the destination for this continent.[160]

Similar sentiments were apparent in a speech Castro gave five years previously at the celebrations for the 100th anniversary of Vladimir Lenin's birth held in the Charlie Chaplin Theatre in Havana. In this he stated, "that without the October Revolution of 1917, Cuba could not have become the first socialist country in Latin America."[161] In addition, more recently in *My Life* Castro has insinuated similarities over the humble beginnings of the Bolshevik party under Lenin in Minsk, Belorussia and the 26th July Movement in the lead up to the attack on the Moncada barracks in the summer of 1953.[162]

Uncertainty over Castro's relationship with Leninism in January 1959 has always existed and a degree of revisionism may be apparent in Castro's speeches of April 1970 and December 1975 cited above, due to the existence and nature of Soviet-Cuban relations when these two speeches were made. The same accusation can also be made regarding the article entitled "La Revolución de Octubre y su Influencia en Cuba" written by Erasmo Dumpierre that was published in *Bohemia* on 21 April 1967 to mark the 50th anniversary of the Russian Revolution. This article charts links between the two countries from the time of the Russian Revolution including the birth of the PCC. In addition, Dumpierre states,

> The influence of the October Revolution reverberated in the subsequent revolutionary fight of the Cuban people, which culminated in the victory of the ideas of Marxist-Leninism in the first socialist country in Latin America. [163]

Moreover, attempts to illustrate the longevity of the relations between the two countries were also evident in both Antonio Núñez Jiménez's, Minister of Agarian Reform, article "Cuba fue conocida en Rusia desde 1530" that was printed in *Bohemia* in April 1962 and "Tres rusos en la Guerra del 95" that was also printed in *Bohemia* on 10 July 1970. This article did not just detail how three Russians, N. Melentiev, E. Konstatinaich, and P. Stretlsov, travelled to Havana onboard the ship "Nicaragua" and fought with Chinese migrants in Antonio Maceo's army, but also contained a cartoon of them fighting for the rebel army. [164] Revisionism does appear to be apparent in this article when compared to "Two months in Cuba in October" printed in the Russian newspaper *Vestnik Evropi* in May 1898, which was written by Stretlsov on his return from Cuba. This portrays a very different picture with Stretlsov detailing how their time in Cuba ended in ignominy as they required the Russian consulate in New York City to send them money so that they could eventually leave Cuba after being imprisoned by the Cuban government. [165]

Although revisionism appeared to be apparent in the works written after 1959 cited above, an interest in the Russian Revolution and Soviet Union most certainly existed in Cuba before the Cuban Revolution. As detailed the Cuban newspaper *The Havana Post* on 8 November 1917 carried the news of the Russian Revolution and an influence of this was also apparent in December 1919 when Salinas, Secretary of the Communist Section of Cuba, asked for membership of the Comintern which was also examined earlier in this chapter.

In May 1919 the journal *Cuba Contemporánea* published the extensive article "El Bolcheviquismo" written by Juan C. Zamora which outlined what the Bolshevik system was and its foundations beginning from the writings of Marx and Engels. [166] Moreover, in August 1919 the same publication printed the article "Evolución del Socialismo Moscovita" written by P. Rodríguez which examined the evolution of the Russian system from the nineteenth century that culminated in the emergence of Bolshevism in the aftermath of the Russian Revolution. In addition, it also provided a description of what a "soviet" was.[167] *Cuba Contemporánea* printed a further article entitled "Que es el Bolcheviquismo?" in October 1920 that attempted to answer the questions of "what is Bolshevism?" and "what is happening in Russia?"[168] Despite these events unfolding in a country far removed from the Caribbean the appearance of such articles and interest in them could have been expected. This occurred due to the fact that the advent of the Bolshevik regime in Russia had sent a seismic shock through the international system in general; it was the first time such a government had come to power and this had occurred in the world's largest country and one of the great European powers. As a result, it would have been more surprising if interest had not been shown in these historic events.

The same is also applicable to the reporting of both Lenin and Stalin's deaths in January 1924 and March 1953, respectively with the reports in *The Havana Post* being highly interesting on each occasion. On 24 January 1924 the report stated,

> The body of Nikolai Lenine, the Bolshevik premier and probably the greatest rebel of this or any generation against the system of security built up over the ages, lay in a silver-rimmed casket on a red carpeted dais in the great glistening hall of the House of Unions in Moscow.[169]

On 6 March 1953 the article began, "It has happened, the thing that the average Russian never let enter his head. Joseph Stalin has died in the Kremlin."[170] Both reports contain an undertone of dislike of the Soviet leader, with the role of the United States in Cuba in this era being significant for this. However, by the time of their deaths both were world leaders with Stalin by 1953 being the head of one of only two global superpowers. This resulted in considerable interest being taken in his death worldwide, with Cuba being no different, due to the impact which it could have on the global political situation of the 1950s.

Interestingly in July 1919 *Cuba Contemporánea* published "La Dictadura del Proletariado" by Mario Guiral Moreno that was slightly different in tone from the articles printed in this publication that were detailed above. It also examines Bolshevism, but suggests that certain parts could be appealing to the Cuban situation. This is significant, and can be linked to both the appearance of left-wing groups on the island and also the interest which the Communist Section of Cuba showed in joining the Comintern in 1919 that was examined earlier in this chapter. As Bolshevism offered an alternative political model compared to traditional ones, again it is not surprising that it received attention in Cuba although its political and economic situation was vastly different from that of Russia.

In the archive of the Secretary to the President of Cuba in the Cuban National Archive a number of notes exist that were sent to Batista in late 1941 regarding the situation between Cuba and the Soviet Union. This included in October 1941 from the Workers Centre in Regla "Máximo Gómez 81" and Nicolas Guillen, the famed Cuban poet who would become prominent within the Institute of Cuban-Soviet Cultural Exchange once it had been created in the summer of 1945.[171] The Second World War seemed to have impacted on this influx of notes sent to the Cuban President as they praised the improvement in relations between the two countries which would culminate in the creation of diplomatic relations in April 1942. Interestingly Batista received a note on 8 October 1941 which stated

> The cultural committee of the Ukrainian, Belorussian and Lithuanian residents of this hospital enthusiastically greet the message of 6 October of support for the Soviet Union and its citizens in their fight against Naz-fasicism.[172]

The effects of World War II were again important, with these people being in Cuba due to a number who left Russia in the aftermath of November 1917, which will be detailed in the next chapter. However, this does not detract from the importance of these notes of support for the Soviet Union which exist in this archive.

These would correspond with the reports of food packages being sent from Cuba to the Soviet Union in the summer of 1941.[173] Moreover, pro-Soviet rallies also took place at this time including on 23 July 1941 in Havana and the National Antifascist League was also formed.[174] In addition, further solidarity with the Soviet Union was shown in April 1943 when in the aftermath of the creation of bilateral diplomatic relations Maxim Litvinov, Soviet charge d'affaires to Cuba, travelled to the island and the National Antifascist League presented him with a gift of 25,000 pesos.[175] Furthermore, reports also exist that on 6 November 1943 at the Capitol Building in Havana a rally to commemorate the Russian Revolution, attended by 6000 people, was organized by this organization while on 22 February 1945 a rally in the Cuban capital was organized in support of the Red Army, which was attended by 5000 people.[176]

In addition to this, the support for the Soviet Union that existed in Cuba at this time is further illustrated by telegrams which were sent to the Soviet Union praising the Soviet efforts in their battle with Nazi Germany. This included on 9 June 1944 when the Antifascist League sent a telegram to Stalin offering their support and solidarity in this fight.[177] Furthermore, on 10 August 1945 the newspaper *Diario de la Marina* published the article "El Comunismo y sus territorios. España, Rusia y Cuba" by the writer and sociologist Dr. Serapio Rocamora. In this article he praises the achievements of the Russian Revolution and describes how it ended the period of "cruel tsarism."[178]

The impact of World War II was undoubtedly important for this pro-Soviet activity in Cuba at this time, but reports of earlier demonstrations having taken place in support of the Soviet regime also exist. This includes a rally on 1 May 1918 to show support for the Russian Revolution.[179] In addition, on 27 January 1924 a meeting was held in the Regla district of Havana to commemorate Lenin's funeral.[180]

World War II impacted on Cuban interest in the Soviet Union yet further and in a similar manner to Melentiev, Konstatinaich and Stretlsov fighting in the Cuban War of Independence in the final years of the nineteenth century, three Cubans in the form of brothers Jorge and Aldo Vivo and Enrique Vilar fought for the Red Army during World War II. The Vivo brothers had first travelled to the Soviet Union in 1934 due to their "internationalism," with interestingly Jorge Vivo having been known to Moscow for some time before this due to the aforementioned report "Save the Lives of Vivo and Ordoqui" that was sent to the Comintern in 1926.[181] On 20 February 1985 Aldo Vivo and Enrique Vilar were awarded the Order of the Fatherland War posthumously.[182] In addition, as detailed in the previous chapter, a permanent exhibit to these three Cubans exists in the Museum of the Great Fatherland War in Moscow, which Raúl Castro visited during his trip to the Russian capital in January 2009.[183]

Even after diplomatic relations between Moscow and Havana had been severed in April 1952 interest and support in the Soviet Union remained in Cuba. This was evident not just in the PSP attending the 19th and 20th Congresses of the CPSU in October 1952 and February 1956, respectively, but also that Cuba Socialist Youth Movement staged a robust defense of the Soviet Union as a result of a highly critical report of the Warsaw Pact invasion of the Hungary in the autumn of 1956 that was printed in *Bohemia*. It describes the report as being full of "monstrous falsifications" and describes *Bohemia* as being a journal of the "capitalists that is at the service of imperialism."[184]

On a number of occasions, links to Lenin and the Russian Revolution were made in Cuba after January 1959. As detailed a degree of revisionism may be apparent in these, but interest in the Russian Revolution, Bolshevism, and the Soviet Union certainly existed on the Caribbean island. This was apparent in the journal articles and newspaper articles cited above, which is not surprising due to the historic nature of these events and that they had taken place in one of the great European powers. This would only increase in significance as the Soviet Union became a superpower. This interest in the Soviet Union was further highlighted by rallies held in Cuba in support of the Soviet Union and other pro-Soviet activity on the island, including notes of support sent to the Cuban President in the early 1940s. The impact of World War II was important for this, but they had commenced from soon after November 1917.

This in combination with the appearance of left-wing groups including the PCC, interest in the Comintern, and the flow of information that was sent from Cuba to this organization's headquarters in Moscow highlights yet further the interest in the Soviet regime and its policies. As the Bolsheviks provided such a radically different political model, this is not overly surprising, but when taken into account with the activities of the Institute of Cuban-Soviet Cultural Exchange created in the summer of 1945, it can be concluded that considerable interest was taken in the Soviet Union and its policies in Cuba in the period between the Russian and Cuban Revolutions.

In addition to this, what can also be inferred is that the Russian Revolution considerably increased Russian and subsequently Soviet interest in Cuba. In chapter 1 it was outlined how Peter the Great had shown some interest in Latin America, and earlier in this chapter it was detailed how Melentiev, Konstatinaich, and Stretlsov had fought in the Cuban Wars of Independence in the final years of the nineteenth century. This interest was very sporadic and in the case of Melentiev, Konstatinaich, and Stretlsov, serendipity appeared to be significant in their presence in Cuba. However, as this chapter has examined in some detail after the Russian Revolution and the creation of the Third International in March 1919 the Soviet leadership took considerable interest in Cuba, which simply had not existed prior to this.

CONCLUSIONS

In the period between the Russian and Cuban Revolutions the radical aspect of Moscow's "dual track" diplomacy took considerable interest in Cuba. This attention can be divided into two distinct periods: the years from the creation of the Third International in March 1919 until the Seventh Congress of this organization in the summer of 1935, and from this point until January 1959 and the victory of the Cuban Revolution. The tactics followed in these two distinct periods were very different from each other, but Moscow showed interest in Cuba during both.

Crucial to this interest was the Comintern's goal of engineering a successful revolution which would help safeguard Soviet security. With regards to the Developing World in general, this interest was in reality focused on the effects that revolutionary activity in the less well developed countries could have for the metropolitan states. This was still applicable to Cuba due to the nature of the island's relationship with the United States throughout this era. In addition, to maximize profits, U.S. companies kept labor costs in Cuba as low as possible with this resulting in increased labor activity throughout the island. This gave Cuba the appearance as a "hot bed" of radicalism, which in turn increased Soviet interest in the island as the chance of revolutionary success appeared greater in Cuba than elsewhere in the region. The outcome was that an unforeseen consequence of Cuban economic dependence on the United States was to increase Moscow's attention in Cuba.

This was most certainly the case in the period up to the summer of 1935 which was dominated by the ultra left position of the "third period" of the Comintern. A considerable number of documents regarding Cuba exist in the organization's archive for these years, illustrating this interest. The flow of information in this archive was predominantly from Cuba to the Soviet Union, but significantly in 1928 the Third International sent direct instructions to the PCC. After this, direct correspondence from the Third International to Cuba may not have taken place with instead the CPUSA being used as a "vehicle" to transmit this information. However, even once the more cautious tactics of the "popular front" were introduced this attention remained due to the fact that PCC, and subsequently PSP, illustrated the "successes" of this policy due to its size and participation in the Cuban political system. This was only aided by the party gaining legal status in the late 1930s, subsequently having the first communist party members in Latin America to hold governmental positions, and ironically the effects of World War II and the Soviet Union's alliance with the United States.

The ideas of statists and constructivism within Soviet foreign policy, due to the traditional Russian fear of insecurity, were significant in this attention as was the Kremlin's adherence to the principles of realism. The outcome was that Moscow could attempt to use revolutionary activity in Cuba to counteract anti-Soviet U.S. policy elsewhere. This included nonrecognition of the Soviet regime by the United States until November 1933, but also after 1945 the onset of the Cold War. In addition, Cuba's geographical location only intensified the importance of the island for the Kremlin, which also resulted in Moscow as the center of the world revolution not being able to ignore the revolutionary activity on the island.

This activity may never have produced a revolutionary outcome in Cuba in the years between 1917 and 1959, but this was simply representative of the Comintern in general as throughout its existence it failed on a global scale to produce a successful revolution. In addition, tension between Moscow and the PSP did exist in the form of problems regarding "Browderism" within the CPUSA, but this does not reduce the importance of the interest which the Soviet Union had in the Cuban party and radicalism on the island in the period between the Russian and Cuban Revolutions.

Interestingly the Soviet Union showed considerable interest in Cuba at the height of "Browderism," with the events in Europe being significant for this as any revolutionary success on the island could be used to counter what Moscow perceived as anti-Soviet U.S. policy in this part of the world. Significantly the ideas of the "popular front" remained important for this because although the Comintern had been disbanded in the summer of 1943 these tactics brought "success" to the PSP in post World War II Cuba. The PSP provided legitimacy for the Cuban political system resulting in it remaining legal for much longer than other communist parties in Latin America. This illustrated both a degree of Cuban political independence from Washington which has not traditionally been thought to have been the case, but also Soviet interest in the island. This is highlighted by the existence of documents within the archive of the Soviet Commissar for Foreign Affairs regarding Cuba in the early 1950s. Significantly these were sent to the very pinnacle of the Soviet ruling elite, including Stalin himself.

Within Cuba, attention also focused on the Russian Revolution and the Soviet Union in general. The island may have been closely allied to the United States in this period, but due to these historic events taking place in one of the great European powers this attention is not surprising. The result was that interest in the Soviet Union existed in Cuba while the radical aspect of the Moscow's "dual track" diplomacy took considerable interest in the Caribbean island. In sum, in the era between the Russian and Cuban Revolutions the Soviet leadership most certainly did not suffer from "geographical fatalism" with regards to Cuba specifically or Latin America in general.

NOTES

1. "Russian Revolutionaries For Immediate Peace," *Havana Post*, November 8, 1917, 1.

2. For a history and dates of the creation of communist parties in Latin America please see Manuel Caballero, *Latin America and the Comintern 1919–1943*, (Cambridge: Cambridge University Press, 1986), 45–53.Rollie E. Poppino, *International Communism in Latin America. A History of the Movement 1917–1963*, (London: Collier-Macmillan Limited, 1964), 59–95 & 224–229.

3. Karen Brutents, *Tridtsat let na Staroi ploshchadi*, (Moscow: Mezhdunarodnye otnosheniia, 1998), 338–360.While in New York City Trotsky spent most of his time in the company of fellow Eastern Europeans and appears not to have met any Latin Americans. I.D. Thatcher, *Leon Trotsky and World War One: August 1914–February 1917,* (Basingstoke: Macmillan, 2000). Lenin had not written directly about Cuba, but he had made reference to the Spanish-American War in 1898 when using it as an example of the inevitability of war in the imperialist system. His other examples had been the Anglo-Boer War in Africa and the Russian-Japanese War of 1904. Vladimir Lenin, *Polnoe sobranie sochienii Tom 28*, (Moscow: Gospolitizdat, 1962), 669. Vladimir Lenin, *Polnoe sobranie sochienii Tom 30*, (Moscow: Gospolitizdat, 1962), 164. Stalin had never written on Cuba and had made very little reference to Latin America as a whole. In 1927 he referred to the growth of the Argentinean economy, but in 1925 in a speech on imperialism he made no reference to Latin America. I.V. Stalin, *Sochineniia Tom 10*, (Gospolitizdat, Moscow, 1949), 275. I.V. Stalin, *Sochineniia Tom 7*, (Moscow: Gospolitizdat, 1947), 269–270. However, Marx and Engels had written briefly on Cuban economic conditions, while in August 1858 in a letter to Engels, Marx wrote that he had received a letter on the slave trade on the island. K. Marx "Bolivar and Ponte" in *Marx and Engels Collected Works Vol 18*, (London: Lawrence and Wishart, 1982), 219–233. "The Part Played by Labour in the transition from Ape to Man" in *Marx and Engels Collected Works Vol 25*, (London: Lawrence and Wishart, 1967), 463. *Marx and Engels Collected Works Vol 140*, (London:

Lawrence and Wishart, 1983), 340. J. Degras, *The Communist International 1919–1943 Documents, Volume 2* (London: Frank Cass & Co Ltd, 1971), 526–548.

4. Poppino, *International Communism in Latin America*, 1964, 153. A.D. Faleroni "Soviet Relations in Latin America" in *The Soviet Union and Latin America*, ed, J.G. Oswald and & A.J. Strover, (London: Pall Mall Press, 1970), p. 10.

5. G.M. Adibekov, E.E. Shakhnazarova, & K.K. Shirinia, *Organizatsionnaia struktura Kominterna 1919–1943*, (Moscow: ROSSPEN, 1997), 21. Roy was Bengali by birth which has always left the accusation that his real interest was Indian independence and he was merely using Mexico as a vehicle to gain access to the Comintern. M. N. Roy, *M.N. Roy's Memoirs*, (Bombay: Allied Publishers, 1964).

6. Stirner was a pseudonym and he was in reality the Swiss born Edgar Woog. Adibekov, *Organizatsionnaia struktura Kominterna*, 1997, 65–66.

7. Adibekov, *Organizatsionnaia struktura Kominterna*, 1997, 98, 101, 111.

8. Caballero, *Latin America and the Comintern*, 1986, 149.

9. Poppino, *International Communism in Latin America*, 1964, 153.

10. Degras, *The Communist International*, 1971, 526–548.

11. Adibekov, *Organizatsionnaia struktura Kominterna*, 1997, 140–146.

12. Caballero, *Latin America and the Comintern*, 1986, p.117. Poppino has also made this point, Poppino, *International Communism in Latin America*, 1964, 158–161.

13. R. Munck, *Revolutionary Trends in Latin America*, Monograph Series, No 17, Centre for Developing Area Studies, McGill University, 8. Eric Ching, "In Search of the Party: The Communist Party, the Comintern and the Peasant Rebellion of 1932 in El Salvador," *The Americas*, Vol 55, No. 2 (Oct. 1998): 204–239.

14. Caballero, *Latin America and the Comintern*, 1986, 48. Barry Carr, "From Caribbean backwater to revolutionary opportunity: Cuba's evolving relationship with the Comintern, 1925–34" in *International Communism and the Communist International 1919–43*, ed. Tim Rees and Andrew Thorpe, (Manchester: Manchester University Press, 1998), 236.

15. Barry Carr, "Mill Occupations and Soviets: The Mobilisation of Sugar Workers in Cuba 1917–1933," *Journal of Latin American Studies*, 28, (1996): 134.

16. Boris Goldenberg, "The Rise and Fall of a Party: The Cuban CP (1925–59):" 63.

17. Carr, "Mill Occupations and Soviets," 1996, 134.

18. Louis A. Pérez, *Cuba and the United States: Ties of Singular Intimacy*, (Athens, Ga: University of Georgia Press, 2003), 173.

19. Pérez, *Cuba and the United States*, 2003, 173.

20. Goldenberg, "The Rise and Fall of a Party," 63.

21. Hugh Thomas, *Cuba or the Pursuit of Freedom.* (London: Eyre & Spottiswoode, 1971), 576.

22. Thomas, *Cuba*, 1971, 576. Poppino, *International Communism in Latin America*, 1964, 81.

23. Thomas, *Cuba*, 1971, 577.

24. Carr, "From Caribbean backwater to revolutionary opportunity," 1998, 236.

25. Carr, "From Caribbean backwater to revolutionary opportunity," 1998, 236.

26. Carr, "From Caribbean backwater to revolutionary opportunity," 1998, 236.

27. Thomas, *Cuba*, 1971, 577.

28. Goldenberg, "The Rise and Fall of a Party," 64. Carr, "From Caribbean backwater to revolutionary opportunity," 1998, 237. Thomas, *Cuba*, 1971, 579–580.

29. Carr, "From Caribbean backwater to revolutionary opportunity," 1998, 237.

30. Letter from Marselo Salinas, Secretary of the Communist Section of Cuba, 6 December 1919. Russian State Archive for Social and Political History (RSA) 495/105/2.

31. "Report on the Cuban Section of Cuba," 21 January 1920. RSA 495/105/2.

32. RSA/495/105/4.

33. "El Sembrado. Periódico Quince rial Ideas, Critica y Combate" RSA/495/105/1.

34. Letter from PCC to Communist International. RSA/495/105/1.

35. RSA/495/105/1.

36. "Report on Cuba," 1926. RSA495/105/1.

37. This would correspond with Thomas's idea that from its creation the PCC "formally accepted the leadership of the Comintern." Thomas, *Cuba*, 1971, 577. Capote has also written that the PCC was in complete line with the Comintern. Orlando Cruz Capote, *The Comintern and Problems of the Cuban Revolution (1925–1935)*, (Moscow: Academia de Ciencias Sociales, 1989), 4. In addition, Gott has also described how from its creation the PCC was "beholden to Moscow." Richard Gott, *Cuba. A new history*, (New Haven: Yale University Press, 2004), 132.

38. Julio Antonio Mella "Información para la Prensa Obrea y Revolución" RSA/495/105/1. A copy of Julio Mella's article "La Provocación Imperialista a los Soviets" that was published in *El Machete* in June 1927 exists in the Fondo Especial in the Cuban National Archive (CNA). In this Mella displays his allegiance to the Soviet Union due to his highly critical comments of the West's attempts to crush the Bolshevik regime from its inception. CNA, Fondo Especial, 6/63, June 1927.

39. Mella "Información para la Prensa Obrea y Revolución" RSA/495/105/1.

40. Letter from PCC to Comintern International, 31 May 1926. RSA495/105/2.

41. "Save the Lives of Vivo and Ordoqui" RSA/495/105/2.

42. Carr, "From Caribbean backwater to revolutionary opportunity," 1998, 237.

43. A number of authors have written of the importance of outside help that the PCC received at this time. Carr, "From Caribbean backwater to revolutionary opportunity," 1998, 237. Goldenberg, "The Rise and Fall of a Party," 64. Thomas, *Cuba*, 1971, 577.

44. Carr, "From Caribbean backwater to revolutionary opportunity," 1998, 237. Goldenberg, "The Rise and Fall of a Party," 64. Caballero, *Latin America and the Comintern*, 1986, 33–36. Poppino interestingly has written, "The Pole, who used the name Abraham or Fabio Grobart, may have been the least obtrusive of the Comintern agents. He went to Cuba in 1927 to organise the Communist underground and spent much of the next two decades as an adviser to the party there." Poppino, *International Communism in Latin America*, 1964, 155.

45. Adibekov, *Organizatsionnaia struktura Kominterna*, 1997, 140–146.

46. Degras, *The Communist International*, 1971, 526–548.

47. Poppino, *International Communism in Latin America*, 1964, 157.

48. Letter from Secretariat of the Communist International to PCC, 5 January 1928, 1. RSA495/105/10.

49. Letter from Secretariat of the Communist International to PCC, 5 January 1928, 2–3. RSA495/105/10.

50. Letter from Secretariat of the Communist International to PCC, 5 January 1928, 6. RSA495/105/10.

51. Letter from Secretariat of the Communist International to PCC, 5 January 1928, 7. RSA495/105/10.

52. Letter from Secretariat of the Communist International to PCC, 13 January 1928. RSA495/105/10.

53. Carr, "From Caribbean backwater to revolutionary opportunity," 1998, 237. Goldenberg, "The Rise and Fall of a Party," 64. Poppino, *International Communism in Latin America*, 1964, 155. Caballero, *Latin America and the Comintern*, 1986, 33–36.

54. Ronald Grigor Suny, "Living in the Hood: Russia, Empire, and Old and New Neighbours,' in *Russian Foreign Policy in the Twenty-first Century and the Shadow of the Past*, ed, Robert Legvold (New York: Columbia University Press, 2007), 57.

55. Kevin McDermott, "Stalin and the Comintern during the 'Third Period', 1928–1933" *European History Quarterly*, Volume 25, (1995): 418.

56. On this policy shift McDermott and Agnew have written, "The adoption by the Sixth Congress in the summer of 1928 of a strident anti-social democratic platform formalized the 'turn to the left' which had been in the making since late 1926 and foreshadowed an onslaught on the 'right-wing deviation' in the international communist movement." Kevin McDermott & Jeremy Agnew, *The Comintern. A History of International Communism from Lenin to Stalin*, (Basingstoke: Macmillan Press Ltd, 1996), 82. Rees and Thorpe have written, "The new line, 'class against class,' was formally promulgated at the ninth ECCI plenum in February 1928." Tim Rees & Andrew Thorpe, "Introduction" in *International Communism and the Communist*

International 1919–43, ed. Tim Rees and Andrew Thorpe (Manchester: Manchester University Press, 1998), 4.

57. Caballero, *Latin America and the Comintern,* 1986, 60–61.

58. Pérez, *Cuba and the United States,* 2003, 185.

59. Pérez, *Cuba and the United States,* 2003, 160.

60. "Informo" 5 September 1930. RSA/495/105/37.

61. Letter from PCC to Communist International, August 1930. RSA/495/105/37.

62. Caballero, Goldenberg, and Capote have all written of the importance of the CPUSA and Caribbean Bureau to the PCC. Caballero, *Latin America and the Comintern,* 1986, pp. 29–31. Goldenberg, "The Rise and Fall of a Party," 64–65. Capote, *The Comintern and Cuban Revolution,* 1989, 5–6. Carr has also written of this, but also that communication with both of these organizations was made easier after the arrival of the Comintern agent "Juan" in Cuba in 1930. Carr, "From Caribbean backwater to revolutionary opportunity," 1998, 238. Furthermore, the close links between the PCC and CPUSA were illustrated by a report signed by Theodore Plecan of the CPUSA stating that a Workers School for Revolutionary Problems in Latin America had been attempted to be created and that relations between workers in the U.S. and Latin America, but particularly Cuba should be encouraged. Theodore Plecan, "Report" 21 January 1931. RSA495/105/138.

63. "Letter of the Central Committee of the CP USA to the Central Committee of the CP of Cuba, 6 November 1930. RSA/495/138 & *The Communist,* Vol X, No 1 (January 1931): 66–73.

64. "Letter of the Central Committee of the CP USA to the Central Committee of the CP of Cuba," (January 1931): 2.

65. "Letter of the Central Committee of the CP USA to the Central Committee of the CP of Cuba," (January 1931): 12.

66. "Letter of the Central Committee of the CP USA to the Central Committee of the CP of Cuba," (January 1931): 12–13.

67. O. Rodríguez, "Our Present Tasks in Cuba," *The Communist,* Vol X, No 6 (*June* 1931):516.

68. Rodríguez, "Our Present Tasks in Cuba," (June 1931): 516.

69. Goldenberg, "The Rise and Fall of a Party," 65.

70. Goldenberg, "The Rise and Fall of a Party," 65. Carr, "From Caribbean backwater to revolutionary opportunity," 1998, 238.

71. Carr, "From Caribbean backwater to revolutionary opportunity," 1998, 240.

72. Carr, "From Caribbean backwater to revolutionary opportunity," 1998, 239.

73. Carr, "From Caribbean backwater to revolutionary opportunity," 1998, 239 & 248.

74. Goldenberg, "The Rise and Fall of a Party," 66.

75. Carr, "Mill Occupations and Soviets," 1996, 135–136. Barry Carr, "Identity, Class, and Nation: Black Immigrant Workers, Cuban Communism, and the Sugar Insurgency, 1925–1934," *Hispanic Historical Review,* 78:1, (1996): 97–99.

76. Carr, "From Caribbean backwater to revolutionary opportunity," 1998, 240.

77. Letter from PCC to CPUSA, 10 May 1933. RSA495/105/76. Significantly Carr has written, "Another black union leader was Sandalio Junco, the PCC's first Negro affairs specialist (and later the founder of Cuban Trotskyism)." Carr, "Identity, Class, and Nation," 1996, 96–97.

78. Carr, "From Caribbean backwater to revolutionary opportunity," 1998, 234.

79. Thomas, *Cuba,* 1971, 618.

80. Goldenberg, "The Rise and Fall of a Party," 66–67. Carr, "From Caribbean backwater to revolutionary opportunity," 1998, 241–247.

81. Carr, "From Caribbean backwater to revolutionary opportunity," 1998, 244. Carr, "Mill Occupations and Soviets," 1996, 157–158. Alexander, *Communism in Latin America,* 1957, 274–275.

82. M.J. Olgin, "X-The Third Period" in Bernard K John, *A Documentary History of the CPUSA, Volume III, United and Fight* (Westport, Conn.: Greenwood Press, 1994), 615.

83. Walter LaFeber, *The American Age. United States Foreign Policy at Home and Abroad since 1750,* (New York: W.W. Norton & Company, 1989), 361–362.

84. Carr, "From Caribbean backwater to revolutionary opportunity," 1998, 247–248.

85. "Report from PCC to Secretary of Comintern International," 4 November 1933, RSA495/105/76.

86. Carr, "From Caribbean backwater to revolutionary opportunity," 1998, 248.

87. Rees & Thorpe, 'Introduction,' 1998, 5. McDermott also states this. McDermott, "Stalin and the Comintern," 1995, 409.

88. Alexander, *Communism in Latin America*, 1957, 276. The resolution of the congress illustrated the PCC's continued loyalty to Moscow as it stated, "The Land of the Soviets has become a powerful industrial country and is the beacon of all the oppressed peoples in the world in their struggle for liberation." "The Present Situation, Perspectives, and Tasks in Cuba. Resolution of the Second Congress of the Communist Party of Cuba." *The Communist*, XIII, No 9 (September 1934): 876.

89. "Obreros, Campesinos, Estudiantes. Capas populares de le población." CNA November 1934, Fondo Especial 8/108/63.

90. Eudocio Ravines, *La Gran Estafa*, (Santiago de Chile: Editorial del Pacifico, Mexico, 1952), 257.

91. Jorge Garcia Montes & Antonio Alonso Ávila, *Historia del Partido Comunista de Cuba*, (Miami: Ream Press, 1970) 168.

92. Adibekov, *Organizatsionnaia struktura Kominterna* , 1997, 182–184. Poppino has written that his appointment was highly important and showed the regard in which Blas Roca was held in Moscow, *International Communism in Latin America*, 1964, 115.

93. Lucillo Batlle, *Blas Roca. Continuador de la Obrara de Balino y Mella*, (Havana: Editorial de Ciencias Sociales, 2005) 141–143.

94. Blas Roca, "Forward to the Cuban Anti-Imperialist People's Front!" *The Communist*, Vol XIV, No 10 (October 1935): 955.

95. Roca "Forward to the Cuban Anti-Imperialist People's Front!" (October 1935): 959.

96. Roca "Forward to the Cuban Anti-Imperialist People's Front!" (October 1935): 959.

97. Regarding PCC attempts to create these general coalitions of Cubans Roca continued, "we formulated a program of simple demands, clear and easily understood, for the masses, which includes their most urgent economic and political demands, under the principal slogans: 'For the Overthrow of the Reactionary Government of Mendieta-Batista,' 'Drive Yankee Imperialism Out of Cuba,' 'Drive Caffrey Out of Cuba.'" Roca, "Forward to the Cuban Anti-Imperialist People's Front!" (October 1935): 961.

98. Roca, "Forward to the Cuban Anti-Imperialist People's Front!" (October 1935): 967. Roca has since spoken of the importance of this conference for the implantation of the "popular front" tactics in Cuba. Batlle, *Blas Roca*, 2005, 143.

99. RSA 495/105.

100. RSA 495/105/158 & RSA 495/105/169.

101. RSA/82/2/1275.

102. RSA/82/2/1275.

103. LaFeber, *The American Age*, 1989, 72.

104. Letter from Blas Roca, General Secretary of PCC, to Central Committee of CPUSA, 6 February 1935. Archive of the Communist Party of United States (CPUSA), 1935, Reel 293, Delo 3803a. Moreover, in December 1934 the CPUSA agreed to help the PCC with this help taking the form of not only financial assistance, but also for the PCC to send three to five "students" to New York so that they could become "acquainted with the editing and managing of a daily newspaper." Archive of CPUSA, 1934, Reel 268, Delo 3441.

105. "Minutes of Small Commission Meeting," 8 July 1935, Archive of CPUSA, 1935, Reel 293, Delo 3803a.

106. "The Seventh World Congress of the Communist International and the Tasks of our Party," *The Communist*, Vol XIV, No 12 (December 1935): 1184.

107. Thomas, *Cuba*, 1971, 707–708.

108. Thomas, *Cuba*, 1971, 709.

109. Goldenberg, "The Rise and Fall of a Party," 72.

110. William Z. Foster, "The Congress of the Cuban Communist Party," *The Communist*, Vol XVIII, (March 1939): 225.

111. Foster, "The Congress of the Cuban Communist Party," (March 1939): 225.

112. Thomas, *Cuba*, 1971, 711.

113. Louis Carlos Prestes represented Brazil as a full member and R. Ghiodi of Argentina was like Blas Roca a candidate member. Adibekov, *Organizatsionnaia struktura Kominterna*, 1971, 209–211.

114. Blas Roca, "Forging the People's Victory in Cuba," *The Communist*, Vol XIX, No 2, (February 1940): 136.

115. Poppino, *International Communism in Latin America*, 1964, 81.

116. Blas Roca, *Los Fundamentos del Socialismo en Cuba*, (Havana: Ediciones Populares, 1961), 133–134. Garcia & Alonso, *Historia del Partido Comunista de Cuba*, 1970, 247.

117. Goldenberg, "The Rise and Fall of a Party," 73. Poppino has also written of the importance of the alliance with Batista for the PCC at the time of the Nazi-Soviet pact. Poppino, *International Communism in Latin America*, 1964, 81.

118. Jules R. Benjamin, *The United States and the Origins of the Cuban Revolution. An Empire of Liberty in an Age of National Liberation*, (Princeton: Princeton University Press, 1990), 103.

119. Benjamin, *The United States and the Origins of the Cuban Revolution*, 1990, 103.

120. Benjamin, *The United States and the Origins of the Cuban Revolution*. 1990, 102.

121. Alexander, *Communism in Latin America*, 1957, 281.

122. Julia E. Sweig, *Inside the Cuban Revolution. Fidel Castro and the Urban Underground*, (Harvard University Press, Cambridge, Massachusetts, 2002), 126. Karol has written that in 1942 the Cuban Communist Party had 87,000 members. Karol, *Guerrillas in Power, The Course of the Cuban Revolution*, (London: Jonathan Cape, 1971), 87.

123. Karol, *Guerrillas in Power*, 1971, 60.

124. Karol, *Guerrillas in Power*, 1971, 270.

125. Garcia & Alsonso, *Historia del Partido Comunista de Cuba*, 1970, 168.

126. For the various debates surrounding the end of the organization please see McDermott & Agnew, *The Comintern*, 1996, 204–211. Interestingly even in 1961 Blas Roca continued to defend the Third International when he wrote, "The Communist International defended the principles of revolutionary Marxism against vulgarities and falsifications of opportunists; it helped in the formation of authentic Marxist workers parties, and fought against fascism. Blas Roca, *Los Fundamentos del Socialismo en Cuba*, 1961, 187.

127. Poppino, *International Communism in Latin America*, 1964, 32–33.

128. Alexander, *Communism in Latin America*, 1957, 283.

129. Pérez, *Cuba Between Reform and Revolution*, 219. This figure for membership of the PSP is only matched by the Chilean Communist Party and exceeded by the Brazilian party who are estimated to have 50,000 and 150,000 members respectively. The Cuban party membership being second only to the Brazilian party is remarkable due to the differences in the size of the two countries' populations. Poppino, *International Communism in Latin America*, 1964, 231.

130. Goldenberg, 'The Rise and Fall of a Party," 76.

131. Alexander, *Communism in Latin America*, 1957, 17. Poppino, *International Communism in Latin America*, 1964, 34–35.

132. Leslie Bethell & Ian Roxborough, "Latin America between the Second World War and the Cold War: Some Reflections on the 1945-8 Conjuncture," *Journal of Latin American Studies*, 20, (1988): 177.

133. Angel Garcia & Piotr Mironchuk, *Raices de las relaciones Cubano Sovieticas*, (Havana, Editorial de Ciencias Sociales, 1988), 131.

134. Jacques Duclos, "On the Dissolution of the Communist Party of the United States," *Political Affairs*, Vol XXIV, Number 7, (July 1945): 656–672.

135. Duclos, "On the Dissolution of the Communist Party of the United States," (July 1945): 656.

136. Duclos, "On the Dissolution of the Communist Party of the United States," (July 1945): 670.

137. Batlle, *Blas Roca*, 2005, 144.

138. Batlle, *Blas Roca*, 2005, 144.

139. The first time a significant member of the PSP is chronicled as being involved in the Institute's activities was when Carlos Rafael Rodríguez, member of the politburo of the PSP, spoke at the event "La URSS y la Cultura," sponsored by the Institute and part of the Seventh Book Festival held in Parque Central in Havana in December 1946. *Cuba y la URSS* Num 18, (January 1947): 31.

140. Goldenberg, "The Rise and Fall of a Party," 77.

141. Alexander, *Communism in Latin America*, 1957, 291.

142. Benjamin, *The United States and the Origins of the Cuban Revolution*, 1990, 106–107. Thomas, *Cuba*, 1971, 752–754 & 757.

143. *Pravda* June 15, 1949, 3.

144. Thomas, *Cuba*, 1971, 767. For the removal of the PSP from the CTC please see Benjamin, *The United States and the Origins of the Cuban Revolution*, 1990, 106–107.

145. Marifeli Pérez -Stable, *The Cuban Revolution. Origins, Course, and Legacy*, (Oxford: Oxford University Press, 1999), 49.

146. Pérez, *Cuba Between Reform and Revolution*, 2006, 219.

147. Report prepared for Vyacheslav Molotov by V. Grigorian, Chairman of the International Department of the Central Committee. 25 November 1950. RSA25/C/2163.

148. Report prepared for Joseph Stalin by Grigorian, 25 November 1950 RSA25/C/2177.

149. Luis Báez, *Conversaciones con Juan Marinello*, (Havana: Casa Editora Abril, 1995), 54–55.

150. RSA 82/2/1797.

151. RSA 82/2/1867.

152. John Edwin Fagg, *Latin America: a general history* (New York: Macmillan, 1977), 603–605.

153. *Daily Worker* 5 August 1953, 1. Gott, *Cuba*, 2004, 159. Karol has written "Throughout, they remained Popular Frontists, advocates of a broad anti-fascist union, built on the model designed by the Seventh Congress of the Comintern," Karol, *Guerrillas in Power*, 1971, 150.

154. Alexander, *Communism in Latin America*, 1957, 293–294.

155. Karol, *Guerrillas in Power*, 1971, 150.

156. Thomas, *Cuba*, 1970, 980–981.

157. Samuel Farber, *The Origins of the Cuban Revolution Reconsidered*, (Chapel Hill: The University of North Carolina Press, 2006), 145 & 156. Alexandr Fursenko & Timothy Naftali, *The Secret History of the Cuban Missile Crisis. "One Hell of a Gamble."* (London: John Murray, 1997), 12. George J. Boughton "Soviet-Cuban Relations, 1956–1960," *Journal of Interamerican Studies and World Affairs*, Vol 16, No 4 (November 1974): 436–453.

158. *Pravda* October 15, 1952, 1–7. *Pravda* February 15, 1956, 1–11. Both Poppino and Garcia and Alonso have argued that Moscow's interest in Latin America was shown by invitations for Latin American communists to travel to Moscow on these occasions during this period. Poppino, *International Communism in Latin America*, 1964, 168–169. Garcia and Alonso have made a similar argument. Garcia and Alonso, *Historia del Partido Comunista de Cuba*, 1970, 444–445. Moreover, the PSP's loyalty to the Soviet Union was further shown in 1950 when Blas Roca wrote, "The people of Cuba have fiercely protested against U.S. imperialist intervention in Korea and hailed with enthusiasm the attitude of the Soviet Union—the great socialist state—which opposes interference in the internal affairs of other countries." Blas Roca, "People of Cuba Fighting Against War, For Democratic Liberties!" *For a Lasting Peace. For a People's Deomocracy*, May 18, 1950, 3.

159. Batlle, *Blas Roca*, 2005, 55.

160. Fidel Castro, "Address to First Congress of the PCC," 17 December 1975, *Primer Congreso del Partido Comunista de Cuba. Memorias* (Havana: Departamento de Orientación Revolucionaria del Comité Central del Partido Comunista de Cuba, 1976), 38.

161. Fidel Castro, "Lenin Centennial Ceremony," Havana Domestic Service in Spanish 0333GMT 23 April 1970, FBIS 19700423.

162. Fidel Castro & Ignacio Ramonet, *My Life*, (London: Allen Lane, 2007), 85.

163. Erasmo Dumpierre, "La Revolución de Octubre y su Influencia en Cuba," *Bohemia*, April 21, 1967, 9.

164. Antonio Núñez Jiménez, "Cuba fue conocida en Rusia desde 1530" *Bohemia*, April 1962, .20–25 & D. Aragon, "Tres rusos en la Guerra del 95," *Bohemia*, July 10, 1970, 16–17.

165. P. Stretlsov "Two Months in Cuba in October," *Vestnik Evropi*, May 1898, Volume 3: 129–166. The same edition of *Vestnik Evropi* published an article on the Spanish-American war in the section "Foreign Review," *Vestnik Evropi*, May 1898, Volume 3: 379–390.

166. Juan C. Zamora, "El Bolcheviquismo," *Cuba Contemporánea*, May 1919, 35–81.

167. P. Rodríguez, "Evolución del Socialismo Moscovita," *Cuba Contemporánea*, Volume XX, August 1919, 481–499.

168. L. Chestoff, "Que es el Bolcheviquismo?" *Cuba Contemporánea*, Volume XXIV, October 1920, 196–211.

169. "Thousands File Past Coffin of Premier Lenine," *Havana Post*, January 24, 1924, 1.

170. "Stalin Dead. Soviet Leader Dies Four Days after a Stroke," *Havana Post*, March 6, 1953, 1.

171. Secretaria de la Presidencia Caja 51, Numero 75, CAN.

172. 8 October 1941, Secretaria de la Presidencia Caja 51, Numero 75, CAN.

173. Angel Garcia, & Piotr Mironchuk, *Esbozo Historica de las Relaciones entre Cuba-Rusia y Cuba-URSS*, (Havana: Academia de Ciencias de Cuba, 1976), 182–184. E.A. Larin, *Politicheskaia istorii Kuba XX Veka*. (Moscow: Visshaya shkola, 2007), 88–90. M.A. Okuneva, *The Working Class in the Cuban Revolution*, (Moscow: Nauka, 1985), 80–81.

174. Garcia & Mironchuk, *Esbozo Histórico de las Relaciones entre Cuba-Rusia*, 1976, 182–183. Okuneva, *The Working Class in the Cuban Revolution*, 1985, 80–81.

175. Garcia & Mironchuk, *Raices de las relaciones Cubano Sovieticas*, 1988, 126.

176. D. Zaikin to Molotov, Havana, 8 November 1943, G.E. Mamedov and A. Dalmau, *Rossiia-Kuba, 1902–2002, dokumenty i materialy*, (Moscow, Mezhdunarodnye otnosheniia, 2004), 57–58. Zaikin to S.A. Lozovskomu, Deputy Commissar of Foreign Relations, Havana, 23 February 1945. Mamedov and Dalmau, *Rossiia-Kuba, 1902–2002*, 2006, 64.

177. Antifascist League to Stalin, Havana, 9 June 1944, Mamedov and Dalmau, *Rossiia-Kuba, 1902–2002*, 61.

178. Serapio Rocamora, "El Comunismo y sus territorios. España, Rusia y Cuba" *Diario de la Marina*, 10 August 1945, CAN Fondo Especial 6/63.

179. *CCCP-Cuba. Documents of Friendship and Socialism*, (Moscow: izdatevl'stvo politicheskoii literatury, 1985), 48.

180. Cuba-URSS *Crónica*, (Moscow: Progreso, 1990), 520.

181. "Save the Lives of Vivo and Ordoqui" RSA/495/105/2.

182. *Granma International Weekly Review*, March 17, 1985, 2.

183. "65 Aniversario de la Gran Victoria," *Edicion de la Embajada de la federación de Rusia en Cuba*, Numero 4, (2010): 28.

184. "Documento impreso de la Juventud Socialista en Respuesta a 'La gran Mentira' de Bohemia," November 1956. CNA, Fondo Especial, Caja o Legajo 14, Numero de orden 121, Fondo 63.

Chapter Three

Diplomacy and Statecraft

As detailed in the previous chapter, Moscow had taken considerable interest in Cuba via the Third International, or Comintern, with the Russian Revolution also having impacted on the island's political landscape. This chapter will examine the other component of the Kremlin's "dual track" diplomacy as it will analyze more traditional forms of diplomatic links that existed between the two countries. Moreover, it will also examine the substantial cultural connections and the limited levels of bilateral trade that had taken place at various times in the period between the Russian and Cuban Revolutions.

The first official contact between Russia and Cuba predates the Russian Revolution and took the form of a short telegram from the Cuban President, Tomas Estrada Palma, to Tsar Nicholas II on 26 March 1902.[1] This, however, was the extent of diplomatic contact at this time and it was not until October 1942 that diplomatic relations between the Soviet Union and Cuba were created. On 5 October 1942 the Cuban Foreign Minister, José Agustín Martínez, sent a telegram to his Soviet counterpart Vyacheslav Molotov requesting that diplomatic relations between Moscow and Havana be created.[2] Regarding this, on 10 October 1942 the Cuban newspaper *The Havana Post* stated,

> The Cuban Government has decided to recognise Russia and establish diplomatic relations with the Soviet Union, Prime Minister Ramon Zaydin revealed yesterday in a speech delivered at the National Theatre during ceremonies feting the anniversary of the Grito de Yara.[3]

EL Mundo's reporting was more celebratory in nature when it stated, "The final culmination of the celebration in the National Theatre to commemorate the Grito de Yara was Prime Minister Dr Zaydin's announcement that diplomatic relations with the Soviet government of Russia were to be created."[4] The importance which Cuba attached to the creation of diplomatic relations was illustrated on 25 October 1942 when the Cuban journal *Bohemia* published the article "La Bandera de Rusa en la cancilleria Cubana" which proudly stated, "Cuba is the second nation of the Americas – the first was the United States – to have relations with the Soviet Union."[5] As stated in chapter 1, diplomatic relations had existed between Moscow and Mexico and Uruguay in the 1920s and 1930s, which had been subsequently broken, but this is not to downplay the significance of the creation of diplomatic relations between Moscow and Havana in 1942.

With the creation of diplomatic relations Maxim Litvinov became the Soviet charge d'affaires to Cuba. This is highly interesting because in the 1930s Litvinov had been the Soviet Commissar of Foreign Affairs before becoming Moscow's ambassador in Washington. In his position as Soviet charge d'affaires to Cuba, Litvinov may not have actually lived on the island, but he was most certainly not a mere party apparatchik. In the immediate aftermath of the creation of bilateral diplomatic relations Litvinov held a number of meetings in Washington with Aurelio Concheso, who would become Cuba's first ambassador to the Soviet Union. Interestingly Litvinov requested the first meeting on 14 October 1942 on the behest of Molotov and on 26 October 1942 Concheso sent a report of this meeting to the Cuban President Fulgencio Batista. In this Concheso reported that Litvinov had asked about the Antifascist League in Cuba. In his reply Concheso had "thought it necessary to explain the political organization on the island" with this including the social-democratic coalition and the role of the Cuban Communist Party (PCC).[6] It appeared that from the inception of diplomatic relations the Soviet Union was showing an interest in the political situation within the island. In addition to this, in April 1943 Litvinov visited Cuba during which he not only met a number of Cuban intellectuals at the Hotel Nacional in Havana, but while in the Cuban capital he also met Batista.[7]

During this visit *Bohemia* published the article "El Embajador Litvinoff en la Habana," written by José Luis Martín, the nature of which is surprising as it mocked the idea that the Third International, or Comintern, was interested in the island and even called Litvinov "fun loving."[8] This content is somewhat unusual, but the inclusion of such material would make it appear that sections of the Cuban population had reservations about the creation of diplomatic relations with Moscow. This may have been a legacy of the Comintern interest in Cuba in the early 1930s, which was detailed in the last chapter, but if these concerns had not existed, *Bohemia* would not have published such an article. Moreover, very interestingly the article also stated that Litvinov had spoken of Soviet interest in trade with Cuba. Vyacheslav Molotov, Soviet Commissar of Foreign Affairs, in August 1939 writing about the importance of trade with Cuba being likely to increase due to the disruption in global trade as a result of the effects of World War II, which were examined in the previous chapter, could partly explain Litvinov's comments, but bilateral trade is a topic that will be returned to later in this chapter.

As stated, Aurelio Concheso became the first Cuban ambassador to the Soviet Union and arrived in Moscow in mid May 1943. On 21 May 1943 Concheso sent a report of his arrival to the Cuban Foreign Minister Emeterio Santovenia in which he grandiosely stated that "the Cuban flag is flying over the capital of the socialist world."[9] He also reported that on 21 May 1943 he had met Mikhail Kalinin, Soviet Head of State, with his description of the meeting including the fact that it had lasted for 20 minutes and that "President Kalinin is a middle aged person whom appears to be in good health. Throughout he displayed warmth and friendliness toward relations with Cuba."[10] Concheso also stated he had emphasized to Kalinin Cuba's desire to fight Nazism. Three days later on 24 May 1943 Concheso presented his credentials as Cuban ambassador to the Soviet Union to Joseph Stalin, with Molotov also being present at the meeting. *Pravda* printed a very short report of this meeting five days later on 29 May 1943.[11]

However, the *Pravda* report does not convey the full details of the meeting because in the archive for the Commissar for Foreign Affairs in the Russian State Archive for Social and Political History in Moscow a transcript of this meeting, which took place in the Kremlin at 2200 on 24 May 1943, exists. The meeting began with Concheso reading a statement from the Cuban government in which he said

> your people in Leningrad just as your armies in the epic battle of Stalingrad, have shown in the will to victory, an unequal heroism and spirit of self-sacrifice that will live forever as an example of humankind. The people of Cuba, loving their liberty for which they fought for decades, have known how to appreciate your titanic efforts, and in initiating the establishment of diplomatic relations between our two countries, have wanted to render tribute and homage to your patriotism and to that of the armies and the people of the Soviet Union. [12]

As this meeting marked the creation of diplomatic relations, and with World War II continuing to engulf Europe, such sentiments from the Cuban government are unsurprising. However, another part of the statement stated,

> the President wishes me to convey to you, the keen interest with which Cuba has followed the course of your Government during the period preceding the war in the effort to create for the People of the Soviet Union a prosperous and happy destiny at peace with all the nations of the world and the horror with which it saw how when these events were achieving success through the collective will and sacrifice of all, the barbarous nazi-fascist aggression in violation of sacred conventions, compelled the Soviet Union to mobilize all its

national resources and energies in order to save, together with the achievement
of your great and human revolution, the very independence of the Soviet
Union and the freedom of the world. [13]

The sentiments toward the end of this section may refer to the greater evil of
Nazism, but those at the start are somewhat surprising as a result of both the
influence which Washington had in Cuban political life and also that prior to
World War II, Washington and Moscow had endured a less than cordial
relationship. It could have been assumed that this would have prevented such
sentiments being contained in this statement. However, diplomatic protocol
may have tempered this, but their inclusion is surprising.

The Cuban government statement read by Concheso was only one part of
the meeting with the remainder of it consisting of the Soviet leader asking the
Cuban ambassador a series of seven questions about Cuba, the nature of
which are highly revealing about Stalin's knowledge of the island. These
questions included "how many people live in Cuba," "how many are of
Spanish descent," "how many soldiers are there in the army" and "what are
Cuba's main exports?" [14] These are far from being the most sophisticated
questions, but the final two would make it appear that the Soviet leader was
attempting to ascertain what the Soviet Union could "acquire" from this new
relationship with Cuba. At the time of this meeting, the early summer of
1943, it was still unclear if the Allies would defeat Nazi-Germany and with
the Soviet Union continuing to encounter food shortages, the nature of Stalin's final two questions is much less surprising.

Although this is the case, the Soviet leader's first two questions to
Concheso are extremely interesting as they were "Tell me, Cuba appears an
independent country, is it not dependent on the United States?" and "are
there Cubans in the American army?" [15] The nature of Stalin's questions
would suggest that he did not possess the most nuanced understanding of
Cuba, but the first two show that he did understand the political role that the
United States played in the island. This may have partly been the result of the
role that the United States played in the creation of diplomatic relations
between Moscow and Havana, which will be detailed later. However, the
first two questions would suggest that the Kremlin's real interest was not
Cuba per se, but the island's relationship with Washington. This agrees with
the ideas of Light, detailed in chapter 1, when she suggested that Soviet
interest in the Developing World really focused on the colonial power or
metropolitan state rather than in the Developing World country itself, with
this still being applicable to Cuba due to its relationship with the United
States.

Due to Stalin's domination of the Soviet political system, with this adhering to the Great Man Theory, his interest was vital for Soviet-Cuban relations. Moreover, Stalin's interest could also result from a legacy of the previ-

ous attention which the Soviet Union, predominantly via the Comintern, had paid in Cuba and the Cuban Communist Party (PCC) prior to this meeting which was detailed in chapter 2 of this book. This included the 1933 general strike which has been described as "the most substantial revolutionary opportunity seen in Latin America before the 1950s."[16] In addition this also comprised the "successes" of the PCC that had been achieved via the "popular front" strategy of the Comintern which had included Juan Marinnello and Carlos Rafael Rodríguez being appointed to Batista's cabinet in the year before Concheso's meeting with Stalin and also Molotov preparing the report "What opinion of the Cuban Government" for the Supreme Soviet in August 1939 that was also detailed in the previous chapter. The importance of Marinnello, and Rodríguez's appointments in 1942 and their impact on Cuban political life for Stalin's interest in Cuba are given more credence since in his report of this meeting, which he sent to the Cuban Foreign Minister Santovenia, Concheso wrote that Stalin, "also had an interest in the activities, which President Batista had engaged in the social sphere, especially rural schools and the increase in citizen's rights last year."[17]

In addition to this, it also appears that Moscow attached more importance to its relationship with Cuba than with other Latin American countries. Stalin conducted a similar meeting with the Mexican ambassador on 20 April 1943 at which he asked a similar number of questions, but unlike in the meeting with Concheso he also asked about Argentina and Chile.[18] The Kremlin's relationship with Mexico may have been strained due to the break in diplomatic relations in January 1930 and the presence of Leon Trotsky in Mexico in the late 1930s, but omitting questions about other Latin American countries in the meeting with Concheso would suggest that Stalin had singled out the Caribbean island in preference to Argentina, Chile, or Mexico. This is all the more interesting due to Cuba being considerably the smallest country both in geographical terms and economically in this quartet.

The importance which the Kremlin appeared to attach to its relationship with Cuba is further illustrated by the fact that on 31 May 1943 Molotov wrote to Concheso regarding his meeting with Stalin. In this Molotov wrote, "Stalin has given me the special mission to thank the president of the Republic of Cuba General Fulgencio Batista for his friendliness toward the Soviet people." Molotov continued, "J.V. Stalin hoped that diplomatic relations between the Soviet Union and Cuba will bring the people of the two countries closer together."[19] Diplomatic protocol may partly explain these sentiments, but on 24 June 1945 Concheso, along with the Chilean, Mexican, and Uruguayan ambassadors, were invited to the celebrations in Red Square to mark the victory in World War II.[20] The result was that a Cuban representative was present at one of the most historic and important days in Soviet history.

This, however, does not explain why diplomatic relations had been created, but in the early to mid-1940s Moscow created diplomatic relations with a
number of countries in Latin America, with the role of the United States in
the region, global events, and the realist paradigm of International Relations
being vital for this process. As detailed in chapter 1, the United States may
not have officially recognized the Soviet Union until 1933, but the unleash-
ing of Operation Barbarossa by Nazi Germany against the Soviet Union and
the Japanese attack on the United States at Pearl Harbour had ultimately
resulted in Moscow and Washington becoming allies in the fight against the
Axis powers. Paterson et al. have described this wartime alliance between
Washington and Moscow as a "marriage of convenience,"[21] but the Kremlin's willingness to join this alliance illustrated the Soviet elites' adherence to
the central tenets of realism, which Grigor Suny believes was evident in the
Soviet leadership's thinking from soon after November 1917. Simply this
alliance had been formed to safeguard the security of the Soviet state and
thus also the Russian Revolution itself as both had been placed in jeopardy
by Operation Barbarossa.

However, a byproduct of this alliance with Washington was the creation
of diplomatic relations between the Soviet Union and a number of Latin
American countries. Bilateral relations between Moscow and Havana followed this trend with the importance of the United States in it being further
illustrated by both the fact that Litvinov had presented his credentials as
Soviet charge d'affaires to the island at the Cuban embassy in Washington,
and also that in the *Havana Post* article of 11 October 1942 which had
announced the creation of diplomatic relations it was stated that,

> It was learned in diplomatic circles last night that negotiations between the
> Cuban government and officials of the Russian embassy in Washington, lead-
> ing to the establishment of diplomatic relations have been going on for some
> weeks.[22]

Moreover, as detailed during Litvinov's trip to Cuba in April 1943, *Bohemia*
had proudly stated that the Caribbean island had been the second country in
the region, the first had been the United States, to create diplomatic relations
with Moscow, further illustrating the importance of the influence which
Washington had had in Soviet-Cuban diplomatic relations. It was this and a
byproduct of the wartime alliance between Moscow and Washington, underpinned by the principles of realism, that had resulted in the creation of diplomatic relations between Moscow and Havana in April 1942.

In August 1943 Litvinov was replaced as Soviet charge d'affaires to Cuba
by Andrei Gromyko. Similarly to when Litvinov became Soviet charge
d'affaires to Cuba, Gromyko presented his credentials not in Havana, but
rather to President Roosevelt of the United States, again highlighting both the

U.S. influence in Cuba at this time and its importance in Soviet-Cuban relations.[23] Again, Gromyko did not live on the island but in December 1943 he did travel from New York City to Havana. During this trip, on which he was accompanied by his wife, he also met Fulgencio Batista, with the *Havana Post* stating, "Although little is known here of the functions planned by the Cuban Government, it is expected the couple will stay at the National Hotel and will be widely feted in the three or four days they expect to remain in the city."[24] Gromyko sent a very brief report of his meeting with Batista to Molotov on 22 December 1943. However, it does not provide a great deal of insight into this meeting and regarding the Cuban leader, Gromyko stated, "He spoke of the Cuban populations support for the Soviet people."[25]

While in Havana, Gromyko also met the Cuban Foreign Minister Emeterio Santovenía and was accompanied to this meeting by Dmitri Zaikin, which is extremely interesting for a number of reasons. Evidence exists that Zaikin had been in Cuba for some time before this meeting because on 8 November 1943 he sent a report to Molotov detailing the nature of the celebrations to commemorate the Russian Revolution that had been held in Cuba. As detailed this included an event held on 6 November 1943 at the Capitol Building in Havana which had been organised by the Antifascist League with Zaikin claiming that 6000 people had attended. He also stated that 400 people were present at the celebrations held at the Soviet embassy in the Cuban capital.[26] Moreover, Zaikin would become the future Soviet representative of the Soviet Society for Cultural Relations with Foreign Countries (VOKS) in Cuba, resulting in him having met members of the Cuban political elite before taking up this position. In addition, the significance of this organization for Soviet-Cuban relations was considerable and thus will be detailed much more fully later in this chapter.[27]

In addition to this, Gromyko's appointment as Soviet charge d'affaires to Cuba is important for the relationship that would develop between the Soviet Union and Revolutionary Cuba in the late 1950s and early 1960s due to the trajectory of Gromyko's future career as he would become the Soviet Minister of Foreign Affairs. This meant that in January 1959 at the time of the Cuban Revolution, a member of the Soviet ruling elite had personal experience of the island that had been acquired from this earlier period.

While diplomatic relations were in existence a series of telegrams were exchanged between the ruling elites. The majority of these were extremely brief and took the form of formal greetings being sent on significant dates for the respective countries. This included Batista sending greetings to Kalinin on the anniversary of the Russian Revolution in 1942 and 1943.[28] This was repeated by the then Cuban President Ramón Grau San Martín in 1944, before on 17 August 1945 he sent congratulations to Kalinin on the Allies victory over Japan in World War II.[29] The fact that such correspondence took place while bilateral diplomatic relations were in existence is not surprising with diplomatic protocol underpinning these exchanges.

This exchange of greetings continued after the end of World War II and interestingly the Kremlin was notified on 27 August 1948 that Carlos Prio Socarras was to become Cuban President. On 4 October 1948 Molotov sent a telegram to the Cuban government accepting the invitation for a Soviet representative to be present at Prio's inauguration.[30] Again, diplomatic protocol would be significant for this. Also in 1949, N.M. Shvernik, Chairman of Supreme Soviet of the Soviet Union, sent greetings to Prio on 19 May 1949 to mark the Caribbean island's national holiday. Prio reciprocated this by sending a telegram to Shvernik on 7 November 1949 on the occasion of the anniversary of the Russian Revolution. He would do this again in 1951.[31]

Bilateral diplomatic relations may still have been in existence at this time, but the correspondence that took place after 1945, and the Cuban invitation for a Soviet representative to be present at Prio's inauguration, are highly interesting. This was due to the fact that they were sent after the end of World War II and the wartime alliance between Moscow and Washington had not just been confined to history but relations between the Soviet Union and United States had rapidly deteriorated. Moreover, as referred to in chapter 2, Bethell and Roxborough have written that in the immediate aftermath of World War II "a marked shift to the right"[32] took place in Latin America, with this only increasing as the 1940s progressed.

As detailed in the previous chapter, this regional political move to the right was repeated within the Cuban political system with cases of intimidation against Cuban Socialist Party (PSP) members and volunteers appearing in the late 1940s, including in April 1947 the PSP radio station *Mil Diez* being taken over by force by the Ministry of Communication.[33] This was very different from the war years when Benjamin believes that local communist parties in Latin America had been highly useful for local governments with their ability to foster anti-fascist sentiment amongst their populations. The PSP was no different, but this abruptly stopped with the end of the war.[34] Soviet-Cuban relations were not immune to the political move to the right within the island as these cases of intimidation also started to impact on the relationship. This was particularly the case in June 1945 regarding Soviet couriers entering Cuba and also in June 1949 a number of Soviet citizens were arrested in Cuba for distributing pro-Soviet literature on the island.[35] Regarding this, *Pravda* printed the article "Anti-Soviet Statement by the President of Cuba," which stated,

Fawning before his masters, the American reactionaries, Socarras permitted himself a number of absurd slanderous attacks against the Soviet Union. He declared that the Soviet Union has a part in the activity of Communist parties in other countries. The Cuban President's anti-Soviet statements merely testify to the pathetic role played by the Cuba's present rulers, who are betraying the interests of their country to American monopolists. It is not surprising that in a country where such statements by the President are possible the police bait and persecute progressive figures and organise police pogroms. At the end of May the police raided the building belonging to a cultural and educational organization of Byelorussians and Ukrainians living in Havana. [36]

This is a scathing attack and most certainly does not use diplomatic language. As a result, it could have been thought that diplomatic relations would have been severed for a number of reasons. This included the political move to the right and the importance of Cuba's relationship with the United States in general and specifically for the creation of diplomatic relations between Moscow and Havana. Moreover, the onset of the Cold War would only have made this more likely. Furthermore, a number of Latin American countries broke diplomatic relations with the Soviet Union in the immediate aftermath of World War II. However, as neither Moscow nor Havana broke diplomatic relations over these two incidents in 1945 and 1949 it highlights the importance of the bilateral relationship for both countries. Moreover, these two incidents appear to be the "exceptions" regarding Soviet-Cuban relations and Soviet citizens in Cuba. This was illustrated by the cordial tone of the correspondence between the two elites which continued at this time. Furthermore, diplomatic relations between the Soviet Union and Cuba remained in place until April 1952.

As discussed in chapter 2 this suggests that at this time Havana enjoyed a degree of political independence from Washington that has not previously thought to have been the case. What was vital for this was, as detailed, the fact that the PSP provided legitimacy for the Cuban political system which in the years immediately after World War II did not only undergo a marked shift to the right but also became increasingly corrupt and violent. [37] This legitimacy would have been lost if the PSP had been outlawed and if this had taken place it would have increased the tension in an already tense situation. The Ramón Grau and Prio governments were not prepared to do this as the PSP remained legal until Batista once again became Cuban President in early 1952. The result was that despite the political move to the right in Cuban politics which had manifested itself in cases of intimidation against the PSP, the party performed a significant role within the Cuban political system in the aftermath of World War II.

This was crucial for Cuban-Soviet relations, but the relationship also mirrored this partial move against the PSP that fell short of outlawing the party, because again it was not Grau or Prio but Batista that "engineered" the severance of diplomatic relations with Moscow in April 1952. This will be detailed more fully later in this chapter, but from 1947 until April 1952 Cuban diplomatic affairs in the Soviet Union were conducted by the Mexican embassy in Moscow as a result of the closure of the Cuban embassy in the Soviet capital.[38] The reason for this appears to be the unfolding Cold War and more precisely the Soviet stance over the question of the Allied occupation of a divided Germany, as documents exist which illustrate the tension which appeared between the Moscow and Havana regarding this. On 27 March 1947 the Cuban Minister of State Rafael González Muñoz contacted the Soviet embassy in Havana criticizing the Soviet action at the Council of Foreign Ministers held in Moscow in March 1947.[39] On 8 April 1947 a meeting between Yakov Malik, Soviet Deputy Commissar for Foreign Relations, and Alberto Espinosa, Cuban ambassador to the Soviet Union, was held in Moscow regarding this. At this meeting Malik acknowledged the tension which had resulted from the unfolding situation in Eastern Europe, but hoped that it would not adversely affect bilateral relations between Moscow and Havana.[40]

The closure of the Cuban embassy in Moscow did not just constitute part of the move to the right which took place in the Cuban political system at this time, but Soviet-Cuban relations had once again been impacted by global events. Moreover, Havana's relationship with Washington and the role of the U.S. in the island would also appear to be important as the United States was most certainly unhappy about the events in Eastern Europe, with Havana's displeasure illustrating its pro-U.S. leanings in many issues. Although this was the case, diplomatic relations were not actually severed by Havana, illustrating a degree of political independence from Washington. Significant for this was both the Grau and Prio government's policies toward the PSP, because it would have been incongruous if Soviet-Cuban diplomatic relations were broken while the PSP provided legitimacy for the Cuban political system. In short, Grau and Prio were unwilling to jeopardize this by pursuing a more aggressive policy against the PSP or breaking diplomatic relations with Moscow.

An unforeseen consequence of the Cuban political situation in the years immediately after World War II was to increase Soviet attention in the island, because the longer the PSP remained legal due to this important role it played within the island's political system and performed well in elections, the Cuban party appeared to highlight the "success" of the "popular front" strategy of the Comintern, outlined in chapters 1 and 2. The Third International may have been disbanded in the summer of 1943, but the PCC and subsequently the PSP continued to adhere to this strategy of working within the local political systems and enjoyed more "success" when compared to other Latin American communist parties. As outlined in chapter 2 this 'success' was in terms of both its membership and political achievements: in 1942 Juan Marinello and Carlos Rafael Rodríguez had been appointed to Batista's cabinet. This led Karol to write that it was "the most important Communist Party in Latin America."[41] Moreover, this continued the trend since the

1920s of the island appearing to be a "hot bed" of left wing activity, in part as a result of economic dependence on the United States. As detailed in the previous chapter the Cuban party may have been closely associated with "Browderism" in the Communist Party of the United States (CPUSA) in 1945 with this appearing to affect its relationship with the Kremlin, but due to its size and "achievements" it would have appeared somewhat unusual if Moscow as the center of the world revolution had ignored either the party or its "successes."

In addition to this, Soviet attention in Cuba was only intensified by the island's geographical location and relationship with the United States. Moreover, any communist success in Cuba could also have repercussions for U.S. investments on the island which would have further increased Moscow's interest in Cuba as these would undermine the United States. By the mid-1940s the Comintern may have been confined to history, but the onset of the Cold War only heightened the Kremlin's interest in the PSP and Cuba as any revolutionary success on the island could be used to counterbalance Washington's anti-Soviet policy elsewhere in the world. As outlined in the previous chapter this was particularly the case with the advent of the Marshall Plan in Western Europe which constituted part of the U.S. desire to contain Soviet influence which had come to prominence after George Kennan's "long telegram" of February 1946. These ideas of containment only fuelled the traditional Russian fear of hostility from outside powers, with this highlighting the significance of both the ideas of statists and constructivism within Moscow's foreign policy. In addition to this, the Kremlin's policies toward Cuba were in accordance with Mearsheimer's ideas that states act to maximize their power at the expense of others, and Grigor Suny's belief that from soon after November 1917 the Soviet leadership displayed realist thinking. In addition, this is also in line with Moscow's policies toward the Developing World in general that were outlined in chapter 1.

The result was that in this period these factors combined to make the relationship, or at least the PSP and consequently diplomatic relations for the Cuban government, important for both Havana and Moscow. For the Cuban government the PSP provided legitimacy for the island's political system, with this in turn only increasing Soviet attention in the island due to the apparent "achievements" of the Cuban party. The Kremlin could utilize any potential revolutionary success on the island to counteract U.S. anti-Soviet policy elsewhere. Realpolitik was fundamental for both Moscow and Havana regarding the bilateral relationship in the immediate aftermath of World War II.

As stated, in the mid to late 1940s it appeared that the Cuban government was displaying a degree of political independence from Washington as the Caribbean island, very much in the U.S. sphere of influence, seemed to be bucking the regional trend with regards to the legality of the PSP. In turn this seemed to be repeated with Cuba's relationship with the Soviet Union. Previously this was not thought to have been the case and appears to be contrary to traditional thinking on Cuban-U.S. relations at this time, as Havana seemed to be pursuing a somewhat different policy with regards to its relationship with Moscow. This is beyond the focus of this book, but this form of political independence, illustrated by both the legal status of the PSP and Cuban-Soviet relations, requires further examination by experts on Cuban-U.S. relations.

Diplomatic relations between Moscow and Havana were terminated on 3 April 1952, a matter of weeks after Batista had become the President of Cuba for the second time, when the Kremlin severed them in the aftermath of Soviet couriers being denied entry to Cuba while carrying a diplomatic pouch. The letter sent from G.E. Formin, Soviet charge d'affaires, to the Cuban Deputy Minister of Foreign Affairs terminating diplomatic relations stated

The USSR Legation in Cuba, on instructions of the Soviet government, considers it necessary to state the following.

> In view of the fact that on March 21, 1952, the Cuban government refused to allow diplomatic couriers of the Soviet Union to enter Cuba and thereby deprived the USSR Legation in Cuba of normal diplomatic contact with the government of the USSR, violating generally accepted diplomatic standards, the Soviet government is withdrawing the USSR charge d'affaires in Cuba and terminating relations with the government of Cuba. [42]

Furthermore, on 8 April 1952 *Literaturnaya Gazeta* published the article "A Soviet View of Cuba," by the journalist Yu. Yartsev. On Batista replacing Prio as Cuban President, Yartsev wrote,

> And so one President has taken over the place of another. What, it may be asked, has changed? Cuba remains as before a colony of the American monopolists, and both Presidents, the old one and the new, are only obedient puppets in their hands. The boss pulls the string—there is a coup in Havana; he pulls again—there is another coup and the next President turns up. There is almost no difference between the Presidents—it is a question of a struggle inside the Cuban ruling elite. [43]

This article is radically different in tone from earlier reporting on Cuba and omits to mention that that both Litvinov and Gromyko had met Batista in 1943. The geopolitical situation may have radically changed in the years between 1943 and 1952, but the break in diplomatic relations was very sudden, illustrated by the fact that the final edition of the Institute of Cuban-Soviet Cultural Exchange's journal *Cuba y la URSS* was published as late as

February 1952.[44] Both the Institute and this journal will be examined more fully in the next section of this chapter.

As with the creation of diplomatic relations in April 1942 the United States and its relationship with Cuba was also significant in its termination. The coup which had returned Batista to power had taken place in early March 1952, meaning that when the relationship was severed at the beginning of the following month, Batista would still have been trying to cement his power within the island. Key to this process was winning the backing of Washington which resulted in the incident with the Soviet couriers being denied entry to Cuba, providing Batista with the perfect opportunity of illustrating to the U.S. administration his pro-American credentials. On this, Thomas has written, "He realized that the circumstances of the cold war gave him new opportunities for ingratiation with the United States."[45]

In the archive for the Commissar for Foreign Relations in the Russian State Archive for Social and Political History in Moscow, there is a communiqué sent from A. Vishnevsky, Secretary to the Central Committee, to Stalin and the other members of the Soviet political elite on 27 March 1952. In this Vishnevsky provides a brief history of the relationship and states "Relations between Cuba and the Soviet Union existed for 10 years and they have been friendly." In this, interestingly he makes no comment on the intimidation of Soviet couriers in 1945 or the arrest of Soviet citizens in Cuba during the summer of 1949 which *Pravda* had been so scathing about. In addition, on the lead up to Batista returning to power he continues "General Batista reported the situation to the United States, which opened up his return to power thus ending the power of Grau Soccarras."[46] Furthermore, Vishnevsky then states that relations with the United States, Europe, and Latin America were the goal of Batista.[47] It would appear that the Kremlin believed that Washington had been complicit in the process which returned Batista to power.

Batista once again becoming the President of Cuba and these turn of events caused problems for the Kremlin in its relationship with Cuba resulting in the Soviet elite reassessing the relationship. This reassessment was illustrated by Vishnevsky's communiqué to Stalin. The re-emergence of such a pro-U.S. Cuban administration appeared to signal the death knell for the "popular front" strategy or other revolutionary activity on the island. In addition, in the extremely tense geopolitical situation of the early 1950s, it would have appeared somewhat unusual for diplomatic relations to continue to exist with a country which was governed by such a pro-U.S. President.

The nature of Havana's relationship with Washington was crucial for the existence of diplomatic relations between the Caribbean island and the Soviet Union in the ten year period from 1942 to 1952. It was this, combined with events geographically distant from the Caribbean and the realist paradigm of International Relations theory that were important for their creation. The impact of World War II had resulted in the wartime alliance between Moscow and Washington being created, with realism being crucial as the Soviet Union's very survival had been placed in jeopardy by Nazi Germany. A byproduct of this alliance was the creation of diplomatic relations between Moscow and Havana. However, it is very interesting that this relationship continued for a number of years after the wartime alliance had ceased to exist, the dramatic deterioration in relations between Moscow and Washington, and the advent of the Cold War. This resulted from the fact that the Grau and Prio governments were unwilling to outlaw the PSP as it provided legitimacy for the corrupt and violent Cuban political system which would have made a break in diplomatic relations with the Soviet Union appear incongruous. This in turn only increased the Kremlin's interest in the island due to the Cuban party's "successes," which could be used by the Kremlin to counter U.S. anti-Soviet policies elsewhere in the world. However, diplomatic relations came to a sudden and abrupt end in the aftermath of Batista becoming Cuban President for the second time as he "engineered" their termination to both cement his power in Cuba and illustrate his pro-U.S. credentials to Washington.

BILATERAL TRADE

As detailed in chapter 2, interest in the Soviet Union in Cuba began from soon after the Russian Revolution, but World War II caused an increase in this to take place. Part of this interest manifested itself in the reports that exist of food packages being sent from Cuba to the Soviet Union with the items being shipped including condensed milk and meat amongst others. Significantly these shipments took place during World War II and are in line with reports of pro-Soviet rallies being held in Havana in the summer of 1941.[48] Furthermore, Hugh Thomas in *Cuba: Pursuit of Freedom* has written that in 1941, "Russia by this time also required Cuban sugar, since the Ukrainian beet fields had fallen to Germany: 70,000 tons a month were sent via the Allies."[49]

The fact that these reports were from during World War II is undoubtedly important and will be analyzed, but this is by no means to suggest that this was the first time that some forms of "trade" between Latin America and the Soviet Union had taken place as 25.2 and 16.5 million rubles worth of trade with Argentina had occurred in 1929 and 1930, respectively.[50] This was the highest level of trade that Moscow conducted with one Latin American country in the years prior to World War II, with it representing a mere fraction of total Soviet global trade. However, it would correspond with the creation of the Soviet trading company Yuzantong in the Uruguayan capitol Montevideo in the late 1920s, further illustrating Moscow's tentative interest in trade with the region. As stated in the previous chapter the accusation has always existed that this trading company was a cover for more covert Soviet operations in the region, but this is not to discount the fact that despite the geographical distance between Latin America and the Soviet Union some levels of trade had taken place, and Moscow had shown some interest in "trade" with the region as a whole before the reports of Cuban food packages and sugar being sent to the Soviet Union during World War II.[51]

Moreover, these reports about Cuban agricultural produce being in the Soviet Union may also explain both Litvinov speaking about the possibilities for bilateral trade while he was in Cuba in April 1943 and also the nature of some of Stalin's questions in his meeting with Aurelio Concheso, the Cuban ambassador to the Soviet Union, in May 1943. As detailed earlier in this chapter, the Soviet leader's final two questions had appeared to indicate that he wanted to ascertain what the Soviet Union could "acquire" from its relationship with Cuba. This was not only due to the food shortages which continued to exist in the Soviet Union in mid-1943, but also because an embryonic "trading" relationship had already existed between the two countries due to the Soviet Union acquiring Cuban sugar two years before this meeting took place.

However, as with the establishment of diplomatic relations in April 1942, the effects of both World War II and also Havana's relationship with Washington were fundamental to Cuban sugar being shipped to the Soviet Union in 1941. As detailed in chapter 2, even before the Soviet Union entered the war, Molotov believed that it would impact on global trade with this increasing the importance of Cuba as a source of sugar. This was only intensified with, as previously discussed, the Nazi invasion of the Soviet Union in June 1941 placing the very survival of the Soviet state in jeopardy with this requiring the Kremlin to acquire allies in its battle with Nazism. This is in complete accordance with the principal tenets of the realist paradigm of international relations that states act to safeguard their own survival. Moreover, Waltz's ideas that "self-help is necessarily the principle of action,"[52] are also highly significant because the Soviet elite believed they must act to safeguard the security of the Soviet state, with this adhering to the ideas of neo-realism. However, this also applies to Thomas's aforementioned quote on page 129 regarding Cuban sugar being in the Soviet Union in 1941 as a consequence of the food shortages that resulted from the Kremlin's loss of Ukrainian agricultural output. This necessitated that Moscow find alternative sources for this important commodity. The alliance between Moscow and Washington may have been created to fight Nazi Germany, but a byproduct of this had been the establishment of both diplomatic relations and trade between the Soviet Union and Cuba as a result of Havana's relationship with the United States.

However, by 1955 when the Soviet Union bought sugar to the value of 32.2 million rubles from Cuba, the geopolitical situation was radically different from the war years. Not only was the wartime alliance between Moscow and Washington dead, but the Cold War was also raging.[53] In addition, diplomatic relations between Moscow and Havana had been severed three years previously. Although this is the case, Garcia and Mironchuk believe that the United States remained key to this sale of Cuban sugar to the Soviet Union due to the influence which Washington continued to play in Cuba. In the early 1950s an issue of overproduction in Cuban sugar arose and a solution to this was the sale of sugar to other countries. Despite the Cold War this even included the Soviet Union. Moreover, the United States had granted Cuba "permission" to make these sales to the Soviet Union.[54]

Washington unquestionably had an important part to play in this transaction, with practical economic reasons also being important, but this Soviet purchase of Cuban sugar also appeared to signify an increased interest in Latin America that the Kremlin began to show in the early 1950s. This is contrary to the ideas detailed in chapter 1 of Andrew and Mitokhin, Miller, and Pavlov that prior to the Cuban Revolution Moscow took little interest in the region, as significantly this commenced while Stalin was still the Soviet leader and before the subsequent change in Soviet foreign policy that took place in the mid-1950s after his death. However, it is in accordance with Light's assertion detailed in chapter 1 that with regards to the Developing World, the Kremlin's policies had begun to become more radical at this time. However, it has been thought that this excluded Latin America. Significant for this Soviet attention was the fact that Moscow could use any revolutionary success on the island to potentially counterbalance anti-Soviet U.S. policy elsewhere in the world. This returns to Soviet interest in Cuba being underpinned by the principles of realism.

Trade appeared to be at the forefront of this interest, with this only increasing in importance due to the regional political move to the right in the years in the immediate aftermath of World War II that had resulted in the break in bilateral diplomatic relations between Moscow and many Latin American countries. This interest was illustrated on 12 March 1955 when *Pravda* printed the article "Demands in Latin America for Expansion of Trade with USSR and People's Democracies," which had highlighted bilateral trade between Brazil and Czechoslovakia, but interestingly also for the wish amongst sections of Latin American society to increase trade with the Soviet Union in an attempt to reduce dependence on the United States. This had mirrored earlier articles published in *Izvestia* on 15 August 1953 and *Komsomolskaya Pravda* on 17 January 1954 that had focused on the desire in Argentina, Chile, and Brazil, respectively, for increased economic links with the Soviet Union.[55] Moreover, on 22 February 1953 a letter from Cuba written by Rojelio del Campo was printed in *Pravda* which stated,

The groundlessness of the assertion that there are no markets for our basic food product besides the United States of America and its satellites became completely evident after a report was widely disseminated in the country about the readiness of the Chinese People's Republic and the European people's democracies to buy a large quantity of sugar from us.[56]

Furthermore, in an *Izvestia* article on 15 August 1953 the journalist M. Mikhailov wrote, "The Soviet government, as was stated at the 5th session of the USSR Supreme Soviet, intends still more persistently to pursue a policy of developing trade between the Soviet Union and foreign countries."[57] In addition, on 22 January 1956 the article "For Expansion of Cooperation between USSR and Latin American Countries," appeared in *Pravda* which was the published transcript of an interview that Nikolai Bulganin, Soviet Prime Minister, gave to the U.S. magazine *Vision.* In this, Bulganin was quoted as having said,

American monopolies are opposing the attempts of Latin American countries to expand their trade relations, particularly with the countries of the socialist camp. As a result, a vast amount of coffee has accumulated in Brazil, sugar in Cuba, lead and zinc in Mexico and tin in Bolivia. By the end of 1955 there were about 200,000 tons of unsold saltpetre in Chile.[58]

Bulganin was not only highly critical of U.S. economic policy toward Latin America, but this interview signalled the Kremlin's apparent interest in the region's raw materials.

As detailed, Soviet interest in trade with Latin America was not a new phenomenon and directly linked to this were the realist and neo-realist paradigms of International Relations, but in particular Waltz's belief that "self-help is necessarily the principle of action."[59] In the 1950s Soviet agricultural production levels were poor, eventually leading to the implementation of the Virgin Land Campaign in an attempt to address this problem, but before its commencement the Kremlin's interest in increased foreign trade in general and Latin America specifically was partly a result of self-help. The Kremlin needed to acquire alternative sources for agricultural products because if they did not, Soviet food security could be questioned. The situation was repeated with the specific case of the 1955 Soviet purchase of Cuban sugar, because this provided a different source of much needed sugar which would partly help alleviate the shortfall in the production of this commodity.

The Soviet purchase of Cuban sugar in 1955 is undoubtedly important for the bilateral relationship prior to the victory of the Cuban Revolution, but it was very much the exception in the 1950s with trade quickly falling to its previous low levels.[60] Cuba's relationship with the U.S. was significant in this process because not only had the U.S. granted "permission" for the 1955 Soviet purchase of Cuban sugar, but the global reaction to the Warsaw Pact invasion of Hungary in October 1956 was also important. Washington was deeply perturbed by the situation in Hungary. However, in November 1956 Cuba, highlighting its close relationship with the United States, tabled a draft resolution at the United Nations (UN) on it. Regarding this draft resolution, D.T. Shepikov, the Soviet representative at the 11th Session of the UN General Assembly, stated in a speech on 19 November 1956 to a plenary session of the General Assembly,

> In attempting to give some credibility to their slanderous allegations, the authors of the Cuban draft resolution glibly refer to mythical "information of official Radio Budapest." However, verification of this charge has shown that Radio Budapest has not broadcast any such information. For this reason the Cuban representative no longer refers to this source today. On what, then, are the provocative fabrications of the Cuban delegate based? On nothing. [61]

In such a tense political situation it would have been somewhat surprising if Moscow had continued to purchase Cuban sugar. The island's relationship with the United States, and global politics in general, had once again impacted on Soviet-Cuban relations. However, and despite this, Garcia and Alonso have written that in late 1957 the Soviet ambassador to Mexico met his Cuban counterpart Oscar de la Torre in the Hotel Prado in Mexico City where they spoke of further Soviet purchases of Cuban sugar. [62] This further illustrates Soviet interest in Cuban sugar. However, no actual purchase took place.

The level of trade conducted between the Soviet Union and Cuba in 1955 may have represented a mere fraction of the total annual sale of Cuban sugar, but the Kremlin had shown interest in Cuban sugar at various times before this. As detailed in chapter 2 this included in August 1939 when Molotov wrote of the importance of Cuban sugar increasing due to the disruptive effects which the onset of World War II would have for the global market. In addition, in July 1949 the Soviet periodical *New Times* published an article by the journalist G. Rubtsov entitled "In Cuba" which focused on the Caribbean island's political and social situation, but began by concentrating on the importance of sugar for the island. Rubtsov details the level of the Cuban sugar harvest and wrote,

> The virtues of Cuban sugar are extolled at every step by huge electric signs and streamers on the streets of the capital. In the cinema, the latest Hollywood hit is preceded by impassioned appeals from sugar and tobacco firms to buy sugar and smoke cigars. [63]

The article may have turned into a polemic about the role of the United States in Cuba with Rubtsov writing, "Colonial dependence on the United States places Cuba entirely at the mercy of the monopolies,"[64] but this does not reduce the significance of the article and its focus on sugar in Cuban society.

As both bilateral diplomatic relations between Moscow and Havana existed at this time and Cuba was also the world's largest sugar producer, this article may be less surprising than it first appears. However, Soviet interest in Cuban sugar production can be dated to December 1921 when the Council of Labour and Defence had debated the possibility of purchasing Cuban sugar, with even the price to be paid being discussed.[65] The sale of Cuban sugar to the new Bolshevik government did not actually take place, but due to the effects of the Russian Civil War it is not surprising that this debate took place.

In 1921 agriculture production in the Soviet Union had been decimated by the civil war with it being so low that even the survival of the Revolution was questioned. This would eventually lead to the implementation of the New Economic Policy (NEP), but in 1921 the Soviet Union desperately needed agricultural products with sugar being no different and at this time Cuba was one of the world's largest sugar producers. Again, as in the 1950s, this once again returns to Waltz's ideas regarding self-help with the Bolshevik elite believing they were required to act to safeguard both their own survival and that of the Revolution. It is therefore less surprising that the Council of Labour and Defence had discussed the possibility of purchasing sugar from one of the world's largest sugar producers. The result was that the realist and neo-realist paradigms of International Relations underpinned the Soviet interest in Cuban sugar production in the early 1920s.

The Soviet Union showed interest in Cuban sugar at various times in the years from 1917 to 1959, with a commonality existing between the different occasions when this attention was apparent. This commonality was poor Soviet agricultural output which required Moscow to acquire sugar from other sources, with Cuba, one of the world's leading sugar producers in this period, providing this alternative. Different reasons underpinned the specific poor Soviet agricultural returns, but it resulted in interest in Cuban sugar being apparent in the early 1920s, during World War II, and the early 1950s, with this being in accordance with realism, neo-realism, and Waltz's ideas of "self help" due to the severe situation that faced the Soviet leadership on these three separate occasions. In addition, Cuba was one of the world's leading sugar producers throughout this period resulting in it being logical that the Kremlin should try and buy Cuban sugar when it faced these shortfalls. Havana's relationship with Washington was also undoubtedly important, particularly during World War II, and also to a lesser extent in the 1955 sale of Cuban sugar to the Soviet Union. However, this does not dilute the significance of the Soviet interest, and purchase, of Cuban sugar prior to January 1959.

CULTURAL LINKS

Regarding formal diplomatic contact between Russia and Cuba it was stated on the opening page of this chapter that this even predated the Russian Revolution with a telegram being sent from the Cuban President, Tomas Estrada Palma, to Tsar Nicholas II on 26 March 1902.[66] In a similar manner, cultural links between the two countries also predate the Russian Revolution with a number of reports of predominantly Russian dancers performing in Cuba. On 13 March 1915 Anna Pavlova became the first Russian to perform in Cuba, returning again in March 1917 to perform at the Sauto Theatre in Havana before spending the whole of the 1918 to 1919 season on the island, during which she not only performed in Havana, but also Santiago.[67] The number of Russians performing in Cuba increased throughout the 1920s and in the 1930s a ballet school was opened in Havana by the Russian Nikolai Yavorski, a former male soloist in Paris, which was attended for a time by the future famed Cuban ballerina Alicia Alonso.[68]

As a result it would appear that cultural links between the two countries have a considerable heritage with this questioning the disparaging manner in which cultural links between them in the period from 1959 to 1991 were often portrayed.[69] However, what is important for these early cultural links are once again Cuba's relationship with the United States and also the Russian Revolution. A number of the Russian performers travelled to the island from the United States with their performances being underwritten by U.S. impresarios. This was certainly the case with Pavlova with the previously mentioned performances, the Russian soprano Maria Kuznechova who performed Carmen in May 1923 having travelled from Key West with this being organized by the U.S. impresario Fortena Gallo, and also in March 1936 when Sol Erok arranged for Tatiana Rjabvshinskaja, Leonid Mjasin, and David Lishin to dance at the Auditorium Theatre in the Cuban capital.[70] As a result, these performances can be perceived as really being part of a "U.S. tour" with Cuba being added to the list of dates due to the close nature of relations between Cuba and the United States at this time, which also impacted on Cuban culture.[71]

In addition to this, other Russian performers in Cuba at this time were exiles from the Russian Revolution. Aleksandra Koshetsa who performed at the theatre Capitolio on the night of 16 February 1924 had left the Ukraine in 1919 while Yavorski had been a former artillery general in the tsarist army before leaving Russia for Belgrade and finally arriving in Cuba in the late 1920s.[72]

However, the same arguments can most certainly not be made with the opening in the summer of 1945 of the Institute of Cuban-Soviet Cultural Exchange in Havana with offices at Number 7 Bernaza Street. This institute evolved from the Institute of Hispanic Cuban Culture which had been created in 1926, with the Institute of Cuban-Soviet Cultural Exchange's first President being the celebrated Cuban anthropologist and intellectual Fernando Ortiz. From August 1945 until February 1952 the Institute published the aforementioned monthly journal *Cuba y la URSS*.

In the first edition of this journal Ortiz wrote that Soviet global influence had increased at an "extraordinary rate" due to the effects of World War II, which he interestingly states began in 1936 with General Franco's insurrection in Spain. [73]

Moreover, this issue also contained a letter dated 12 August 1945 from Vladimir Kemenov, the Soviet art historian and chairman of the Board of the All-Union Society for Cultural Relations with Foreign Countries, which stated, "The Soviet intellectuals, who are in agreement with the foreign cultural relations of the Soviet Union, are delighted with the creation of the Institute of Cuban-Soviet Cultural Exchange and the journal *Cuba y la URSS*." [74] He continues that this would be vital for the exchange of creative ideas in the fields of science and art. [75] Such sentiments by Kemenov and Ortiz in the first issue of *Cuba y la URSS* may not be surprising. However, they appear to almost justify the creation of the Institute, but as diplomatic relations continued to exist at this time, its creation and the publication of the journal are less surprising than would first appear.

In a number of issues of this journal attempts were made to show the longevity of cultural links between the two countries. This began as early as the second edition in an article entitled, "La amistadad de los Ajedreasitas Rusos y Cubanos," written by Anatoli Kafman. This article focuses on the invitation sent to the Russian chess Grandmaster Miguel Chigoin to participate in a competition at the Chess Club of Havana in January 1899. [76] Moreover, to illustrate the links between Russia and the region as a whole, a report was published in December 1945 that the Venezuelan revolutionary Francisco Miranda had been in Russia in September 1786. [77] With these appearing so soon after the creation of the Institute such articles could been seen in the same light as Ortiz and Kemenov's comments in the first edition of *Cuba y la URSS* as a way of "explaining" or justifying the Institute's endeavors due to the traditional perception of lack of contact between the Soviet Union, and before it Russia, with Cuba and Latin America as a whole.

The journal also carried advertisements encouraging people to join the Institute at a cost of $1 per year. For this, members received monthly copies of *Cuba y la URSS* and also gained access to the various functions organized by the Institute which included film screenings and recitals of Russian music. [78] This advertisement also illustrated the way in which the Institute and the journal operated. The Institute organized a number of events and cultural evenings highlighting the Soviet Union, its culture, and achievements since the Russian Revolution. In addition to this, the Institute also conducted Russian language courses and had a library of Russian music for the use of its members.[79] Throughout the time in which it was in circulation, *Cuba y la URSS* in the main published two types of articles: ones that focused on Soviet cultural exhibitions within Cuba and others on the Soviet Union and its achievements. Each of these will be examined in turn.

The events and cultural evenings began very soon after the Institute's creation with the Soviet film "1812" being shown at the Institute on 18 July 1945, while in December 1946 the Institute sponsored a pavilion at the Seventh Book Festival held in Parque Central in the Cuban capital. Nikolai Ludomviski, second secretary of the Soviet embassy, attended this while, as detailed previously, Carlos Rafael Rodríguez, member of the politburo of the PSP, spoke at the event "La URSS y la Cultura," which had been organized to coincide with the book fair.[80]

A number of other Soviet films were shown at various times in the period from the summer of 1945 until March 1952, with many being shown at the cinema Gris in Havana. This included on 7 May 1946 when three different Soviet films were shown with the first two concentrating on the Soviet re-public of Mongolia and the last one being "1 de Mayo en Moscú."[81] On 14 May 1947 the Soviet film "La Muchada 217" was shown at the same cinema, while on 20 October 1948 at the Riviera Theatre a documentary on Soviet youth was screened.[82] This was followed on 11 March 1949 with the docu-mentaries "Un Dia en la Union Sovietica" and "Nuestra Juventud" being shown at the Valdés Rodríguez Municipal Theatre in the Vedado district of the Cuban capital.[83]

In addition to the screenings of these Soviet films a number of cultural evenings celebrating Soviet culture were also organized by the Institute. On 5 November 1949, once again in the Valdés Rodríguez Municipal Theatre, a celebration for the anniversary of the Russian Revolution took place with a "homage" to the Soviet Union and its culture. The music was organized by Enrique González Mantici, the famed Cuban musician.[84] Moreover this was repeated in 1950 with a concert entitled "Homenaje a la Cultura Soviética. Selecto Programa Musical."[85]

Furthermore, the Institute sponsored numerous exhibitions in the Cuban capital often including photographic exhibitions illustrating Soviet life. From 16 to 27 January 1947 a photograph exhibition entitled "Exposición de Moscú" was held in the Salón de los Pasos Periodos in the Cuban Capital Building. Moreover, the March 1947 edition of *Cuba y la URSS* contained photos of this exhibition.[86] Furthermore, from 28 October to 4 November 1948 at the Casa de la Cultura in Havana the exhibition "La Mujer en la URSS" which showcased the achievements made by women in the Soviet Union since the time of the Russian Revolution was held.[87] During the fol-lowing month a photographic exhibition that contained 400 photographs enti-tled "Enseñanza para Ejercer los Derretíos Democracia en la URSS" was held at the Club Cultura Deportivo Metalúrgico. At this Carlos Rafael

Rodríguez spoke.[88] In August 1949 the same venue hosted another exhibition that contained a similar number of photographs which concentrated on Soviet culture while in April 1950 at the College of Masters in Havana a photographic exhibition that focused on the Soviet education system was held.[89]

In the early summer of 1950 the Institute organized a series of conferences to celebrate the achievements of the Soviet Union, but also the fifth anniversary of the Institute's creation. In May 1950 this included the conference "La URSS, Socialismo y Cultura" at which the Cuban poet Nicolas Guillen spoke.[90] This highlighted Guillen's interest and sympathies for the Soviet Union because as detailed in chapter 2 he had written to Batista in 1941 praising the improvements in the relationship between Moscow and Havana which were taking place due to the considerable impact of World War II on it. In the month following Guillen's article three further conferences were held with Juan Marinello, former head of the Cuban Communist Party, speaking at the conference on 21 June 1950 at the Patriotic Club that focused on Soviet theater, cinema, and dance. Furthermore, to celebrate this fifth anniversary a cocktail party was organized which was attended by Serafin Durin, Cultural Attaché of the Soviet embassy in Havana.[91] Moreover, regarding the success of the Institute in the previous five years, the August 1950 edition of *Cuba y la URSS* stated, "The circulation of *Cuba y la URSS* continues to be healthy and grow from day to day."[92]

The second main type of article which appeared in *Cuba y la URSS* were ones which highlighted Soviet achievements in all aspects of society. This included in April 1946 an article by the Central American writer Luis Cardoza Aragón who had attended the 1 May 1946 celebrations in Moscow in which he outlined them. In addition, he had also visited Lenin's mausoleum and glowingly wrote "Lenin appears almost god-like encased on a crystal of rock. It is fantastic how lifelike his body appears. Lenin's godliness lives and will always for the workers of the world."[93] Furthermore, in the summer of 1947 an interview with Y. Kogan, vice minister of the Soviet car industry, was published while the same edition also printed an article that focused on the pediatric hospital in Leningrad.[94] The August 1950 edition of this journal included the articles "La Universidad del Estado de Kazajstan" written by Tuelgeun Tazhibaiev, Rector of the Kazakhstan State University, and one written by Liudmila Dubrovina, Director of Education for Child Literature, on publications in the Soviet Union written by children.[95] In November 1950 and July 1951 articles focusing on Soviet television and radio written by V. Renard, second engineer of Central Moscow Television, and Nikolai Sabetski, respectively, were printed.[96]

Furthermore, in February 1951 the article "La protección al trabajo de los jóvenes obreros de la URSS" was printed while in November of that year an article which focused on Maxim Gorki written by A. Tarasenkov, subdirector of the Soviet journal *Novi Mir* was published.[97] Soviet cultural achievements were also highlighted including in the article "El Pació de Cultura de los Mineros de Karaganda" which was printed in the November 1951 edition of *Cuba y la URSS*, while in January 1951 an article consisting of photographs of the Lenin Museum in Moscow was published.[98]

In addition to this, periodically *Cuba y la URSS* also published articles about Soviet sport. This included in April 1948 when the article "50 anos de rusos boxeo" written by Valentin Durov was published, and in October 1950 in a special edition the journal printed a 28 page article that focused exclusively on Soviet sport. This covered a wide variety of different sports, including athletics, with the article also containing a number of photographs.[99]

Apart from the content of these articles, what is also highly interesting is the stature within Soviet society of the people who were writing some of them. In the aforementioned article on the Soviet car industry, Kogan was the vice-minister of the Soviet car industry. Moreover, in August 1948 the article "Nuestro Aporte a la Ciencia Mundial" was published, written by Sergei Vavilov, President of the Soviet Academy of Sciences, and in January 1950 a portion of the article written by I.A. Vlasov, President of the Presidium of the Soviet Union, entitled "J.V. Stalin creado del Estado Socialista Soviética multinacional" was printed.[100] A number may have been reprints of articles that originally appeared in Soviet publications, but this does not detract from the fact that *Cuba y la URSS* contained material written by prominent people within Soviet society including even the President of the Presidium of the Soviet Union.

The Institute's activities and content of *Cuba y la URSS* give rise to the fundamental question of how the Institute was acquiring its articles, films, information and photographs. The answer to this question returns to the ideas of soft power, and Gould-Davies' belief that "The Cold War was, in essence, a struggle between ideas," [101] with culture being significant to the "central requirement for Soviet foreign policy: to fragment and diminish the power of the Western bloc,"[102] which were detailed in chapter 1. Key for Soviet-Cuban relations was the role within Soviet foreign policy of propaganda with Nye having written,

> The Soviet Union also spent billions on an active public diplomacy program that included promoting its high culture, broadcasting, disseminating disinformation about the West, and sponsoring antinuclear protests, peace movements, and youth organisations.[103]

With relation to propaganda, Barghoorn has stated that it was significant within Soviet foreign policy from soon after November 1917 with Moscow utilizing it "as a political instrument for the survival and advancement of Soviet power."[104] In addition, this can also be linked to Tsygankov's ideas of the importance of civilizationists, who believed that Russian values were superior to Western ones, within Russian foreign policy that were detailed in chapter 1. Gould-Davies has written that with regards to Moscow and Washington's use of propaganda in the years immediately after the end of World War II "each side sought to penetrate the other's polity while denying access to its own."[105] In addition, in his February 1946 "Long Telegram" George Kennan wrote

> Everything must be done to advance the relative strength of USSR as a factor in international society. Conversely, no opportunity must be missed to reduce strength and influence, collectively as well as individually, of capitalist powers.[106]

Kennan believed both that this included the Developing World and that the Kremlin would utilize culture and try to infiltrate various groups in order to achieve its goals.[107]

The ideas of Soviet soft power, with propaganda at its forefront, is key to understanding both the creation of the Institute of Cuban-Soviet Cultural Exchange and also Moscow's interest in Cuba at this time. In the years immediately after the end of World War II the Soviet elite must have believed that the Cuban polity was ripe for penetration, because if they had not, the Institute simply would not have been created. The size and "successes" of the PSP, including in 1942 having two cabinet ministers within Batista's government, were crucial for this belief, as was the perception of Cuba as being a "hot bed" of labor radicalism in part resulting from adverse affects of Cuban economic dependence on the United States. This only increased in importance due to the geographical location of the island and its relationship with the United States. Furthermore, if the Soviet Union was successful in penetrating the island's polity it would have resulted in increasing Soviet influence in Cuba while reducing U.S. influence, which is in accordance with Mearsheimer's ideas on realism that states attempt to maximize their own power while simultaneously reducing the power of their adversaries. In addition to this, these "achievements" could potentially be used to counteract what the Kremlin perceived as anti-Soviet U.S. policy elsewhere in the world. The result was to highlight the significance of the realist paradigm of international relations for the Soviet interest in Cuba at this time. However, this questions the ideas that Soviet soft power never extended beyond its military borders or that after World War II Moscow severed cultural exchanges with the United States due to these Soviet activities in Washington's "soft underbelly."[108]

The fact that the Soviet Society for Cultural Relations with Foreign Countries (VOKS) was active in Cuba at this time is highly important. Writing about Soviet financial assistance to Latin American communist parties in the 1920s, Poppino has argued that this assistance was directly related to Moscow's perception of revolutionary potential in the respective countries.[109] The geopolitical situation in the mid-1940s may have been very different from the mid-1920s, but in a similar manner VOKS would only have become active in Cuba if the Kremlin believed that revolutionary potential existed on the island. This illustrates the importance which Moscow attached to both Cuba in general and more specifically spreading pro-Soviet material on the island, as does Radio Moscow broadcasting programs about the Soviet Union to Cuba on frequencies of 19, 31, and 41 meters.[110]

VOKS had been created in August 1925 with Article 1 of its statutes stating "to cooperate in the establishment and development of scientific and cultural relations between institutions, public organizations and individual scientific and cultural workers in the U.S.S.R. and those of other countries."[111] However, Ludmila Stern has written, "From its creation, VOKS began to manifest an underlying political agenda – that of promoting the Soviet system in the West by means of cultural cover."[112] The organisation's representative in Cuba was Dmitri Zaikin with the May 1946 edition of *Cuba y la URSS* stating that at a celebration in the Lonchamp suite of the Hotel Sevilla in Havana, Ortiz had met with Zaikin and his wife and that the discussions had been fruitful.[113]

As previously detailed, intriguingly Zaikin had accompanied Gromyko to his December 1943 meeting with the Cuban Foreign Minister Santovenía held during Gromyko's trip to the island. This is important as it resulted in Zaikin having met a number of the Cuban ruling elite before he took up his position as the head of VOKS on the island. In addition, Zaikin had been in Cuba for some time before taking up this appointment. This was illustrated by the reports he had sent on the situation in Cuba to the Soviet ruling elite, with this including Molotov, which even predate this December 1943 meeting with Santovenia. These reports highlight both the fact that the Soviet elite were in receipt of information regarding Cuba, and also that it appeared that Zaikin was the Kremlin's trusted "man in Havana." This resulted from both his presence on the island from soon after the creation of diplomatic relations in October 1942 and the nature of the reports he had sent to the Soviet Union, which focused on much more that merely bilateral cultural relations. It could also suggest that the Soviet Union's interest in cultivating cultural ties with Cuba did not start with the creation of the Institute of Cuban-Soviet Cultural Exchange in the summer of 1945, but from soon after bilateral diplomatic relations had been formalized due to Zaikin's presence in Cuba and position within VOKS.

Moreover, during Gromyko's December 1943 trip an exhibition depicting the Soviet Union in times of Peace and War had been staged in the Salón de los Pasos Periodos in the Capital building in Havana.[114] The staging of this exhibition and the one in January 1947 in the capital building that was detailed earlier in this chapter show the importance which the Cuban government attached to its relationship with the Soviet Union, as these exhibitions were being held in one of the most significant buildings in Havana.

However, after the creation of the Institute of Cuban-Soviet Cultural Exchange it can be concluded that it was Zaikin and his associates who were supplying both the information, and photographs that were subsequently published in *Cuba y la URSS*, and also films and documentaries that were being shown at various cinemas throughout Havana. Moreover, but perhaps unsurprisingly the Soviet embassy in Havana also appeared to be involved with this.[115] This is important, but the significance which Moscow attached to the work of the Institute was illustrated at the beginning of 1950 when Eugenio Mitskevich, the director of VOKS, sent "warm greetings" to the Institute and its members.[116]

The Comintern may have been disbanded two years before the Institute of Cuban-Soviet Cultural Exchange was created, but instead of this slowing Soviet interest in Cuba, it appeared to increase as was evident due to the Institute's creation in the summer of 1945 and the content and nature of *Cuba y la URSS*. Although this was the case, what is interesting is that in the previously detailed activities of the Institute, *Cuba y la URSS* did not report the involvement of prominent members of the PSP in them until January 1947 when Carlos Rafael Rodríguez had addressed the event "La URSS y la Cultura" in December 1946, which had taken place during the Seventh Book Fair held in Parque Central in Havana, and had been organized by the Institute.[117] This appears somewhat unusual because it could have been expected due to the nature of both the Institute's work and content of *Cuba y la URSS* that prominent PSP members would have been heavily involved in these activities from their commencement in the summer of 1945. As previously state, this may have resulted from a legacy of the PSP's association with the end of "Browderism" in the CPUSA in 1945 that was detailed in the previous chapter.

As previously detailed, any tensions which had existed between Moscow and the PSP over its association with "Browderism" quickly evaporated with the size and "success" of the Cuba party being important in the Kremlin's interest in the Caribbean island. This resulted in the relationship being beneficial for both the Soviet and Cuban governments due to the aforementioned important role that the PSP continued to play in the island's political system at this time. Furthermore, Soviet activities in Cuba were in line with the "popular front" strategy and mirrored VOKS activities in other countries. It was standard practice for this organization to cultivate ties with people who may be sympathetic toward the Soviet Union or at least had been involved in "dissenting" politics. This was repeated in Cuba with the prominence of the radical intellectual Fernando Ortiz within the Institute. It is very interesting that Antonio Núñez Jiménez, who would both fight in the guerrilla war of the late 1950s and become the Minister of Agrarian Reform in the Revolutionary

Government of the 1960s, was also active within the Institute by the time of its closure.[118]

Moreover, due to the nature of U.S.-Cuban relations, the involvement of VOKS in the island can be perceived as part of the battle of "hearts and minds" which Gould-Davies believes was significant during the Cold War.[119] In addition to this, VOKS activities could have resulted in Soviet influence on the island increasing while simultaneously reducing U.S. influence. This adheres to Mearsheimer's work regarding realism that countries attempt to maximize their own power at the expense of others. Furthermore, any revolutionary success on Cuba could potentially be utilized by Moscow to counter what it perceived as anti-Soviet U.S. policy elsewhere in the world. At the end of World War II, Europe may have remained the global focus of international relations, but this only increased the importance of Cuba for the Kremlin due to these effects of realism. Moreover, the significance of Cuba for Moscow at this time was further highlighted by the fact that this Institute was opened at the very moment that tension between Moscow and the PSP existed due to the effects of "Browderism" in the CPUSA. Problems may have existed with the Cuban party, but this had not reduced the Kremlin's considerable interest in Cuba, illustrated by this Institute's creations and the involvement of VOKS with it. However, this is very different from traditional thinking about the relationship between Moscow and Havana prior to 1959 or Soviet foreign policy in general toward Latin America, which at this time was thought to be dominated by the principles of "geographical fatalism."

The vast majority of the activities and work of the Institute may have been to increase the Soviet influence and prestige in Cuba, but this did not mean that the "cultural flows" were all in one direction as *Cuba y la URSS* printed various reports of Cuban cultural exhibits being held in the Soviet Union. In the very first edition of this journal in August 1945 the article "Pintura Cubana en Moscú" by N. Yaborskaia was published. This article focused on an exhibition of Cuban art held in the Cuban embassy in Moscow, which included paintings by Esteban Valderrama and Ramón Loy, and was attended by amongst others V. Kamenev, the Soviet Minister for Cultural Relations with Foreign Countries.[120] In November 1945 an article entitled "La Exposicion de Arte Cubano en Moscú" appeared which stated it was hoped that an exhibition of Cuban art, sculpture, and free drawings could be organized in the Soviet capital.[121] The June and July 1946 editions of *Cuba y la URSS* printed the articles "Arte Cubano en la URSS" and "Pintura Cubano en Moscú," respectively, which focused on this exhibition with the June article stating that the invitation for this to take place had been sent by VOKS. The July edition stated that it was envisaged the exhibition would be held in the Moscow Museum of Western Art, and would include paintings by amongst others Carlos Enríquez, Wilfredo Lam, Felipe Orlando, and Domingo Ravenet and sculptures by Teodoro Rames Blanco, Manuel Rodolfo Tardo, and Marta Arjoria.[122]

The plans for this exhibit appeared to be well formed, but it was not until the summer of 1948 that these paintings and other works of art actually left Cuba. In the November 1948 edition of *Cuba y la URSS* the article "Obras cubanos Expuestas en Moscú" was printed which included a picture of the crate containing these works of art being loaded onto a ship in Havana harbor. The article also stated that it was with "great satisfaction" that this crate had been sent to the Soviet Union.[123]

It may have taken some time for these paintings to actually leave Cuba, but this exhibition and the aforementioned one in the Cuban embassy in Moscow in 1945 were by no means the only Cuban exhibitions which had taken place in the Soviet capital. In 1946 it was reported that an exhibition of Cuban Architecture had been held in Moscow. Once again this had been the result of an invitation from VOKS with the exhibit concentrating on the growth and urbanization of Havana since the early seventeenth century. José Luciano Franco, President of the Institute's Section on Urbanism, organized the drawings and photographs that were sent which included photographs from the Cuban National Archive of the construction of Havana harbor. The photographs that were sent to Moscow were described as "magnificent" with a number of prominent people attending this exhibition including the Soviet Vice President of the Academy of Architecture, Alabain, and the Vice President of the Committee for Architecture and member of the Council of Ministers of the Soviet Union, Rubanenkov.[124]

In addition, in 1949 the Soviet Union of Writers invited Nicolas Guillen to the Soviet Union while toward the end of 1951 VOKS invited Enrique González Mantici, President of Cuban National Institute of Music, and his wife to Moscow.[125] This invitation was extended to Mantici and his wife while they were in Leipzig, having previously travelled to Berlin for the Grand Festival of World Youth for Peace. While in the Soviet capital they met Tijon Jrennikov, Secretary of the Union of Soviet Composers. The January 1952 edition of *Cuba y la URSS* published an interview with Mantici once he had returned to Cuba with much of it reading in a similar manner to a travel log with the Cuban musician describing the museums and libraries that he had visited, which included the Moscow Opera Theatre. He appears to have almost been "seduced" by the Soviet capital as not only does he refer to the modern nature of the museums and the fact that many concentrated on World War II, but also that it appeared that the Soviet population had a great interest in culture. Regarding Moscow in general, Mantici is quoted as having said, "There is much to say that is good about the Soviet capital, where you can witness the best of human mankind."[126]

Interestingly, while he was in Moscow, Mantici was invited to conduct the Moscow Radio Orchestra with the performance being broadcast to Latin

America and throughout the Soviet Union. Moreover, the February 1952 edition of *Cuba y la URSS* printed the article from the journal *Soviet Music* that reported Mantici's appearance on Soviet radio. The result was that over seven years before the victory of the Cuban Revolution a Cuban had performed on Soviet national radio with this highlighting the considerable cultural links that had existed between the two countries at this time.[127]

Mantici's visit, and the other Soviet invitations for Cubans to visit the Soviet Union, is important for a number of reasons. They illustrate that the "cultural flows" between the two countries that were taking place were not all in an east to west direction and also a number of these were after the Cuban embassy had been closed in the Soviet capital in 1947. It would appear that this had not had a dramatic negative effect on the cultural links between Moscow and Havana. Moreover, Mantici's visit appears particularly significant because on 11 August 1951 Molotov signed the papers which authorized VOKS to invite him to the Soviet Union.[128] This document is highly important as it illustrates the importance which the Kremlin attached to its relationship with Cuba and the work of the Institute in Havana, as the invitation was not authorized by a mere party apparatchik, but instead the Soviet Commissar of Foreign Affairs.

The Soviet Union's considerable interest in Cuba had therefore been evident while Stalin was the Soviet leader, which is significant for a variety of reasons. It appeared that Moscow very much desired a global presence before March 1953 which is important as it has traditionally been thought that this only commenced with the foreign policy changes which were implemented in the aftermath of Stalin's death. Moreover, this also questions the idea that prior to January 1959 the Soviet Union suffered from "geographical fatalism" with regards to its relationship with Cuba. In addition, the Caribbean island also appeared to be bucking the regional trend with regards to its relationship with Moscow as Cuba appeared to be continuing to enjoy cordial relations with the Soviet Union while most Latin American countries had severed bilateral ties in the immediate aftermath of World War II.

Although this is the case, as previously detailed some tensions did appear in the relationship in the period while the Institute of Cuban-Soviet Cultural Exchange was open but most noticeably on two occasions. The first resulted in Zaikin sending a letter to the Cuban Minister of State, Gustavo Cuervo Rubio, on 29 January 1945 complaining about the treatment that Soviet couriers entering the country had received.[129] The second occurred four years later and illustrated both the Cuban authorities' unease at Soviet activity on the island, and also the importance which the Kremlin associated with this relationship due to the arrest of a number of Ukrainians and Byelorussians for continuing to spread pro-Soviet literature throughout Cuba. The Soviet government was unhappy at this turn of events with the sharp response from *Pravda* being quoted earlier in this chapter.[130]

In the archive for the Commissar for Foreign Relations in the Russian State Archive for Social and Political History, documents exist on both these arrests and also a report of a meeting between the KGB and the Cuban secret police regarding them that was sent from the KGB officer Abakomov to Molotov on 3 May 1949. It was subsequently forwarded to Stalin, Mikoyan, and Beria.[131] The existence of this document is hugely important as it not only further proves that the very top of the Soviet ruling elite was receiving information about the Caribbean island in the 1950s, but also that KGB personnel had been present in Cuba prior to the Cuban Revolution. KGB interest in Cuba at this time is further illustrated by the report which Zaikin sent to the KGB on 8 November 1945 in which he detailed the celebrations in Havana for the Russian Revolution and criticizes the article "Socialism versus Capitalism" which had been printed in the Cuban newspaper *Marina*. Zaikin describe this paper as not just being right wing but even "falangist."[132] A KGB presence, and interest in the island, may not have been completely unexpected as a result of Soviet citizens living and working in Cuba; this had certainly occurred in Mexico in the 1920s when bilateral relations between Moscow and Mexico City had been in existence, but these documents prove beyond doubt that the KGB had been active and taken interest in Cuba prior to January 1959.[133]

Cultural links between the two countries not only predated the Cuban Revolution, but even the Russian Revolution. However, the original contacts were more the result of serendipity, Cuba's relationship with the United States, and the fact that many of the Russian performers had fled Russia in the aftermath of November 1917. However, the situation was very different at the end of World War II when the Institute of Cuban-Soviet Cultural Exchange was created in Havana, and published the monthly journal *Cuba y la URSS*. Both existed until April 1952 and the termination of bilateral diplomatic relations. The "cultural flows" were in both directions with the Kremlin taking considerable interest in these as evident by the involvement of VOKS. This interest was underpinned by the prevalence of left-wing politics on the island illustrated by the size and 'successes' of the PSP, but the nature of Cuban-U.S. relations was also important, not least from some effects of Cuban economic dependence on the United States. If Soviet cultural influence increased on the island it would simultaneously reduce U.S. influence. The Kremlin could also utilize revolutionary success on the island to counterbalance what it perceived as anti-Soviet U.S. policy elsewhere in the world. The importance of Cuba in general for the Kremlin, but particularly the cultural links, was illustrated by the fact that this Institute was opened and VOKS involvement in the island commenced at the time when tension existed between Moscow and the PSP due to the effects of "Browderism" in the CPUSA. In short, Soviet cultural interest in Cuba was highly important for

Moscow and was driven by the central tenets of the realist paradigm of international relations.

DE-STALINIZATION AND CHANGES IN SOVIET FOREIGN POLICY

As detailed, bilateral diplomatic relations between Moscow and Havana came to a sudden and shuddering end in April 1952 over the issue of Soviet couriers being denied entry to the island. This also had the effect of closing the Institute of Cuban-Soviet Cultural Exchange in the Cuban capital and ending the cultural links that had existed between the two countries. However, Moscow did buy sugar from the Caribbean island in 1955, but as stated this appeared very much a "one-off" as in 1956 the levels of trade quickly fell again.

This deterioration in the relationship coincided almost perfectly in time with the changes in Soviet foreign policy that occurred in the aftermath of Joseph Stalin's death. This is somewhat ironic as these changes, highlighted by Nikita Khrushchev's speech at the 20th Congress of the Communist Party of the Soviet Union (CPSU) are often perceived as having sparked the Kremlin's interest in the Developing World. [134]

Although this is the case, the Soviet Union did take some interest in Cuba in the period between the break in diplomatic relations in April 1952 and the victory of the Cuban Revolution in January 1959. However, this interest was at a very much reduced level compared to the years 1945 to 1952 and predominantly took the form of articles periodically appearing in the Soviet press. The exceptions to this were the aforementioned Soviet purchase of Cuban sugar in 1955 and two years later reports exist of the Cuban ballerina Alicia Alonso performing in the Soviet Union, including at the Bolshoi Theatre in Moscow. [135] Alonso's performances appeared more a return to the reports of Russian dancers performing in Cuba before World War I rather than the "systematic" nature of the cultural links in the period from 1945 to 1952 when the Soviet government had been heavily involved in them.

The Soviet newspaper reports which do exist at this time may not be large in number but their content is still revealing. In these Batista is referred to in various forms including a "U.S. puppet" with P. Yeronin in "The Big Stick Again!" writing "Batista is not really President of Cuba; he is the watch-dog for American investment." [136] Moreover, on 5 February 1957 *Pravda* printed the article "Bloody Atrocities in Cuba" written by V. Vasilchikov. In this he stated,

> Recently all honest people have been appalled by the monstrous crimes committed by the Cuban dictator Batista, who, in one night, without indictment or trial, shot 21 prominent progressive leaders in Cuba. Fulgencio Batista, or, as

he is called in America, the "Child of Wall Street sugar magnates," recently brought disgrace to Cuba.[137]

The anti-Batista nature of these articles is not surprising due to his role in the break in diplomatic relations between the two countries in April 1952 and his pro-United States credentials.

In a similar manner in September 1957 *New Times* published V. Tikhmenev's article "Sweeping the Dirt Under the Rug," which began by stating,

> "Soviet agents are responsible for the uprising against the Government," that irresponsible statement comes from President Batista of Cuba. There is nothing new in it. The reactionary faction in the West have time and again resorted to similar absurd allegations in order to sidetrack attention from their own aggressive plans and intentions. Who knows, they might discover "Soviet agents" conspiring on the Moon!"[138]

Not only does Tikhmenev ridicule Batista's statement, but his article very clearly illustrates that the more cordial period of relations between the two countries which existed while diplomatic relations were in existence were very much confined to history.

In relation to this, the above quoted articles that painted Batista in an unflattering light were also highly critical of the role of the United States in Cuba with many providing figures for U.S. investment in the island.[139] Again, this may have been expected, but what may be less so is the detail provided about the Cuban internal situation with this including both the insurgency and even labor relations.[140] In March and April 1956 the newspaper *For a Lasting Peace. For a People's Democracy*, published in Bucharest and the organ of the Information Bureau of the Communist and Workers Parties, printed two articles entitled "Strike Struggle in Cuba" and "Unity of Action of Cuban Working People." The first article listed the strikers' pay demands while the second one concentrated on the situation within the Las Villas Province on the island.[141] The fact that these last two articles were published in the organ of the Information Bureau of the Communist and Workers Parties was significant as this newspaper published articles not written by Soviet journalists but rather by people from the countries that the articles focused on. In particular, the two above cited articles were written by Blas Roca and Lazaro Pena who had both held the position of General Secretary of the PSP.[142] Interestingly, *New Times* in the autumn of 1958 within the section entitled "People in the News" printed an article about Fidel Castro and the situation in Cuba. This article did not only include a photograph of Castro, but stated

> Fidel Castro, a prominent leader of the insurgent force in Oriente Province, was born in 1927. His father was a wealthy planter and he was educated at the

Jesuit Dolores College in Santiago de Cuba and the Belen College in Havana. He studied law and social sciences at the University of Havana. Even in those university years Castro was active in the revolutionary movement.[143]

The article continued with an account of his failed attack on the Moncada barracks on 26 July 1953, subsequent trial, imprisonment, and exile in Mexico before turning to the situation in Cuba in 1958.[144] The article may have been fairly short, but its content is remarkable due to its detail of Castro's early life and revolutionary activities.

On 3 January 1959 *Pravda* printed the article "Cuba is Fighting, Cuba Will Win!" by V. Levin that reported Batista's flight from Cuba and stated "On January 1 1959, the dictatorship of this henchman of America collapsed under blows of the rebel movement."[145] Its tone may be similar to many of the other articles that had appeared in the Soviet Union regarding Cuba, but it is substantially longer, at over 1400 words, than previous articles and although Castro is not actually mentioned, it has considerable detail about the unfolding situation on the island. Its penultimate paragraph states

> The Cuban people have drunk the dregs of bitter suffering and they cannot be cheated or frightened off. The patriots have the firm attention of carrying the liberation through to the end. "If the American Marines land in Cuba," declared the insurgent radio, "we will fight them as we fought Batista's soldiers."[146]

This would appear to coincide with George Boughton's analysis of the Soviet press reporting on Cuba in his article "Soviet-Cuban Relations 1956–1960" in which he wrote of the importance of the changes to Soviet foreign policy implemented in the aftermath of Stalin's death for Soviet interest in Cuba. In relation to this he stated that throughout 1957 "Soviet policy makers began to look more closely at Cuban events."[147] He continues that Soviet policy underwent change in late 1957 and early 1958 with the aim being "to create conditions within Cuba favourable to the development of normal, especially commercial, relations between the two countries."[148]

In 1958, with the outcome of the guerrilla war uncertain, whether the increase in Soviet press reporting on Cuba illustrated this goal of Soviet policy toward the island is perhaps debatable. However, what appears significant was Herbert Matthews' trip to the Sierra Maestra in February 1957 to meet Fidel Castro with the subsequent article "Cuban Rebel Is Visited in Hideout" being printed on the front page of the *New York Times* on 24 February 1957.[149] Not only did this article disprove the idea that Castro had been killed, but the number of articles in the Soviet press on Cuba increased from this point onward.

Moreover, much of the reporting which did take place quoted articles printed in North America. In the autumn of 1957 *International Affairs* printed the article "Cuba in Flames" by M. Kremnyov in which when writing about civil resistance in Cuba he wrote, "The American Press, for instance, reported that four mines went off in Havana on June 12. One of them damaged a power station."[150] In December 1957 *New Times* published an article under the same title in which the *New York Herald Tribune* correspondent Hogan is cited.[151] The following year *International Affairs* published "The Big Stick Again!" written by P. Yeronin in which he quoted the Mexican magazine *Manana* but he also wrote "The American journal *Business Week* wrote that Batista himself had received $60 million in bribes in return for profitable concessions and privileges granted to various American companies."[152] In the summer of 1958 *New Times* in the section entitled "International Notes" cited the *New York World-Telegram* with relation to the situation in Cuba.[153] The aforementioned article by Levin that was published by *Pravda* on 3 January 1959 also references the *New York Herald Tribune, New York Times Magazine*, and the *New York Times* itself.[154]

In addition to this, in November 1957 *International Affairs* published "Cuba Aflame" by A. Burlakin in which he quotes the *Wall Street Journal* and also writes, "Describing the situation in Cuba, the American journalist Matthews likened Batista to a man fighting a rear-guard action while standing on the brink of a precipice."[155] In "Tottering Dictator" published in *New Times* in March 1958 Matthews' 18 February article in the *New York Times* is cited, while in April the same publication printed "The People and the Dictator" which referenced the *Wall Street Journal* and quoted the U.S. journal *Christian Science Monitor*. Furthermore it stated "Herbert Matthews of the *New York Times* wrote on March 29 that Havana was ripe for an uprising. Though the capital was outwardly calm, he said, the atmosphere was so tense it would not take much to blow the lid off."[156]

It would appear that the Soviet expertise on Cuba was not being acquired from an analysis of the actual situation within the island, but rather a reading of the U.S. press reports on Cuba. This is not to downplay the importance of the Soviet press reporting on Cuba as knowledge of the island did evidently exist within the Soviet Union, but it is a very different situation from the early 1950s when the top echelons of the Soviet ruling elite were receiving periodic reports on the Cuban situation.

Moreover, no documents regarding Cuba after the telegram ending diplomatic relations on 2 April 1952 exist in the archive for the Commissar for Foreign Affairs in the Russian State Archive for Social and Political History in Moscow. This may have been expected, but documents had existed in this archive before April 1942 when diplomatic relations had been created, most noticeably in August 1939. However, this practice of Moscow utilizing the U.S. media to acquire knowledge of Cuba continued even after January 1959. The KGB officer Nikolai Leonov has stated that even in April 1961 the KGB listened to U.S. radio reports during the Bay of Pigs invasion.[157] This is indicative of the situation regarding Soviet knowledge of Cuba in the period from the end of diplomatic relations in April 1952 to the victory of the Cuban Revolution that some interest in and knowledge of the island existed in the Soviet Union, but this was by no means to suggest that this was as systematic as had been the case before April 1952.

In the immediate aftermath of the victory of the Cuban Revolution the close personal relationship that Leonov had formed with Raúl Castro prior to 1959 was significant for relations between Moscow and Havana as the KGB officer was chosen to act as Mikoyan's interpreter during his February 1960 trip to Cuba due to his friendship with Raúl and his knowledge of the island. This friendship had been formed more by chance than by design as the two had met during 1953 as they travelled by ship from Genoa to Latin America, with Leonov also subsequently meeting Fidel Castro in Mexico during 1956. Again, this appears very different from the situation prior to April 1952 when the Soviet Commissar of Foreign Affairs had been in receipt of the documents which the Soviet ruling elite were receiving on the Cuban situation. [158]

CONCLUSIONS

Moscow's more traditional form of its "dual track" diplomacy existed with Havana in the period between the Russian and Cuban Revolutions and took the forms of formal diplomatic relations, trade links, and cultural ties. For all three, the island's relationship with the United States and the realist and neo-realist paradigms of International Relations theory were important.

Bilateral diplomatic relations existed for almost a ten-year period from April 1942 until March 1952. Crucial for their creation was the alliance that had been formed between Moscow and Washington during World War II. This alliance had been vital for the Kremlin as the Russian Revolution's very survival had been placed at risk by the German invasion of June 1941. A bi-product of this alliance was the creation of Soviet-Cuban relations. As a result, both Cuba's relationship with the United States and realism under-pinned the creation of formal diplomatic relations. Although this was the case, they existed until March 1952, a number of years after the end of the wartime alliance and the onset of the Cold War. Many Latin American countries had broken diplomatic relations with Moscow, but Cuba was not one of them. The role of the PSP in Cuban political life was important for this as it provided legitimacy for the turbulent political system. Cuban politics may have moved to the right in the immediate aftermath of World War II, but as long as the PSP remained important for the political system the Cuban government were not prepared to break relations. Moreover, this displayed a level of political independence from the United States which has not traditionally thought to have been the case. However, this situation dramatically changed in March 1952, a matter of weeks after Batista had returned to power, when the Cuban President "engineered" a break in relations as he cemented his power in Cuba and illustrated his pro-U.S. tendencies to Washington.

However, this situation from 1945 to 1952 also had the effect of increasing Soviet attention in the island due to the Cuban party's apparent "achievements." This continued the perception of the Caribbean island as a "hot bed" of radicalism, which had partly resulted from the effects of Cuban economic dependence on the United States, but had been important in stimulating Soviet interest in Cuba from the 1920s. However, in the mid-1940s Moscow could potentially utilize the PSP's "successes" to counteract anti-Soviet U.S. policy elsewhere in the world, which in the Cold War setting of the time was crucial to this interest. In short, realism was key to Moscow's attention in the island.

In the period prior to January 1959 the Soviet Union had both shown an interest in Cuban sugar and even purchased it on various occasions. The most attention was shown in the early 1920s, during World War II, and in 1955 with a commonality existing between all three. This commonality was poor Soviet agricultural output which had arisen for various reasons, but on each occasion Moscow turned to Cuba for the purchase of sugar. This was logical due to the Caribbean island's place as one of the world's leading sugar producers, but realism and neo-realism were also important due to the severity of the situation which necessitated the need for Moscow to find alternative sources of this important commodity. In the cases of World War II and 1955 the role of the United States was also significant, but this is not to detract from the fact that prior to January 1959, Cuban sugar had been shipped to the Soviet Union.

The Kremlin gave considerable attention to cultural ties between the two countries, illustrated by the creation of the Institute of Cuban-Soviet Cultural Exchange in the summer of 1945 and the journal *Cuba y la URSS* being published monthly until March 1952. Significantly this Institute was opened and VOKS commenced operating on the island when tension between Moscow and the PSP existed due to "Browderism" within the CPUSA, but this only further highlighted the importance of Cuba for the Kremlin. The cultural flows were in both directions, but Moscow's interest was highlighted by the prominence of VOKS on the island. At the center of this was the hope that these cultural links could increase Soviet influence on the island, which would simultaneously reduce U.S. influence. This was vital in the embryonic Cold War, but again returns to realism and the significance of Cuba's relationship with the United States. Moreover, the size and "success" of the PSP, partly resulting from adverse effects of Cuban economic dependence on the United States for the island's workers, were also important as this made the Kremlin believe that the Cuban population was ripe for such cultural penetration, because if this had not been the case, the Institute would never have been created and VOKS would not have been active on the island.

What is also highly interesting is that in this period the top echelons of the Soviet elite were receiving information about the internal situation within Cuba while diplomatic relations existed. Moreover, the KGB had also been active within Cuba in the years from 1942 until 1952. This flow of information may have come to an end with the termination of diplomatic relations in March 1952, but interest in Cuba continued in the Soviet Union although at a reduced level. This was illustrated by Soviet press reports on the island, which in some cases were highly detailed with even a short report on Fidel Castro being published in the autumn of 1958. However, these reports were often based on U.S. press reporting on Cuba, but this is not to downplay the considerable links, or interest that Moscow had taken in Cuba.

In addition, the traditional forms of the Kremlin's "dual track" diplomacy listed on the previous pages question a number of long-held beliefs regarding Moscow's foreign policy at this time. This includes that Moscow's desire to have a global presence commenced with the changes made to Soviet foreign policy in the aftermath of Stalin's death in March 1953 as the Soviet Union had been attempting this while Stalin was still alive. In addition, it also questions the ideas that the Kremlin suffered from "geographical fatalism" with regards to Latin America as a whole and Cuba specifically prior to the victory of the Cuban Revolution, and that after World War II the Soviet Union withdrew from its cultural links with the United States due to its involvement in the U.S.'s "soft underbelly." In sum, Moscow's more traditional form of its "dual track" diplomacy had taken considerable interest in Cuba in the period between the Russian and Cuban Revolutions.

NOTES

1. G. E. Mamedov and A. Dalmau, *Rossiia-Kuba, 1902–2002, dokumenty i materialy*, (Moscow, Mezhdunarodnye otnosheniia, 2004), 13.

2. José Agustín Martínez to Vyacheslav Molotov, Havana, 5 October 1942, Mamedov and Dalmau, *Rossiia-Kuba, 1902–2002, 2004*, 37.

3. "Cuban Government to Recognize Russia, Zaydin Announces," *Havana Post*, October 11, 1942, 1.

4. *El Mundo* October 11, 1942, 1.

5. "La Bandera de Rusa en la cancilleria Cubana," *Bohemia* October 25, 1942, 31.

6. Mamedov and Dalmau, *Rossiia-Kuba, 1902–2002*, 2004, 37–39.

7. José Luis Martín, "El Embajador Litvinoff en la Habana," *Bohemia*, April 18, 1943, 46–48 & 50.

8. Martín, "El Embajador Litvinoff en la Habana," 47.

9. Aurelio Concheso to Emeterio Santovenia, Cuban Foreign Minister to Moscow, Moscow, 21 May 1943. Mamedov and Dalmau, *Rossiia-Kuba, 1902–2002*, 2004, 46.

10. Mamedov and Dalmau, *Rossiia-Kuba, 1902–2002*, 2004, 46–47.

11. *Pravda*, May 29, 1943, 3.

12. Russian State Archive for Social and Political History (RSA) 4558/111/349.

13. RSA 4558/111/349.

14. RSA 4558/111/349. Moreover, Stalin's interest in the Cuban economy, trading partners, and the nature of its exports was highlighted by Concheso in a report which he sent to Santovenia on 29 May 1943 detailing his meeting with the Soviet leader. Concheso to Santovenia, Moscow, 29 May 1943. Mamedov and Dalmau, *Rossiia-Kuba, 1902–2002*, 2004, 52–53.

15. Telegram from Concheso to Santovenia, Moscow, 29 May 1943. Mamedov and Dalmau, *Rossiia-Kuba, 1902–2002*, 2004, 52–53.

16. Manuel Caballero, *Latin America and the Comintern 1919–1943*, (Cambridge: Cambridge University Press, 1986), 48. Barry Carr, "From Caribbean backwater to revolutionary opportunity: Cuba's evolving relationship with the Comintern, 1925–34" in *International Communism and the Communist International 1919–43*, ed. Tim Rees and Andrew Thorpe (Manchester: Manchester University Press, 1998), 234.

17. Concheso to Santovenia, Moscow, 29 May 1943. Mamedov and Dalmau, *Rossiia-Kuba, 1902–2002*, 2004, 53.

18. RSA 558/11/350.

19. Molotov to Concheso, Moscow, 31 May 1943. Mamedov and Dalmau, *Rossiia-Kuba, 1902–2002*, 2004, 54.

20. A. Sizonenko, "USSR-Latin America: Diplomatic-Technical Aspects of the War Years Relationship," *America Latina*, No 5, (May 2010): 20.

21. Thomas G. Paterson, J. Gary Clifford, & Kenneth J. Hagan, *American Foreign Policy. A History since 1900*, (Lexington: DC Heath & Company, 1983), 295. Walter LaFeber, *The American Age. United States Foreign Policy at Home and Abroad since 1750*, (New York: W.W. Norton & Company, 1989), 389.

22. "Cuban Government to Recognize Russia," *Havana Post*, October 11, 1942, 1.

23. *Havana Post*, December 18, 1943, 1.

24. *El Mundo*, December 21, 1943, 2. *Havana Post*, December 18, 1943, 1.

25. A. Gromyko to Molotov, Havana, 22 December 1943, Mamedov and Dalmau, *Rossiia-Kuba, 1902–2002*, 2004, 60.

26. D. Zaikin to Molotov, Havana, 8 November 1943, Mamedov and Dalmau, *Rossiia-Kuba, 1902–2002*, 2004, 57–58.

27. "Visito Gromyko al Ministro de Estado" *El Mundo*, December 21, 1943, 2.

28. F. Batista to Kalinin, Havana, 8 November 1942 and 7 November 1943. Mamedov and Dalmau, *Rossiia-Kuba, 1902–2002*, 2004, 40 & 57.

29. R. Grau to Kalinin, Havana, 7 November 1944 and 17 August 1945. Mamedov and Dalmau, *Rossiia-Kuba, 1902–2002*, 2004, 63 & 66. On 21 October 1944 Zaikin had also sent a report to A. Ya Vyshinskomu, Deputy Commissar for Foreign Relations, detailing that Grau had become Cuban President and that in the parade which followed his inauguration the Soviet flag had proudly flown alongside the flags of Cuba, the United States, Great Britain, and China. D. Zaikin to Vyshinskomu, Havana, 21 October 1944, Mamedov and Dalmau, *Rossiia-Kuba, 1902–2002*, 2004, 63.

30. Raúl Gonzalez to Molotov, Havana, 27 August 1948. Mamedov and Dalmau, *Rossiia-Kuba, 1902–2002*, 2004, 75. Molotov to Raúl Gonzalez, Moscow, 4 October 1948, Mamedov and Dalmau, *Rossiia-Kuba, 1902–2002*, 2004, 76.

31. N.M. Shvernik to Prio, Moscow, 19 May 1949. Prio to Shvernik, Havana, 7 November 1949, Prio to Shvernik, Havana, 3 November 1951, Mamedov and Dalmau, *Rossiia-Kuba, 1902–2002*, 2004, 77, 83.

32. Leslie Bethell & Ian Roxborough, "Latin America between the Second World War and the Cold War: Some Reflections on the 1945–8 Conjuncture," *Journal of Latin American Studies*, no. 20, (1988): 177.

33. Jules R. Benjamin, *The United States and the Origins of the Cuban Revolution. An Empire of Liberty in an Age of National Liberation*, (Princeton: Princeton University Press, 1990), 106–107. Hugh Thomas, *Cuba or the Pursuit of Freedom*. (London: Eyre & Spottiswoode, 1971), 752–754 & 757.

34. Benjamin, *The United States and the Origins of the Cuban Revolution*, 1990, 102–103.

35. *Pravda*, June 15, 1949, 3.

36. *Pravda*, June 15, 1949, 3.

37. Thomas, *Cuba*, 1971, 773. Louis A. Pérez, *Cuba and the United States: Ties of Singular Intimacy*, (Athens, Ga: University of Georgia Press, 2003), 233.

38. Angel Garcia & Piotr Mironchuk, *Raices de las relaciones Cubano Sovieticas*, (Havana, Editorial de Ciencias Sociales, 1988), 131–132.

39. Telegram from González to Soviet embassy in Havana, 27 March 1947, Mamedov and Dalmau, *Rossiia-Kuba, 1902–2002*, 2004, 69–70. The March 1947 meeting was the second which had focused on how a divided Germany should be ruled by the Allied powers, but neither meeting had been able to find an agreement between the former wartime allies. William Keylor, *A World of Nations. The International Order Since 1945*, (Oxford: Oxford University Press, 2003), 32–33.

40. Report of meeting between Malik and Espinosa. Mamedov and Dalmau, *Rossiia-Kuba, 1902–2002*, 2004, 72–73.

41. K.S Karol, *Guerrillas in Power. The Course of the Cuban Revolution*, (London: Jonathan Cape, 1971), 60.

42. Mamedov and Dalmau, *Rossiia-Kuba 1902–2002*, 2004, 84–85.

43. Yu. Yartsev, "A Soviet View of Cuba," *Literaturnaya Gazeta*, April 8, 1952, 37.

44. The final edition of the journal was *Cuba y la URSS* Number 76, February 1952. In this final edition an article entitled "Valiosa iniciativa: Llamamiento en favour de la amistad cubano-sovietica" was published which was signed by 65 different people including Mantici, Alberto Alonso, the director of Cuban National Ballet, and highly interestingly Dr. Antonio Núñez Jiménez who was the President of the Cuban Caving Society. This article stated, "The grave international tension, which each day makes relations between the great powers more dangerous, could cause a new and terrible war, that will affect all men and women and annihilate peace and increases from day to day the chances of our the friendship between our peoples being severed. But we are convinced that far from being a threat to our country, the Soviet Union is a force for peace because its politics and actions illustrate the friendship with our people and our collective efforts can reduce the chance of war; because we are convinced that the advantages and possibilities for the Cuban people resulting from these exchanges will help our development, but the decision to cut these which begun approximately on 15 February will have consequences for the Cuban people. This is not just propaganda, as many are against Soviet ideology. However, we know that without the selfless actions of the Soviet government that the situation regarding sciences, art and culture, but also changes in industry, has helped the lives of workers, farmers, students and professors; this is the basis of social security and the basis of Soviet foreign policy." *Cuba y la URSS*, Num 76, (February 1952): 35–36.

45. Thomas, *Cuba*, 1971, 779.

46. RSA 27/11/1952.

47. RSA 27/11/1952.

48. Angel Garcia & Piotr Mironchuk, *Esbozo Historica de las Relaciones entre Cuba-Rusia y Cuba-URSS*, (Havana: Academia de Ciencias de Cuba, 1976), 182–184. E.A. Larin, *Politicheskaia istorii Kuba XX Veka*. (Moscow: Visshaya shkola, 2007), 88–90. Moreover, while Litvinov was in Cuba in April 1943 he was presented with a gift of 25,000 pesos by the National Antifascist League. Garcia & Mironchuk, *Raices de las relaciones Cubano Sovieticas, 1988*, 126.

49. Thomas, *Cuba*, 1971, 728. M.A. Okuneva, *The Working Class in the Cuban Revolution*, (Moscow: Nauka, 1985), 80–81.

50. *Vneshniaia torgovlia SSSR statisticheskii sbornik 1918–1966*, (Moscow: "Mezdunarodnye otnosheniia," 1967), 13.

51. Caballero, *Latin America and the Comintern*, 1986, 117.

52. Kenneth Waltz, *Theory of International Politics*, (New York: Random House, 1979), 111.

53. *Vneshniaia torgovlia SSSR*, 1967, 68–69.

54. Garcia and Mironchuk, *Raices de las relaciones Cubano Sovieticas* , 1976, 141–142.

55. "Demands in Latin America for Expansion of Trade with USSR and People's Democracies," *Pravda*, March 12, 1955, 4. M. Mikhailov, "Soviet-Argentine Trade Agreement," *Izvestia*, August 15, 1953, 4. O. Ignatiev, "A Movement Prompted by Reality," *Komsomolskaya Pravda*, January 17, 1954, 4.

56. Rojelio del Campo, "Fruits of an Antinational Policy," *Pravda,* February 22, 1953, 4.

57. Mikhailov, "Soviet-Argentine Trade Agreement," 1953.

58. "For Expansion of Cooperation between USSR and Latin American Countries," *Pravda,* January 22, 1956, 5.

59. Waltz, *Theory of International Politics*, 1979, 111.

60. *Vneshniaia torgovlia SSSR*, 1967, 68–69.

61. *Pravda*, November 20, 1956, 4.

62. Jorge Garcia Montes & Antonio Alonso Ávila, *Historia del Partido Comunista de Cuba,* (Miami: Ream Press, 1970), 518–519.

63. G.Rubtsov, "In Cuba," *New Times,* No 7 (1949): 23, & 23–26.

64. Rubtsov, "In Cuba," 23–24.

65. "Protocol Number 275 of the Council of Labour and Defence," 9 December 1921. Mamedov and Dalmau, *Rossiia-Kuba, 1902–2002,* 2004, 29.

66. "Protocol Number 275," Mamedov and Dalmau, *Rossiia-Kuba, 1902–2002,* 2004, 13.

67. M.A. Rossiiskii, *Rossiia zarbezh'e na Kuba. Strancy istorii,* (Moscow: Veche, 2002), 8–13.

68. Rossiiskii, *Rossiia zarbezh'e na Kuba,* 2002, 22. For a more complete list of performances by Russians in Cuba in this period please see I.U. V. Pogosov, *Vmeste na vse vremena,* (Moscow: Molodaiaa Gvardiia, 1988).

69. Yuri Pavlov, former head of the Latin American Directorate of the USSR Foreign Ministry, has written regarding cultural links between the Soviet Union and Cuba, "Culturally, Russian, Ukrainians, Byelorussians, and other nations of the USSR were too different and far from the Cubans to develop a strong affinity and kinship during the long period of their political friendship. Common ideology was a poor substitute to its growth…Soviet-Cuban cultural ties were superficial." Yuri Pavlov, *Soviet-Cuban Alliance 1959–1991* (New Brunswick: Transaction Publishers, 1994), 249.

70. Rossiiskii, *Rossiia zarbezh'e na Kuba,* 2002, 8–13, 33 & 142. For the cultural links between Cuba and the United States please see Pérez, *Cuba and the United States,* 2003, 202–236.

71. Pérez, *Cuba and the United States,* 2003, 123–148.

72. Rossiiskii, *Rossiia zarbezh'e na Kuba,* 2002, 24 & 166–167.

73. *Cuba y la URSS*, Num 1, (August 1945): 1.

74. *Cuba y la URSS*, Num 1, (August 1945): 2–3.

75. *Cuba y la URSS*, Num 1, (August 1945): 2–3.

76. Anatoli Kafman, "La amistadad de los Ajedreasitas Rusos y Cubanos," *Cuba y la URSS,* Num 2, (September 1945): 5–6.

77. "Francisco Miranda en Rusia," *Cuba y la URSS,* Num 5, (December 1945): 20–22.

78. *Cuba y la URSS*, Num 6, (June 1946): 31.

79. In November 1948 a new Russian language course was advertised which was due to begin at the Institute. *Cuba y la URSS,* Num 38, (November 1948):53 & *Cuba y la URSS,* Num 56, (May 1950): 53.

80. *Cuba y la URSS,* Num 1, (August 1945): 24. *Cuba y la URSS,* Num 19, (February 1947): 30–32 & *Cuba y la URSS,* Num 18, (January 1947):31.

81. *Cuba y la URSS,* Num 1, (August 1945): 24. *Cuba y la URSS,* Num 5, (May 1946): 30.

82. *Cuba y la URSS,* Nums 22–23, (May-June 1947): 35–36 & *Cuba y la URSS,* Num 39, (December 1948): 53.

83. *Cuba y la URSS,* Num 44, (May 1949): 51.

84. *Cuba y la URSS,* Num 51, (December 1949): 51.

85. "Homenaje a la Cultura Soviética. Selecto Programa Musical." *Cuba y la URSS,* Num 61, (October 1950): 31.

86. "Exposición de Moscú," *Cuba y la URSS,* Num 20, (March 1947): 16–18.

87. "La Mujer en la URSS," *Cuba y la URSS,* Num 39, (December): 53.

88. "Enseñanza para Ejercer los Derretíos Democracia en la URSS," *Cuba y la URSS,* Num 40, (January 1949): 53.

89. *Cuba y la URSS,* Num 49 (October 1949): 53 & *Cuba y la URSS,* Num 55, (April 1950): 53.

90. "La URSS, Socialismo y Cultura" *Cuba y la URSS,* Num 56, (May 1950): 53.

91. *Cuba y la URSS,* Num 57, (June): 53.

92. *Cuba y la URSS,* Num 59, (August,): 9.

93. Luis Cardoza Aragón, "La Fiesta de los Trabajadores en Moscu," *Cuba y la URSS,* Num 33, (April 1948): 4.

94. *Cuba y la URSS,* Nums 22–23, (May–June 1947): 40–41 & 16–17.

95. Tuelgeun Tazhibaiev, "La Universidad del Estado de Kazajstan" *Cuba y la URSS,* Num 59, (August 1950): 42. Liudmila Dubrovina, "Las Publicanes para nina," *Cuba y la URSS,* Num 59, (August 1950): 21–22.

96. V. Renard, "La Television Sovietica," *Cuba y la URSS,* Num 62, (November 1950): 14–16. Nikolai Sabetski, "Alexandr Popov, inventor de la Radion, *Cuba y la URSS,* Num 69, (July 1951): 8–10.

97. "La protección al trabajo de los jóvenes obreros de la URSS," *Cuba y la URSS,* No 64, (February 1951): 41. A. Tarasenkov, "Maximo Gorki, padre de la literature sovietica" *Cuba y la URSS,* Num 73, (November 1951): 37–39.

98. "El Pació de Cultura de los Mineros de Karaganda," *Cuba y la URSS,* Num 73, (November 1951): 26–30. "El Museu V.I. Lenin" *Cuba y la URSS,* Num 75, (January 1952): 25.

99. Valentin Durov, "50 anos de rusos boxeo" *Cuba y la URSS,* Num 35, (August 1948): 49. *Cuba y la URSS,* Num 61, (October 1950): 1–28.

100. Sergei Vavilov, "Nuestro Aporte a la Ciencia Mundial," *Cuba y la URSS,* Num 35, (August 1948): 49. I.A. Vlasov, "J.V. Stalin creado del Estado Socialista Soviética multinacional," *Cuba y la URSS,* Num 52, (January 1950): 8–11.

101. Nigel Gould-Davies, "The Logic of Soviet Cultural Diplomacy," *Diplomatic History,* Vol 27, No.2, (April 2003): 195.

102. Marshall D. Shulman, *Stalin's Foreign Policy Reappraised,* (Boulder: Westview Press, 1985), 10.

103. Joseph S. Nye, Jr, *Soft Power. The Means to Success in World Politics,* (New York: PublicAffairs, 2004), 73.

104. Frederick C. Barghoorn, *The Soviet Cultural Offensive. The Role of Cultural Diplomacy in Soviet Foreign Policy,* (Princeton: Princeton University Press, 1960), 32.

105. Gould-Davies, "The Logic of Soviet Cultural Diplomacy," 2003, 196.

106. 861.00/2-2246, "The Charge in the Soviet Union (Kennan) to the Secretary of State," http://www.gwu.edu/~nsarchiv/coldwar/documents/episode-1/kennan.htm (accessed 14 April 2012).

107. "The Charge in the Soviet Union (Kennan) to the Secretary of State."

108. Gould-Davies, "The Logic of Soviet Cultural Diplomacy," 2003, 197–198. The German author Josef Joffe believed that Soviet culture did not extend beyond its military borders. Nye, *Soft Power,* 2004, 11.

109. Rollie E. Poppino, *International Communism in Latin America. A History of the Movement 1917–1963,* (London: Collier-Macmillan Limited, 1964), 159.

110. "Emisiones de Moscu para La America Latina," *Cuba y la URSS,* Num 21 (April 1947):29.

111. Quoted in O.D. Kameneva, "Cultural Raprochment: The USSR Society for Cultural Relations with Foreign Countries," *Pacific Affairs,* Volume 1, Num 5 (October 1928): 6.

112. Ludmila Stern, "The All-Union Society for Cultural Relations with Foreign Countries and French Intellectuals, 1925–29" *Australian Journal of Politics and History,* Volume 45, Number 1 (1999): 109.

113. "Homenaje al encargado de negocios de la URSS, SR Dimitri Zaikin," *Cuba y la URSS,* Num 5 (May 1945): 30.

114. "Visito Gromyko al Ministro de Estado" & "Se Verifico le Clausura de la Exposicion Sobre le Rusia Roja," *El Mundo,* December 21, 1943, 2. In a report sent to V.G. Dekanozovu, Deputy Commissar for Foreign Relations, Concheso stated that 30,000 people had visited this exhibition. Concheso to Dekanozovu, Havana, 11 December 1943, Mamedov and Dalmau, *Rossiia-Kuba, 1902–2002,* 2004, 59–60.

115. V.P. Jastrebova, member of the Soviet delegation in Cuba, to the Institute of Cuban-Soviet Cultural Exchange, Havana, 20 June 1946. Mamedov and Dalmau, *Rossiia-Kuba, 1902–2002*, 2004, 68–69.

116. "Felicitación de los Intelectuales Soviéticos con motive deal an Nuevo," *Cuba y la URSS*, Num 53 (February 1950): 53.

117. *Cuba y la URSS*, Num 18, (January 1947): 31.

118. Stern, "The All-Union Society for Cultural Relations," 1999, p.101. Dr. Antonio Núñez Jiménez had signed "Valiosa iniciativa: Llamamiento en favour de la amistad cubano-sovietica" which had appeared in the final edition of *Cuba y la URSS*. *Cuba y la URSS*, Num 76, (February 1952): 35–36.

119. Gould-Davies, "The Logic of Soviet Cultural Diplomacy," 2003, 195.

120. N. Yaborskaia, "Pintura Cubana en Moscú," *Cuba y la URSS*, Num 1, (August 1945): 2.

121. "La Exposicion de Arte Cubano en Moscú," *Cuba y la URSS*, Num 3, (October 1945): 18.

122. "Arte Cubano en la URSS," *Cuba y la URSS*, Num 6, (June 1946): 28. "Pintura Cubano en Moscú," *Cuba y la URSS*, Num 7 (July 1946): 16–17.

123. "Obras cubanos Expuestas en Moscú," *Cuba y la URSS*, Num 38, (November 1948): 53.

124. "Exposiciones Cubana de Arquitectura y Urbanismo en la URSS," *Cuba y la URSS*, Num 4, (April 1946): 28.

125. *Cuba-URSS Cronica*, (Moscow: Progreso, 1990), 520.

126. "Un Músico Cubano Visita La Unión Soviética," *Cuba y la URSS*, Num 75, (January 1952): 4.

127. "Un Músico Cubano" 1952, 3–5. "En la Sección de Música de la VOKS," *Cuba y la URSS*, Num 11, (November 1951): 51.

128. RSA 25-C-1491.

129. Garcia and Mironchuk, *Raices de las relaciones Cubano Sovieticas*, 1988, 131.

130. *Pravda*, June 15, 1949, 3.

131. RSA 82/2/1275.

132. Zaikin to KGB, Havana, 8 November 1945. Mamedov and Dalmau, *Rossiia-Kuba, 1902–2002*, 2004, 67. "Falangist" refers to the right-wing Spanish party Falange Española de las Juntas de Ofensiva Nacional Sindicalista which had been created in the 1930s.

133. In the aftermath of the break in Soviet-Mexican relations in January 1930 Spenser has written that evidence was found in the former Soviet embassy of spying activities. Daniela Spenser, *The Impossible triangle. Mexico, Soviet Russia and the United States in the 1920s*, (Durham: Duke University Press, 1999), 187.

134. Please see amongst others: Christopher Andrew & Vasili Mitrokhin, *The World Was Going Our Way. The KGB and the Battle for the Third World*, (New York: Basic Book, 2005), 27. Nicola Miller, *Soviet Relations with Latin America 1959–1987*, (Cambridge: Cambridge University Press, 1989), 5–6. Pavlov, *Soviet-Cuban Alliance*, 1994, 2. Alexandr Fursenko & Timothy Naftali, *The Secret History of the Cuban Missile Crisis. "One Hell of a Gamble."* (London: John Murray, 1997), 12. Samuel Farber, *The Origins of the Cuban Revolution*. 144.

135. *Cuba-URSS Cronica*, 1990, 520.

136. *International Affairs* Num 7 (1957): 115. P. Yeronin "The Big Stick Again!" *International Affairs*, No 9 (1958): 97.

137. V. Vasilchikov, "Bloody Atrocities in Cuba," *Pravda*, February 5, 1957, 4.

138. V. Tikhmenev, "Sweeping the Dirt Under the Rug," *New Times*, Num 40 (1957): 18.

139. Burlakin stated "ten years ago U.S. investment in Cuba totaled $550m; today they are close to $800, the third largest in Latin America after Venezuela and Brazil." A. Burlakin, "Cuba Aflame," *International Affairs* Num 11, 1957, p.113. "The People and Dictator" *New Times*, No 15 (1958): 22. V. Levin, "Cuba is Fighting, Cuba Will Win!" *Pravda*, January 3, 1959, 3.

140. For insurgency please see: "The People and the Dictator," *New Times*, Num 15 (1958): 22. "Cuba in Flames" *New Times*, no 50 (1957): 21–22, "Tottering Dictator" *New Times*, Num 10, (1958): 21–22. V. Vasilchikov, "Bloody Atrocities in Cuba," *Pravda*, February 5, 1957, 4.

141. Lázaro Pena "Strike Struggle in Cuba," *For a Lasting Peace. For a People's Democracy,* March 23, 1956, 6. "Unity of Action of Cuban Working People," *For a Lasting Peace. For a People's Democracy,* April 17, 1956, 4.

142. Blas Roca, "People of Cuba Fighting Against War, For Democratic Liberties," *For a Lasting Peace. For a People's Democracy,* May 18, 1950, 3.

143. "Fidel Castro" *New Times,* Volume 34 (1958): 31–31.

144. "Fidel Castro" *New Times,* Volume 34 (1958): 31–31.

145. V. Levin, "Cuba is Fighting, Cuba Will Win!" *Pravda,* January 3, 1959, 3.

146. Levin, "Cuba is Fighting," 3.

147. George J. Boughton, "Soviet-Cuban Relations, 1956–1960," *Journal of Interamerican Studies and World Affairs,* Vol 16, No 4 (November 1974), 438.

148. Boughton, "Soviet-Cuban Relations, 1956–1960," 1974, 438.

149. Herbert Matthews, "Cuban Rebel Is Visited in Hideout," *New York Times,* February 24, 1957, 1.

150. M. Kremnyov, "Cuba in Flames," *International Affairs,* Num 7 (1957): 116. *International Affairs* Num 11(1957): 112–113.

151. *New Times,* Num 50 (1957): 22.

152. Yeronin, "The Big Stick Again!" *International Affairs,* Num 9 (1958): 97.

153. *New Times,* Num 28 (1958): 19.

154. Levin, "Cuba is Fighting," *Pravda,* January 3, 1959, 3.

155. A. Burlakin, "Cuba Aflame," *International Affairs,* Num 11 (1957): 112–113.

156. "Tottering Dictator," *New Times,* Num 10, (1958): 21. "The People and the Dictator," *New Times,* Num 15 (1958): 22.

157. Fursenko & Naftali, *The Secret History,* 1997, 93.

158. N.S. Leonov, *Lixoletye* (Moscow: Mezhdunarodnye otnosheniia, 1995), 29–37.

Chapter Four

Final Thoughts on the "Disappearing" Relationship

In the opening chapter of this book Christopher Andrew and the former KGB archivist Vasili Mitrokhin have been quoted as having written in their book *The World Was Going our Way: The KGB and the Battle for the Third World*,

> For over forty years after the Bolshevik Revolution, Moscow doubted its own ability to challenge American influence in a continent which it regarded as the United States' backyard. [1]

This was most certainly the traditional perception of the Kremlin's interest in Latin America as a whole prior to the victory of the Cuban Revolution. Moreover, with regards to Cuba specifically the sentiments of this quote were perhaps even intensified due to the island's geographical proximity to the United States and the nature of the relationship between Washington and Havana. It has been thought that this only changed in January 1959 with the emergence of Fidel Castro's new regime in Cuba. However, this was far from the case with the Bolshevik leadership taking an interest in the island from soon after the Russian Revolution in November 1917. On taking power the new government in Russia employed a form of "dual track" diplomacy consisting of the highly radical policies of the Third International, or Comintern, and also the more formal forms of traditional diplomacy. Both aspects of this "dual track" diplomacy showed interest in Cuba.

The Bolshevik leadership believed that the Russian Revolution was only the first of many revolutions which would eventually lead to the spread of socialism on a global scale. In order to achieve this, in March 1919 the Comintern was created in Moscow. The primary focus of this organization may have been Europe, but interest in the Developing World was also taken. However, this attention was not in this part of the world per se, but rather the effect which revolutionary activity in the less developed countries could have for the metropolitan states. This was underpinned by the idea that if the Comintern was successful in "engineering" another revolution it would help safeguard Soviet security as the Bolshevik regime would no longer be the sole socialist regime in the world. In sum, this returns to the key tenets of the realist paradigm of International Relations theory that states act to preserve their own survival.

Both of these ideas were key to the attention which the Comintern took in Cuba. This interest can be divided into two distinct stages with the first being from the time of the organization's creation until the summer of 1935 and its Seventh Congress, and the second from this point onward. The tactics of the Third International were very different in these two stages, but interest was taken in Cuba during both.

A number of documents exist in the Comintern archive housed in the Russian State Archive for Social and Political History in Moscow regarding Cuba. These commence as early as December 1919, almost six years before the creation of the Cuban Communist Party (PCC) in August 1925. At this time the correspondence which took place may have all been in a west to east direction from Cuba to the Soviet Union, but the Comintern most certainly had information regarding Cuba and the situation on the island. After its creation the PCC quickly gained membership to the Comintern and rapidly began to hold significant positions within the organization's structure. This included gaining candidate membership of the Central Bureau at the Sixth Congress of the Comintern held in 1928, significantly the first congress after the PCC's creation.

The year 1928 was highly important for Latin America as a whole because it was in this year that the region was "discovered" by the organization, with it appearing that it was receiving more attention from the Third International. With regards to Cuba specifically, 1928 was also significant not just because it gained candidate membership of the Central Bureau of the Comintern, but it was also in this year that information began to be sent from the Third International headquarters in Moscow to Cuba. This was highly significant as it was detailed information on the tactics which the Cuban Party should employ, illustrating both the knowledge which the organization had on the internal situation on the island and their interest in it. Critically this was during the highly radical "third period" of this organization which desired a class against class struggle.

Crucial for this interest was the island's relationship with Washington and in particular Cuban economic dependence on the United States. The upshot of this was that any revolutionary success in Cuba could have consequences economically for the U.S. due to the level of economic investments in the island and the intertwined nature of the two economies. As a result, this Soviet interest in Cuba was similar to their interest in the Developing World in general; i.e. that it was the consequences for the metropolitan states of revolutionary activity in the less developed countries that underpinned this interest. This was still applicable to Cuba due to the nature of Cuba-U.S. relations at this time. In addition, Cuba would have appeared as a "hot bed" of left-wing activity due to labor unrest concerning amongst other things low pay and poor working conditions. This would only have increased Soviet attention in Cuba with ironically this resulting from these effects of Cuban economic dependence on the United States.

Comintern attention in Cuba was particularly high in the summer of 1933 when it appeared that a genuine revolutionary opportunity was about to come to fruition. Direct correspondence between the organization and the PCC may not have taken place, but instead this was conducted via the Communist Party of the United States (CPUSA). This only further highlights the importance of the island's close relationship with the United States in Soviet interest in Cuba. In addition, Comintern agents were also active on the island at this time.

This revolutionary opportunity may not have been realized, but it did not herald the end of Comintern interest in Cuba. Correspondence continued, particularly via the CPUSA, and the PCC was also present at the meeting in Moscow in late 1934 which began to usher in the very different tactics of the "popular front" strategy which were formalized at the Comintern's Seventh Congress in the summer of 1935. These were vastly different from the previous "third period" and called for communist parties to work within the local political systems. By adhering to this change in tactics the PCC was not only able to gain legal status in Cuba in the late 1930s, but it would eventually lead to Juan Marinello and Carlos Rafael Rodríguez being appointed to Fulgencio Batista's cabinet in 1942. This was truly historic as they were the first members of any communist party in Latin America to achieve such appointments. Moreover, this also further increased the interest of Moscow in Cuba as they illustrated the "success" of the "popular front" tactics and highlighted the apparent revolutionary potential on the island. This was only aided by the size of the membership of the Cuban Socialist Party (PSP) which in 1945 was only exceeded in Latin America by the Brazilian Communist Party. However, even before these appointments, Vyacheslav Molotov, Soviet Commissar of Foreign Affairs, sent the text "Independent Cuba" to *Noticias de Hoy* in late 1939. This is highly important as it illustrated not just the Comintern, but also the Soviet ruling elites' interest in the PCC before the creation of diplomatic relations and during the "popular front" stage of the Third International.

The revolutionary potential on the island was highly significant for the Kremlin as it could be used to counter what it perceived as anti-Soviet U.S.

policies elsewhere in the world. This included attempts to crush the Bolshevik regime in its infancy, the nonrecognition of the Soviet Union until 1933, and the eventual onset of the Cold War in the mid to late 1940s. This is not just in accordance with the core tenets of realism, but due to the traditional Russian fear of aggression from outside powers also constructivism and Tsygankov's ideas of the importance of statists within Soviet foreign policy. The geographical proximity of the island to the United States and the nature of Cuban-U.S. relations only increased Soviet attention in Cuba.

The interest which the Comintern took in Cuba suffered from the same problems and issues which blighted the organization in general, chiefly the sporadic nature of the correspondence which took place. Moreover, the activity in Cuba failed to produce a successful revolution, but this was by no means unique as the Comintern failed to achieve this once throughout its history. Although this is the case, it does not detract from the considerable interest which the radical aspect of Moscow's "dual track" diplomacy took in Cuba during both the "third period" and "popular front" stages of the Third International, with the Cuban party illustrating the "success" of this latter stage. The attention which the Third International played in Cuba was driven by the general principles that underpinned Soviet attention in the Developing World. That was the effects that revolutionary activity could have for the metropolitan states with this still being applicable to Cuba due to the nature of Cuban-U.S. relations. At the core of this were realism, constructivism, and the ideas of statists within Moscow's foreign policy as these policies were ultimately designed to try and safeguard Soviet security. Moreover, the island's geographical location and relationship with the United States only intensified the Comintern's interest in Cuba.

The Comintern was disbanded in the summer of 1943, but the Cuban Socialist Party (PSP) continued to adhere to the principles of the "popular front." This was important for the way in which it was able to provide legitimacy for the corrupt Cuban political system of the mid to late 1940s. Ironically this took place when tension between the Cuban Party and Moscow existed due to the PSP's close association with the end of "Browderism" in the CPUSA. This tension did not last long, but the important role that the PSP played in the Cuban political system occurred despite harassment against the Party's membership. This also impacted on formal diplomatic relations between the two countries which existed at this time because, despite the Cuban embassy in Moscow being closed in early 1947 due to Cuban displeasure at the Soviet stance over how a divided Germany should be governed, it would have been incongruous for the Cuban government to completely sever these relations while the PSP played this important role in Cuban politics. This was illustrated in October 1948 when Molotov accepted the Cuban regime's invitation for a Soviet representative to be present at Carlos Prios Socarras's inauguration as Cuban President. The result was that

Cuba seemed to be bucking the regional trend at this time of breaking diplomatic relations with the Soviet Union. The upshot of this was that Cuba appeared to be enjoying more political independence from Washington than may have previously been thought.

Some Russian interest in Cuba had taken place even before the Russian Revolution, but this had been very sporadic and increased considerably after November 1917 and particularly once the Third International had been created in March 1919. Cuban interest in Russia mirrored this as it also increased after the Russian Revolution with interest being shown in the Comintern as early as 1919 and the PCC joined this organization on its inception in the summer of 1925. The number of newspaper articles and reporting on the unfolding events in Russia was both fairly substantial and detailed. This was unsurprising due to the historic and truly unique nature of these events which were taking place in one of the great European powers. After January 1959 both governments made a number of links between the Russian and Cuban Revolutions. However, a degree of revisionism may have been apparent in these, but this is not to downplay the Cuban attention which focused on Russia after November 1917.

As stated, the more formal aspect of the Kremlin's "dual track" diplomacy also showed considerable interest in Cuba in the period prior to the Cuban Revolution. Formal bilateral diplomatic relations were created on 10 October 1942 with Havana's relationship with Washington, events far removed from the Caribbean, and the realist paradigm of International Relations theory all being important. Crucially, diplomatic relations were created during World War II and once the Soviet Union had formed an alliance with the United States to fight the greater evil of Nazism. Moscow had joined this alliance as the very survival of the Soviet state had been placed in jeopardy by Nazi Germany. This adhered to the central tenets of realism, but a byproduct of this alliance had been the creation of diplomatic relations with Cuba. The importance of the United States to this was illustrated by the fact that the first Soviet charge d'affaires to Cuba, the former Soviet Commissar for Foreign Affairs, Maxim Litvinov, had presented his credentials not in Havana but instead at the Cuban embassy in Washington. Moreover, his successor Andrei Gromyko, the future Soviet Foreign Minister, presented his own credentials to U.S. President Franklin D. Roosevelt. The result was that due to both the formation of this alliance, which was underpinned by realism, and also the nature of Cuban-U.S. relations, formal diplomatic relations between Moscow and Havana had been created.

Considerable importance appeared to be attached to this relationship as while Soviet charge d'affaires both Litvinov and Gromyko travelled to Cuba during which they met the Cuban President Fulgencio Batista. This is significant as the Soviet Union was not being represented by mere party apparatchiks but rather by a former Soviet Commissar for Foreign Relations and a future Soviet Foreign Minister. Moreover, very quickly after his arrival in Moscow the Cuban ambassador to the Soviet Union, Aurelio Concheso, met members of the Soviet ruling elite. On 21 May 1943 Concheso met Mikhail Kalinin, Soviet Head of State, and three days later on 24 May 1943 attended a personal appointment with Joseph Stalin in the Kremlin to present his credentials as Cuban ambassador to the Soviet Union. In this meeting the Soviet leader appeared to have a degree of knowledge regarding Cuba and interestingly in particular the island's relationship with the United States. Due to Stalin's domination of the Soviet political system which is in accordance with the Great Man Theory, both the fact that Concheso had been granted a personal meeting with Stalin and the Soviet leader's apparent knowledge of the island were important for the attention which the Kremlin focused on its relationship with Cuba.

In addition to this, official correspondence also took place with a number of telegrams being exchanged by the very top echelons of both ruling elites. This included Batista sending telegrams to Kalinin on the anniversary of the Russian Revolution in 1942 and 1943. The exchange of telegrams continued after the end of the wartime alliance between Moscow and Washington and the onset of the Cold War. Again, this highlights the apparent political independence from the United States which the Caribbean island displayed in the mid to late 1940s.

The role of the United States in combination with the impact of World War II and the Kremlin's adherence to the principles of realism and neo-realism were also crucial for Cuban sugar being sold to the Soviet Union in the early 1940s. The Nazi invasion of the Soviet Union in the summer of 1941 did not just jeopardize Soviet security militarily, but its food security was also placed at risk. This resulted from the German army gaining control of the Ukraine which produced much of the Soviet agricultural output. This necessitated the Kremlin finding alternative sources of agricultural products with Cuba providing much needed sugar, with this again adhering to both the central tenets of realism that states try to safeguard their own security and also Waltz's ideas of "self-help." The wartime alliance and the nature of Cuban-U.S. relations eased these transactions.

A number of these factors were also important for Cuban sugar being sold to the Soviet Union in 1955. Soviet agricultural production was again poor, resulting in Moscow needing to find alternative sources of sugar. Again this was in accordance with realism and neo-realism, but it was also logical that the Soviet Union would buy sugar from Cuba as the island was one of the major global sugar producers at this time. In addition, an issue of overproduction had arisen in Cuba which could be partly solved by selling sugar to third party countries, including the Soviet Union. Moreover, the U.S. had been "consulted" about this transaction. This once again highlighted the significance of the United States in Soviet-Cuban relations.

However, the Bolshevik leadership had shown interest in Cuban sugar much earlier than this when in December 1921 the Council of Labour and Defence had debated the price that it would pay for Cuban sugar. Once more the Soviet Union was blighted by poor agricultural output in the early 1920s with again Moscow believing that Cuba could provide a source of sugar. The Soviet awareness of the importance of Cuban sugar was further shown in 1939 with Molotov's belief that Cuba would become more important for the Soviet Union due to the disruption in the global trade that resulted from World War II. This was borne out by the Soviet purchase of Cuban sugar in 1941 outlined above. However, commonalities exist between these three different times when Soviet interest in Cuban sugar took place prior to January 1959: poor Soviet agricultural output which necessitated alternative sources being found with this adhering to the principles of realism and neo-realism.

Evidence of Russian dancers performing in Cuba even predate the Russian Revolution, but again the island's relationship with the United States was important for these. Many of these performances were organized by U.S. impresarios and can be perceived as part of a "U.S. tour" as many travelled to the island from the United States. However, in the summer of 1945 the Institute of Cuban-Soviet Cultural Exchange was opened in Havana which subsequently resulted in both the publication of the monthly journal *Cuba y la URSS* and the involvement of the Soviet Society for Cultural Relations with Foreign Countries (VOKS) in Cuba. In addition to publishing *Cuba y la URSS* the Institute also organized amongst other things cultural evenings and film screenings devoted to the Soviet Union and its achievements. Moreover, it also ran Russian language classes. This drew the attention of a number of prominent Cubans who had been involved in "dissenting" politics on the island, not least the radical intellectuals Fernando Ortiz and Nicolas Guillen, but also highly interestingly Antonio Núñez Jiménez, the future Minister of Agrarian Reform in the Cuban Revolutionary Government of the 1960s.

This is highly important as the creation of the Institute, its activities, and the involvement of VOKS illustrate the considerable interest which the Soviet Union had in Cuba at this time. In addition, it also highlights that Moscow must have believed that an interest in the Soviet Union existed amongst the Cuban population, because if this had not been the case simply the Institute would not have been opened. The size and "successes" of the PSP, which resulted from adhering to the Comintern's "popular front" tactics, would have been important in this, as would the reports of pro-Soviet rallies being held on the island during World War II. It is very interesting that the Institute was opened at the time when apparent tension existed between the Kremlin and the PSP due to the effects of "Browderism" within the CPUSA. This was illustrated by the fact that it took until December 1946 for *Cuba y la URSS* to report prominent PSP member involvement in the Institute's activities. Although this is the case, the opening of the Institute in the summer of

1945 only further highlighted Soviet interest in Cuba at this time despite the tension which existed with the PSP.

The ideas of civilizationists that Russian and Soviet values were superior to Western ones were important for the Institute's creation, but so was realism as the Institute sought to increase Soviet prestige in Cuba which would simultaneously have the effect of reducing U.S. prestige. This was the underlying goal of VOKS on a global scale with its involvement in Cuba being no different. In the ideological battle of the Cold War this was highly important and highlights the reach of Soviet soft power in the years immediately after the end of World War II. In addition, it also illustrates that Moscow desired global influence much earlier than has traditionally been thought and while Stalin was still Soviet leader. It is very significant that this took place as the wartime alliance between Moscow and Washington was coming to an end and the subsequent onset of the Cold War. Europe may have remained the focus of geopolitics, but revolutionary activity in Cuba could be utilized by the Kremlin to counterbalance what it perceived as U.S. anti-Soviet policies, which after World War II focused on containment, most noticeably with the implementation of the Marshall Plan to prevent the spread of socialism in Europe.

The majority of the Institute's activities were centered on expanding Soviet prestige in Cuba, but in the seven years that it operated, Cuban exhibitions also took place in the Soviet Union. This included ones that focused on Cuban art and in April 1946 also Cuban architecture. Moreover, at the end of 1951 VOKS invited Enrique González Mantici, President of the Cuban National Institute of Music to the Soviet Union. During his stay in the Soviet capital he conducted the Moscow Radio Orchestra with the performance being broadcast on radio to Latin America and throughout the Soviet Union.

The involvement of VOKS is important in itself, but this is further increased as it meant that a number of Soviet citizens were living and working in Cuba during the seven years from 1945 to 1952. This brought tension to the relationship between the two governments when in June 1949 a number of Soviets were arrested for spreading pro-Soviet literature on the island, again showing the significance which Moscow attached to increasing its prestige in Cuba at this time. However, these arrests also brought a very strong response from *Pravda*.[2] Although this was the case, the importance of this event is heightened because in the archive of the Soviet Commissar of Foreign Relations in the Russian State Archive for Social and Political History a document exists on these arrests and the subsequent meeting which took place between Cuban secret police and KGB personnel regarding it. This unequivocally proves that the KGB was active in Cuba before January 1959. Moreover, the KGB's interest in Cuba is further shown by the reports which Dmitri Zaikin, head of VOKS on the island, sent to this organization in late 1945.

In addition to this, these documents also prove that the very pinnacle of the Soviet leadership was receiving information on Cuba. During his time in Cuba Zaikin sent a number of reports regarding the situation on the island to a variety of the Soviet ruling elite including Molotov. Furthermore, the documents in the archive of the Soviet Commissar of Foreign Relations that focused on Cuba were circulated amongst the leading members of the Soviet politburo including Joseph Stalin himself. Moreover, on 11 August 1951 Molotov signed the papers to invite Mantici to the Soviet Union. It appears that not only were the very pinnacle of the Soviet political elite receiving information on Cuba, but also that they were directly involved in the decision-making process regarding the relationship.

It appeared that Cuba had received more attention from the Soviet Union than other Latin American countries, including from the Third International but also Stalin himself due to the nature of his meeting with Concheso on 24 May 1943. In this the Soviet leader only asked the Cuban ambassador questions about the island while in a similar meeting with the Mexican ambassador in April 1943, he had also asked about Argentina and Chile. The importance of Cuba for the Kremlin resulted from a combination of its geographical position, the island's relationship with the United States, and the fact that it appeared to be a "hot bed" of left-wing activity, illustrated by the size and "success" of the PSP and labor radicalism. Ironically this radicalism had been an unforeseen consequence of Cuban economic dependence on the United States.

On 27 March 1952 Stalin received a report written by A. Vishnevsky, Secretary to the Central Committee, outlining the political situation in Cuba, but its primary focus was Batista's return to power. This is crucial because it showed the concerns that the Soviet Union had regarding Batista in the lead up to the break in diplomatic relations in April 1952. The new Cuban President, illustrating his pro-United States credentials to Washington, "engineered" this break resulting in it being simply impossible for Moscow to continue having formal diplomatic relations with Havana. Moreover, Batista's return to power also caused the Cuban political system to move further to the right with this appearing to reduce the likelihood of revolutionary success on the island, thus reducing Soviet interest in it. Ironically this occurred just prior to Stalin's death and the subsequent changes to Soviet foreign policy that have traditionally been thought to have sparked Soviet interest in the Developing World.

Very quickly after April 1952 traces of the relationship disappeared to the extent that it seemed almost to never have existed. In addition, the knowledge of Cuba within the Soviet Union that had been accrued over a number of years was lost. However, some interest remained in the Caribbean island, which was most noticeable in Soviet press reporting on Cuba. The number of articles on Cuba increased in the late 1950s and in the autumn of 1958 *New*

Times even published a report on Fidel Castro.[3] However, what was crucial for these reports was the publication of Herbert Matthews' article "Cuban Rebel Is Visited in Hideout" in the *New York Times* on 24 February 1957.[4] It was from this point that Soviet press reports on Cuba increased when in reality the Soviet articles were a summation of the reports on Cuba that were published in the U.S. press. Although this was the case, this is not to downplay the importance of these reports on Cuba as it illustrated Soviet interest in the unfolding situation on the island in the late 1950s.

Prior to January 1959, a multifaceted relationship between Moscow and Havana had existed with both parts of Moscow's "dual track" diplomacy taking considerable interest in the island. Cuba's geographical location and relationship with the United States was vital for Soviet interest in the island. An unforeseen consequence of Cuban economic dependence on the United States had been to increase labor radicalism on the island, with this only heightening Moscow's focus on Cuba. This radicalism was also apparent in the size of the PCC and subsequently the PSP. The Cuban party's adherence to Moscow's policies also brought it "success" particularly during the "popular front" stage of the Comintern with this only further increasing Moscow's attention in Cuba. In addition, the role of constructivism, realism, neo-realism, and the ideas of civilizationists and statists within Soviet foreign policy were important for Soviet attention in Cuba. Realism impacted on this due to Moscow's desire to increase Soviet influence on the island which would simultaneously reduce U.S. influence. Importantly this could be used to counter what the Kremlin perceived as anti-Soviet U.S. policy elsewhere in the world. In addition, the need for self-help as a result of poor agricultural output at various times in this period resulted in neo-realism being important.

Moreover, Soviet attention in Cuba began a number of years before the changes to Soviet foreign policy that were implemented in the aftermath of Stalin's death. This challenges the assumption that prior to 1959 the Kremlin had suffered from "geographical fatalism" with relation to Cuba specifically, or Latin America generally. The Soviet Union desired a global presence, and had considerable interest in Cuba much earlier than previously thought with this taking place while Stalin was still Soviet leader. This has implications for thinking on both Soviet foreign policy in general and also the Cold War on a global scale. Furthermore, this interest in Cuba was not consigned solely to the years while the Comintern was in existence as it continued, and even increased, after this organization had been disbanded in 1943. Highly significantly this occurred as hostilities in Europe began to come to an end in 1945 and the subsequent onset of the Cold War. This gives credence to the idea that Moscow could use radicalism in Cuba to counter anti-Soviet U.S. policy elsewhere. Key to this increase were the cultural links which took place with this also questioning the idea that after World War II the Soviet Union reduced its cultural links with the United States due to these activities in the

U.S.'s "soft underbelly." In addition, this also challenges the belief that Soviet soft power did not extend beyond its borders. Moreover, it also calls into question the negative perception of the cultural links between the two countries after 1959.

The existence of this multifaceted relationship in the period between 1917 and 1959 is important for the study of the relationship that developed between Moscow and Havana after the Cuban Revolution. Significantly a future Soviet Foreign Minister had been the Soviet charge d'affaires to Cuba resulting in him having personal experience of the island. In addition, a number of the reasons that would underpin the development of the post 1959 relationship had also been important for the one that existed prior to this. These have been returned to a number of times throughout this book and include the geographical location of the island, its relationship with the United States, and the importance of realism within Soviet foreign policy. This is significant as it makes the development of the post 1959 relationship appear less strange despite the geographical distance between the two countries. Moreover, commonalities exist between the two distinct eras prior to and after the Cuban Revolution with the upshot being that the relationship that developed after 1959 can be perceived as more of a re-commencement of relations rather than the creation of a completely new relationship.

POST 1959 BILATERAL RELATIONS AND THE "DISAPPEARING" RELATIONSHIP

After January 1959 the relationship between Moscow and the new revolutionary government in Havana developed very quickly. Only 10 days after Fidel Castro's guerrillas had been victorious the Kremlin recognized the new government in Havana before in February 1960 Anastas Mikoyan, Deputy Prime Minister of the Soviet Union and in 1960 the great Kremlin political survivor, travelled to Cuba. During this visit he placed a wreath at the monument to José Marti in the Cuban capital, but the primary purpose of his trip was to open a Soviet exhibition on science, technology, and culture. At this he stated "I hope that this exhibition will also be a means of expanding economic, cultural and other types of cooperation between our peoples."[5] Before leaving the island he signed a bilateral trade agreement which gave the Cuban government a $100m credit at an interest rate of 2.5 percent for the purchase of Soviet goods. In addition, Moscow also agreed to purchase 425,000 tons of Cuban sugar.[6]

This agreement and Mikoyan's visit were highly significant as it signalled both the great interest which Moscow had in the Cuban Revolution, but also the recommencement of relations between the two countries after January 1959. Over the next 30 years the relationship would develop to unprecedented levels and impinge on all parts of society in both countries. Moreover, Mikoyan also became Cuba's chief champion within the Soviet ruling elite and was the first member of the "Cuban lobby" which would impact on the relationship throughout its existence, but was particularly important in the late 1980s and early 1990s when the relationship felt the full force of the reform processes instigated in the Soviet Union by Mikhail Gorbachev.[7]

Formal diplomatic relations between Moscow and Havana were re-established on 8 May 1960 and on 9 July 1960, in light of Washington cutting its commitment to buy Cuban sugar; the Kremlin agreed to purchase the 700,000 tons that the U.S. had refused to buy. On this Nikita Khrushchev said "Let Americans refuse to buy Cuban sugar. We shall be glad to buy it...If the Americans don't want to eat Cuban sugar, it will be a pleasure for Soviet people to eat it."[8] In December 1960 Moscow increased this commitment to 2.7 million tons, while during the following year further trade agreements were signed which expanded the portfolio of goods which constituted these transactions.[9]

The burgeoning relationship was by no means purely economic because significantly in his speech on 9 July 1960, Khrushchev did not just talk about Cuban sugar, but he also addressed U.S. aggression toward the Cuban Revolution. On this Khrushchev stated

> It should not be forgotten that the United States is now not at such an inaccessible distance from the Soviet Union as formerly. Figuratively speaking, in case of need, Soviet artillerymen can support the Cuban people with rocket fire should the aggressive forces in the Pentagon dare to start intervention against Cuba.[10]

This Soviet and Cuban fear did come to fruition in April 1961 with the U.S. backed exile invasion of the Bay of Pigs. This operation may have failed but it led Castro on 18 April 1961 to extol the socialist nature of the Cuban Revolution before on 2 December 1961 the Cuban leader proclaimed himself, and thus the revolution, to be Marxist-Leninist.[11] By the end of 1961 the Cuban Revolution may have been about to celebrate its third anniversary, but it had also spectacularly left the U.S. sphere of influence and entered the Soviet one due to the rapid development of relations between Moscow and Havana in the three year period from January 1959 onward.

In January 1959 the development of such a relationship between Moscow and Havana had not been envisaged or expected despite the multifaceted relationship which had existed between the two countries prior to the Cuban Revolution which has been the focus of this book. Moreover, commonalities between the relationship before and after 1959 exist. The geographical location of Cuba and its relationship with the United States had always been fundamental to Soviet interest in the island from the 1920s onward. This continued after 1959 with the Revolution's anti-American nature and subsequent deteriorating relationship with Washington only increasing Moscow's interest in it.[12] After January 1959 Moscow faced Chinese accusations of revisionism, which meant in a similar manner to the 1930s and 1940s the Soviet Union simply could not ignore the revolutionary potential on the island if it wished to continue to be perceived as the center of the socialist world.

The change in Soviet foreign policy instigated in the aftermath of Joseph Stalin's death has, as detailed, often been thought to have sparked Moscow's interest in the Developing World in general and Latin America specifically. As has been argued throughout this book, Moscow's interest in Cuba began long before this change in Soviet foreign policy, but it was undoubtedly important for the relationship that developed after January 1959.

Moreover, Soviet-Cuban relations after 1959 were only aided by Khrushchev's risk-taking personality and the close personal relationship that quickly developed between the Soviet leader and his young Cuban counterpart. In addition, by January 1959 the Soviet ruling elite consisted of middle aged career politicians and not heroes of the November 1917 Revolution. This resulted in many of them being captivated by events in Cuba and its Revolution's young vibrant leadership.[13]

As detailed, the island's geographical location and relationship with the United States were fundamental for the attention which the Cuban Revolution received from the Soviet ruling elite. When this is combined with both the timing of its victory, at the height of the Cold War, and the changes to Soviet foreign policy instigated in the mid-1950s, the time was right for Moscow to acquire an ally in the western hemisphere, especially one in such a geostrategically significant location. The result of the continuing presence of the new regime in Havana and Moscow's relationship with it was that it illustrated to the United States that the Soviet Union was a global rival that could challenge U.S. hegemony in both Latin America and even Cuba. This returns to Mearsheimer's principal ideas of realism that countries attempt to increase their own power at the expense of others, again providing a link to the pre-1959 relationship between Moscow and Havana.

Uncertainty over the nature of the Cuban Revolution may have existed in 1959, but what was clear was that the new government in Havana wanted to change its relationship with the United States. Castro would later comment, "We would not in any event have ended up as close friends. The U.S. had dominated us for too long."[14] In addition, the removal of the Arbenz government in Guatemala in 1954 by U.S.-backed exiles, which Che Guevara had personally witnessed, when combined with hostility toward the Cuban Revolution that culminated in the Bay of Pigs invasion, makes Castro's proclamation in December 1961 that he was Marxist-Leninist appear logical.[15]

The Cuban leader would have hoped that this would result in increased Soviet security guarantees, as he would have been aware that for ideological reasons the Kremlin could not allow Washington to topple the first communist regime in the region, especially one in such a significant geographic location. His declaration that he was Marxist-Leninist was designed to increase the pressure on the Soviet elite as a result of this situation. This displayed the strong prevalence of realist pragmatism which has been evident in the Cuban ruling elite from January 1959 onward.[16] It also resulted in the general principles of realism being important for Cuban interest in the Soviet Union, and thus further highlights the significance of this for the relationship in general and thus provides another commonality with the pre-1959 relationship. Moreover, the new Cuban government were drawn to the Soviet economic and political models with Soviet economic assistance also being appealing. This was only aided by the fact that some within the new Cuban ruling elite had shown interest in the Soviet Union before 1959, including both Raúl Castro and Antonio Núñez Jiménez. The outcome was that the relationship that quickly developed between Moscow and Havana after the Cuban Revolution was mutually beneficial to both countries.

Soviet-Cuban relations after 1959 developed to unprecedented levels with a number of reasons and pressures explaining this. Many of these were unique to the late 1950s, but similarities with the pre-1959 relationship also exist. Although this is the case, as stated, in 1959 the rapid development of the relationship in this manner had not been envisaged or expected. Writing in his memoirs about the Cuban Revolution Nikita Khrushchev has stated, "The whole situation was very unclear. The man Fidel appointed to be president was someone we'd never heard of."[17] Khrushchev's sentiments are repeated by Aleksandr Alekseev who was the first Soviet citizen to be granted a visa to travel to Cuba after January 1959. In an interview he later stated "I could not understand what kind of revolution this was, where it was going."[18] It appeared that the Kremlin had little knowledge or understanding of the events unfolding on the Caribbean island. This gives rise to the fundamental question of what had happened to the knowledge regarding Cuba that had been built up in the Soviet Union over a period in excess of 30 years before January 1959. Simply the multifaceted pre-1959 relationship appeared to have disappeared.

Throughout this book the ideas that Moscow suffered from "geographical fatalism" with regards to Cuba prior to January 1959 and that it was the changes to Soviet foreign policy made in the aftermath of Stalin's death that sparked Soviet interest in the Cuban Revolution have been challenged. This is not to say that these foreign policy changes were not important for the development of the relationship after 1959, but conversely to this, they are also key to understanding why the relationship that existed between the two countries in the period between the Russian Revolution and the Cuban Revolution appeared to have vanished after January 1959.

Fundamental to this was Moscow's decision in the mid-1950s to back national liberation movements in the hope of acquiring a presence in the Developing World. It was this in combination with the fact that the victory of the Cuban Revolution had been achieved by a national liberation movement that partly explains the disappearance of the pre-1959 relationship. Moscow may have been unsure of what type of revolution had occurred in the Caribbean, but as the bilateral relationship with Havana rapidly developed and Soviet financial assistance increased, the Kremlin could portray this burgeoning relationship as displaying the correctness of this foreign policy change. This was highly significant in the Cold War setting in which these events were played out, for Soviet prestige in the Developing World in general and also to counter Chinese accusations of revisionism. Moreover, Cuba's geographical location only increased the importance of the island for Moscow.

Writing about the 1930s Gott has stated,

> The alliance between the Communists and Batista was understandable in the context of the time, but was jeered at by the middle-class radicals. The heirs to the upheavals of 1933, and the legend of the Communist Party perfidy remained widespread until long after 1959.[19]

Gott may have been writing about the perception of the PSP within Cuba, but this was also important for the relationship with Moscow after January 1959, as was the Cuban Party's loyalty to Moscow from its inception in August 1925. This alliance with Batista had only originated due to the PCC and subsequently the PSP adhering to Moscow's tactics, and in particular those of the "popular front" of the Third International. Moreover, this alliance also partly explains how the PSP had been able to provide legitimacy for the Cuban political system in the 1940s. As argued in chapters 2 and 3 of this book, this alliance increased Soviet attention in Cuba in the 1930s and 1940s as it displayed the "successes" of their policies at this time, but after 1959 the situation was very different. This was only made worse by the fact that, again due to following Soviet policy, the PSP at best had played a marginal part in the victory of the Revolution and had also famously described Castro's attack on the Moncada barracks in July 1953 as "putchism."[20]

In short, as Moscow showed increasing interest in the Cuban Revolution and its young leaders, both the role of the PSP in Cuban society and also the relationship between the two countries before 1959 became politically highly sensitive for the Kremlin. This was particularly the case as the new regime in Havana, which it very quickly began to court, wanted to fundamentally change the very political system which the PSP, through adhering to Moscow's tactics, had helped provide legitimacy for in the immediate aftermath of World War II.

Moreover, after January 1959 Batista in both the Soviet Union and Cuba became symbolic of the corrupt pro-U.S. "pseudo republic" which the victory of the Revolution had ended.[21] The PSP's former close association with the Cuban dictator, which originated due to adhering to Moscow's tactics, after the Cuban Revolution had to be "removed" from the relationship. This was illustrated by the fact that in his memoirs Andrei Gromyko may have written about being the Soviet charge d'affaires to Cuba and even visiting the island in December 1943, but he makes no mention of his meeting with Batista.[22] Post January 1959 the outcome of earlier policies which had brought "success" to the PSP and the attention of the Kremlin, changes to Soviet foreign policy in the mid-1950s, and the process which had brought the victory of the Cuban Revolution had made this simply impossible to talk or write about. After the Cuban Revolution, revisionism appeared to have impacted greatly on the pre-1959 relationship. In sum, the PSP and the pre-1959 relationship had fallen victim of both the political situation on the island and changes to Soviet foreign policy.

This was repeated regarding the role of the Cuban Party within the Comintern. In 1971 *Outline History of the Communist International,* the definitive history of this organization written in the Soviet Union was published.[23] In this Cuba is only mentioned three times. These are on the creation of the PCC in 1925, with relation to the policy changes implemented in 1934, and regarding the Cuban party gaining legal status in the late 1930s.[24] On this it is stated,

> A popular-revolutionary bloc was formed in Cuba in 1937 on the initiative of the Communists. It consisted of the Communist Party, trade union organizations and peasant leagues. This bloc compelled the government to make certain concessions to the workers and to give legal status to the Communist Party and the revolutionary trade unions.[25]

This may be historically accurate, but it is also incomplete due to the omission of the fact that it was Batista who had granted the PCC legal status. This history of the Comintern was written under ideological constraints with the result being that if this had been included it would have shown that the outcome of Moscow's policies was the PCC's alliance with Batista. After January 1959 this was simply politically impossible to do.

A similar process occurs in other books published in the Soviet era. In V.V. Volskii's *USSR-Latin America 1917–1967* published in 1967, the author writes about the PCC gaining membership to the Comintern, but then details the organization's activity in Latin America as a region and not Cuba.[26] The Cuban author Orlando Cruz Capote also avoids referring to the

PPC's alliance with Batista in the 1930s by simply stopping his historical account in 1935, two years before this association began.[27] The book *Cuba-URSS: Cronica* published in Moscow in 1990 goes even further as it chronicles any contact between the two countries from as early as the sixteenth century regardless of how superficial the contacts may appear, but simply no mention of the PCC or Batista is provided.[28]

The avoidance of the close association between the Cuban party and Batista is further highlighted by the book *Rossiia-Kuba i Sovetskia-Kuba svjazi XVIII: XX vekov* in which A. Aleksandropov writes a chapter on Soviet-Cuban relations from the 1920s to the 1940s without once mentioning Batista.[29] Similarly in *Vmeste na vse vremena* the Seventh Congress of the Comintern in 1935, Jorge Vivo fighting in World War II, and N. Melentiev, E. Konstatinaich, and P. Stretlsov all fighting in the Cuban War of Independence are written about, but not the PCC and its alliance with Batista.[30] Simply this alliance was avoided by referring to events before and after it. Again the association between the PCC and Batista is not referred to in either the aforementioned article "La Revolución de Octubre y su Influencia en Cuba," published in *Bohemia* on 21 April 1967 or by Garcia and Mironchuk in *Raices de las relaciones Cubano Sovieticas* despite Livinov's trip to Cuba in 1943 being detailed. His meeting with the Cuban President during this visit and the exchange of official telegrams which took place at this time, which were examined in chapter 3, are simply omitted.[31] This is also apparent in the speech which Blas Roca gave to the Eighth National Congress of the PSP held in August 1960. Much of his report displays significant revisionism, particularly regarding the events of 26 July 1953.[32] However, this also takes place with his comments regarding the Soviet Union. Roca thanks the socialist bloc countries for their help and support after January 1959 and he even praises the achievements of the Soviet Union. However, no mention of the pre-1959 relationship between either the Cuban party or the island and the Kremlin is made. On reading the report it would appear that the relationship between the two countries began with the Cuban Revolution and not from soon after the Russian Revolution.[33]

A re-writing, or more accurately a non-writing, of the history of the pre-1959 relationship began almost immediately after January 1959. Key to this was the fact that the victory of the Cuban Revolution had been achieved by a national liberation movement and that Moscow could use its backing for the new regime in Havana to display the correctness of its foreign policy changes of the mid-1950s. Also highly significant was the Cuban party's relationship with Batista in the 1930s and 1940s and the fact that it had played at best a peripheral role in the victory of Fidel Castro's national liberation movement. Prior to 1959, the PSP and before it the PCC may have loyally followed Moscow's policies, but ironically the outcome of these very policies which had attracted Soviet attention at the time also meant that after 1959 it became impossible for political and ideological reasons for the Kremlin to refer to them as its relationship with the new government in Havana blossomed. The pre-1959 relationship was overtaken by events and became the victim of Soviet foreign policy changes in the mid-1950s, which resulted in it apparently disappearing.

This disappearance took place very quickly after January 1959 as relations between Moscow and Havana quickly developed, but it has traditionally been thought that the honeymoon period of the relationship after the Cuban Revolution came to a sudden end due to the events of the last two weeks of October 1962. Regarding this, Khrushchev has written "Our relations with Cuba, on the other hand, took a sudden turn for the worse."[34] This mainly originated due to the Kremlin conducting bilateral negotiations with Washington that brought a resolution to the missile crisis, with this offending Cuban nationalism. Furthermore, it resulted in Mikoyan receiving a very frosty reception from his Cuban hosts when he visited the island in November 1962.[35]

Although this is the case, Castro travelled to the Soviet Union twice in an eight-month period in May 1963 and January 1964. Both were historic as the 1963 visit was his first to the Soviet Union, during which he received a hero's welcome, while during the second he signed the first 5-year trade agreement between the two countries.[36] This guaranteed Cuban economic security for 5 years, hardly the action of two countries which were experiencing a strained relationship. However, and conversely to this, Castro's feelings of betrayal over the events of October 1962 were only intensified, because it was only during his May 1963 trip that he learned of the agreement made in October 1962 between Moscow and Washington for the removal of the U.S. missiles in Turkey. In addition, this had only happened by accident when Khrushchev had mistakenly referred to it during a conversation between the two leaders.[37]

The signing of the 5-year trade agreement in January 1964 was highly significant as it was from this point that Cuban radicalism increased which led to tensions in the relationship between Moscow and Havana. This was illustrated in February 1965 when in a speech at Algiers, Ernesto Guevara was not just highly critical of the Soviet Union in general, but also accused the Kremlin of degeneration and even conducting imperialism toward the Developing World.[38] The differences between Moscow and Havana were further apparent in February 1966 at the First Tricontinental Conference held in the Cuban capital. This was attended by representatives from Africa, Asia, and Latin America with the proceedings being highly radical and very different from the more cautious Soviet policies of the time.[39]

In April 1966 Armando Hart, a member of the politburo and secretary of the Central Committee for the PCC, represented Cuba at the 23rd Congress of the CPSU held in Moscow. In his speech Hart exalted the outcomes of the

First Tricontinental Conference, but highlighting the differences between Cuban and Soviet policies his speech was met with total silence.[40] These differences were further illustrated by the radical nature of both Castro's May Day speech at the Plaza de la Revolución, and the First Congress of the Organization for Latin American Solidarity (OLAS) held in Havana in August 1966. Castro graphically demonstrated the tension between the two countries when in November 1967 he ignored the 50th anniversary celebrations of the victory of the Russian Revolution by not personally attending them.[41]

Tension undoubtedly existed, mainly because neither country fully understood each other with particularly Moscow failing to understand the importance of nationalism within the Cuban Revolution, which had been seriously offended by the outcome of the last two weeks of October 1962. In addition, Havana believed both that Soviet society was suffering from degeneration and also that a radical foreign policy could help safeguard its security by moving the attention of the capitalist world away from the Caribbean.[42]

Although this was the case, the relationship was never severed because a variety of pressures had materialized which would have made this problematic for both countries. This included the 5-year trade agreement signed in 1964 and the level of investment which Moscow had already lavished on Cuba which would have simply been lost if the relationship was severed. In a similar manner the Cuban Missile Crisis further increased the pressure on the Kremlin regarding the Cuban Revolution because the Soviet elite had defended their actions by stating that Cuban security had been safeguarded by the outcome of the missile crisis. If a permanent break in relations had occurred this would have been lost which would have left the Kremlin open to further Chinese accusations of revisionism, and also delivered a considerable blow to Soviet prestige in the Cold War.

The tension between Moscow and Havana began to recede in 1968 partly as Cuban internal and external radicalism began to wane. This was graphically illustrated by Guevara's death in October 1967, but an argument has always existed that the Kremlin coerced Havana into this.[43] Castro backing the Warsaw Pact invasion of Czechoslovakia in August 1968 was indicative of the improvement of relations between Moscow and Havana.[44] However, even as Cuba moved back into the Soviet fold, Castro highlighted the distinctive nature of the Cuban Revolution to the Kremlin. He did this in a "secret speech" which he delivered to the Central Committee of the PCC in January 1968 when he was highly scathing of Mikoyan's behavior during his trip to the island in November 1962. Moreover, a microfaction led by Anibal Escalante was uncovered and subsequently convicted of improper activity with the Soviet embassy in Havana that could be detrimental to the Cuban Revolution. This was highly significant not only due to the nature of the charges which Escalante and his associates were found guilty of, but also because Escalante had been a former leader of the PSP before 1959.[45]

Cuba may have been moving back toward the Soviet fold, once again highlighting the prevalence of realist pragmatism within the Cuban leadership, but Castro had sent a very clear message to the Kremlin that it was not going to be able to dictate the terms of this rapprochement. Moreover, it also appeared that some within the Cuban ruling elite continued not to fully trust parts of the pre-1959 PSP as they had been used to send this highly important, but blunt message to the Kremlin. Before the Cuban Revolution the PSP may have been highly loyal to the Kremlin, but after January 1959 this impacted negatively on both Soviet-Cuban relations and also partly explains the disappearance of the pre-1959 relationship.

In the 1970s the tension that existed between Moscow and Havana in the second half of the previous decade receded as the bilateral relationship improved. Furthermore, the Cuban Revolution underwent a "sovietization" process. In the summer of 1972 not only did Castro visit the Soviet Union for the first time in eight years, but Cuba also gained membership to the Council for Mutual Economic Assistance (CMEA).[46] Illustrating the improved relationship, in January 1974 Leonid Brezhnev became the first Soviet premier to visit Latin America when he travelled to Cuba. Moreover, in the following year the First Congress of the PCC was held at which, as previously detailed, Castro spoke of the importance of the Russian Revolution for the Cuban Revolution. Significantly a new constitution, which very closely resembled the Soviet one, was also ratified at this congress. In addition, also during 1975 Cuba became involved with the Soviet Union in Africa and in early 1980 the Caribbean island was one of the few countries to back the Warsaw Pact invasion of Afghanistan. This was despite Castro being the President of the Non-aligned Movement.[47] By the dawn of the 1980s Cuba was very much an integral part of the socialist bloc.

At the start of the 1980s the island remained geostrategically important for the Kremlin, particularly as superpower tension heightened with the inauguration of Ronald Reagan as the President of the United States. The upshot was that realism continued to be significant in Moscow's interest in Cuba, as had been the case since the time of the Russian Revolution. Moreover, the relationship had impacted on all sections of society in both countries with some 8,000 Cubans a year studying in the Soviet Union and 140 educational centers having been built on the island with Soviet assistance.[48] However, as the decade progressed, tension reappeared in the relationship as a result of reform processes introduced in both countries which appeared to be fundamentally dissimilar in nature to one another. The campaign for rectification of errors in Cuba was vastly different from the reforms instigated by Mikhail Gorbachev in the Soviet Union. Although this was the case, both the Soviet and Cuban reforms had the same ultimate goal: the improvement of socialism.

This may have been the hope, but the Soviet reforms began to impact adversely on Soviet-Cuban relations. Key to this was *perestroika's* failure to reinvigorate the Soviet economy with this having negative knock-on effects for the Cuban economy due to the intertwined nature of the two economies. Moreover, in the late 1980s the terms of trade also began to turn against Cuba.[49] In addition, g*lasnost* resulted in the appearance of criticism of the Cuban Revolution within the Soviet Union while as superpower relations improved, due to "new thinking" in Soviet foreign policy, the geostrategic importance of Cuba for the Kremlin fell.[50] In short, the realist principles that had underpinned much of Soviet interest in Cuba from 1917 onward began to recede in significance.

The impact of these reforms cannot be overestimated, but Cuba was partly shielded from their effects by the "Cuban lobby" acting as a "break" to them. The removal of this "break" was graphically illustrated on 11 September 1991, when less than one month after the defeat of the August 1991 coup in Moscow, which had comprised many of Cuba's closest allies in the Soviet elite, Gorbachev announced the removal of the final Soviet troops from the island. This was truly historic, but was done without prior consultation with the Cuban government. The Cuban regime was deeply unhappy at this announcement, and their resentment was further increased due to the fact that it had been made during a joint press conference with U.S. Secretary of State James Baker.[51]

By the end of 1991 Soviet-Cuban relations were fundamentally different from March 1985 when Gorbachev had become General Secretary of the CPSU. However, it was only with the implosion of the Soviet Union in December 1991 that the 30-year relationship came to a sudden end. During the following year relations between Russia, the legal successor to the Soviet Union, and Cuba seemed to be virtually nonexistent with diplomatic relations but little else of the relationship appearing to survive. However, from the mid-1990s onward relations began to improve, which had not been expected or predicted by experts at the time. A variety of reasons explain this upturn including a huge legacy from the Soviet era, changes to Russian foreign policy, and unforeseen consequences of the Cuban economic reforms of the early to mid-1990s which resulted in Russian companies wishing to invest in Cuba. In 1996 this resulted in Russia being Cuba's largest trading partner, which experts in 1992 had certainly not foreseen or predicted.[52]

Russia may have been overtaken by other competitors in the Cuban economy, before the year 2000 most noticeably Canada and Spain and in the twenty-first century China and Venezuela, but Russian-Cuban relations remain robust. This was illustrated by both Vladimir Putin and Dmitry Medvedev visiting Cuba in December 2000 and November 2008, respectively and, as detailed on the opening page of this book, Raúl Castro making his first visit to Moscow in over 20 years in January 2009.[53] Moreover, the Cuban President returned to the Russian capital in July 2012, when he once again met both Putin and Medvedev.[54] Furthermore, in 2008 a Russian Orthodox Church was opened in the Cuban capital while Russia was the "guest of honor" at the 2010 International Book fair held every February in Havana.[55]

The nature of the relationship that continues between Moscow and Havana more than 20 years since the end of Soviet-Cuban relations may not have been expected in the early 1990s, but in the final years of the first decade of the twenty-first century a new process within it commenced. Very interesting is the fact that both governments began to make increasing reference to the relationship that existed between Moscow and Havana prior to January 1959, which has not only been the focus of this book, but had also disappeared after the victory of the Cuban Revolution. This was most notable during Raúl Castro's trip to the Russian capital in January 2009 when, as stated, he paid homage to the brothers Jorge and Aldo Vivo and Enrique Vilar who fought for the Red Army during World War II at the permanent exhibit at the Museum of the Great Patriotic War.[56] However, it has also been noticeable with the publication of such books as *Rossiia zarbezh'e na Kuba: Strancy istorii in 2002*. This book charts bilateral cultural links between the two countries from even before the Russian Revolution. In addition, in May 2011 the photographic exhibition "Chronicle of the Great Fatherland War 1941–1945" was opened in the Museum of the Revolution in Havana.[57] This was important in itself, but has connotations with the photographic exhibitions which formed such an important part of the workings of the Institute of Cuban-Soviet Cultural Exchange that operated in the Cuban capital in the years from 1945 to 1952 and were examined in detail in the previous chapter.

Both Moscow and Havana appear to be attempting to highlight their long intertwined histories that began before the victory of the Cuban Revolution. This did not even happen in the late 1960s when it could have been expected due to the rapprochement which took place between the two countries at this time. However, in the twenty-first century it is becoming increasingly significant because as both countries' populations become younger, large numbers of Russians and Cubans were either born after the end of Soviet-Cuban relations in December 1991 or can no longer remember the halcyon days of the relationship. Over time this will only become increasingly important as Russian-Cuban relations appear likely to remain unchanged for at least the short to medium term. This means that the significance of the multifaceted pre-1959 relationship, which has challenged a number of traditional assumptions including the Kremlin suffering from "geographical fatalism" but disappeared after the victory of the Cuban Revolution, has re-emerged to remain important in the contemporary bilateral relationship between Moscow and Havana.

NOTES

1. Christopher Andrew & Vasili Mitrokhin, *The World Was Going Our Way. The KGB and the Battle for the Third World*, (New York: Basic Book, 2005), 27.

2. *Pravda*, June 15, 1949, 3.

3. "Fidel Castro," *New Times*, Volume 34, (1958): 31–32.

4. Herbert Matthews, "Cuban Rebel Is Visited in Hideout," *New York Times*, February 24, 1957, 1.

5. *Pravda*, February 7, 1960, 7. *Pravda*, January 11, 1959, 7.

6. *Pravda*, February 16, 1960, 6.

7. Mervyn J. Bain, *Soviet-Cuban Relations 1985 to 1991. Changing Perceptions in Moscow and Havana*. (Lanham: Lexington Books, 2007), 74–75 & 94–96.

8. *Izvestia*, July 10, 1960, 10. *Pravda*, May 8, 1960, 1.

9. *Pravda*, December 21, 1960, 21–22. *Izvestia*, September 22, 1961, 21–22.

10. *Pravda*, July 10, 1960, 2.

11. *Revolución*, December 2, 1961, 1.

12. Aleksandr Fursenko & Timothy Naftali, *"One Hell of a Gamble." The Secret History of the Cuban Missile Crisis*, (London: John Murray, 1997), 2. Peter Shearman, *The Soviet Union and Cuba*, (London: Routledge & Kegan Paul, 1987), 5–11.

13. This also happened to Mikoyan who would later state, "You Americans must realize what Cuba means to us old Bolsheviks. We have been waiting all our lives for a country to go communist without the Red Army. It has happened in Cuba, and it makes us feel like boys again." Samuel Farber, *The Origins of the Cuban Revolution. Reconsidered* (Chapel Hill: The University of North Carolina Press, 2006), 147.

14. Wayne Smith, *The Closest of Enemies. A Personal and Diplomatic Account of U.S.-Cuban Relations Since 1957*, (New York: W.W. Norton & Company, 1987), 144.

15. Ernesto Guevara, *The Motorcycle Diaries. A Journey Around South America*, (London: Fourth Estate, 1995), 61–64. D.E. Schulz, *The Cuban Revolution and the Soviet Union*, (Ohio University PhD Thesis, 1977), 14–19.

16. Michael Erisman, *Cuba's Foreign Relations in a Post-Soviet World*, (Gainseville: University Press of Florida, 2000), 25–26.

17. Nikita Khrushchev, *Khrushchev Remembers*, (Boston: Little, Brown and Company, 1970), 489.

18. Fursenko and Naftali, *"One Hell of a Gamble,"* 1997, 27.

19. Richard Gott, *Cuba. A new History*, (New Haven: Yale University Press, 2004), 143.

20. *Daily Worker*, August 5, 1953, 1.

21. Gott, *Cuba*, 2004, 113. For the Soviet press reporting on Batista please see the final section of chapter 3.

22. Andrei Gromyko, *Pamiatnoe Kniga Pervaya*, (Moscow: Politizdat, 1988), 389–398.

23. A.I. Sobolev, *Outline History of the Communist International* (Moscow: Progress Publishers, 1971).

24. Sobolev, *Outline History of the Communist International*, 1971, 232, 368 & 430.

25. Sobolev, *Outline History of the Communist International* , 1971, 430.

26. V.V. Volskii, *SSSR i Latinskaia Amerika 1917–1967*, (Moscow: Mezhdunarodnye otnosheniia, 1967). 70.

27. Orlando Cruz Capote, *The Comintern and Problems of the Cuban Revolution (1925–1935)*, (Moscow: Academia de Ciencias Sociales, 1989).

28. *Cuba-URSS Cronica*, (Moscow: Progreso, 1990).

29. A. Aleksandropov, "Sovetskia-Kuba otnosheniya i 20–40-e godi" in *Rossiia-Kuba i Sovetskia-Kuba svjazi XVIII: XX vekov* (Moscow: Nayka, 1975), 132–146.

30. *Vmeste na vse vremena* (Moscow: Molodaia gvardiia, 1988).

31. Erasmo Dumpierre, "La Revolución de Octubre y su Influencia en Cuba," *Bohemia*, April 21, 1967, 4–9. Angel Garcia & Piotr Mironchuk, *Raices de las relaciones Cubano Sovieticas*, (Havana, Editorial de Ciencias Sociales, 1988).

32. Blas Roca, *The Cuban Revolution. Report to the Eighth National Congress of the Popular Socialist Party of Cuba*, (New York: New Century Publishers, 1961), 40–44.

33. Roca, *The Cuban Revolution.* 1961, 73–74, 76–94.

34. Khrushchev, *Khrushchev Remembers,* 1970, 461.

35. Document 1, Cuban Record of Conversation, Mikoyan and Cuban Leadership, Havana 4 November 1962 in *Cold War International History Project Bulletin,* Issues 8–9 Winter 1996/ 1997, Washington DC: Woodrow Wilson International Center for Scholars, Issues 8–9, (Winter 1996–1997) , 339–342.

36. *Pravda,* January 23, 1964, 1. *Pravda,* April 28, 1963, 1.

37. James Blight & Philip Brenner, *Sad and Luminous Days. Cuba's Struggle with the Superpowers after the Cuban Missile Crisis,* (Lanham: Rowman & Littlefield Publishers, 2002), 35–85.

38. Ernesto Guevara, "Discurso en el Segundo Seminario Económico de Solidaridad Afroasiática" in *Ernesto Che Guevara escritos y discursos, 7,* (Havana: Editorial De Ciencias Sociales), 341–354.

39. *Granma,* February 7, 1966, 1.

40. *Pravda,* April 2, 1966, 7.

41. Fidel Castro, *Fidel Castro Speaks* (London: Allen Lane The Penguin Press, 1969), 161–180.

42. Blight & Brenner, *Sad and Luminous Days,* 2002, 99–104. Erisman, *Cuba's Foreign Relations,* 2000, 80–82.

43. Blight & Brenner, *Sad and Luminous Days,* 2002, 121–126.

44. *Granma,* August 24, 1968, 2–4.

45. Blight & Brenner, *Sad and Luminous Days,* 2002, xxiii & 132–137.

46. *Pravda,* June 28, 1972, 1–2. For the "sovietization" process of the Cuban Revolution please see: Carmelo Mesa-Lago, *Cuba in the 1970s, Pragmatism and Institutionalization,* (Albuquerque: University of New México Press, 1974).

47. Erisman, *Cuba's Foreign Relations,* 2000, 103–104. *Pravda,* January 31, 1974, 5. *Granma,* December 19, 1975, 2–7.

48. V. Lavrentyev, 'USSR-Cuban Brotherhood and Cooperation', FBIS LD182341 Moscow Domestic Service in Russian 0615 18 April 1985.

49. Bain, *Soviet-Cuban Relations,* 2007, 85–87.

50. For the type of articles that appeared in the Soviet Union regarding Cuba please see: Vladislav Chirkov, "An Uphill Task" *New Times,* 33, (17 August 1987): 16–17.

51. *Izvestia,* September 12, 1991, 1.

52. For analysis of the post-1992 relationship please see: Mervyn J. Bain, *Russian-Cuban Relations Since 1992. Continuing Camaraderie in a Post-Soviet World.* (Lanham: Lexington Books, 2008).

53. Stanislav Kondrashov, "Language of Gestures in Putin's Diplomacy," *Vremya,* December 22, 2000, 3. "Russian truck maker Kamaz considering production in Cuba," 2008, RIA Novosti, 21 November, http.www.rian.ru/Russia/20081121 (accessed 23 November 2008). "La colaboración cubana-rusa ha cobrado un nuevo dinamismo," 2009, Trabajadores January 30, http://www.trabajadores.cu/la-colaboracion-cubano-rusa (accessed 3 February. 2009).

54. Yaima Puig Meneses, "Intensa y muy útil visita de trabajo." Juventud Rebelde, 12 July 2012, www.juventudrebelde.cu . (accessed 17 July 2012).

55. "The Russian Orthodox Church" http//www/granma.cu/2008/octubre/mier22 (accessed 4 November 2008).

56. '65 Aniversario de la Gran Victoria,' *Edicion de la Embajada de la federación de Rusia en Cuba,* Numero 4, (2010):28.

57. M.A. Rossiiskii, *Rossiia zarbezh'e na Kuba: Strancy istorii* (Moscow: Veche, 2002). *El Ruso Cubano, Boletín Informativo de le Embajada de le Federación de Rusia,* No 59, (9 July 2011): 5–6.

Index

Agrupacion Comunista de la Habana, 33
Agustín Martínez José, 77
Alekseev, Aleksandr, 134
Alonso, Alicia, 96, 108
Andrew, Christopher, 20, 92, 121
Arbenz, Jacob, 61, 133
Asociación de Buen Gobierno, 33
August 1933 coup, 14. *See also* Caribbean
Bureau; CPUSA; "Sergeants Revolt; "
third period; Welles

Baker, James, 141
Baliño, Carlos, 33, 34
Batista, Fulgencio, 2, 65, 78, 99; 1952
Coup, 60; relations with United States,
14; correspondence with Soviet Union,
83, 126; "popular front", 51–52, 54,
101, 135, 136; break in diplomatic
relations with Soviet Union, 58, 60, 85,
88, 89, 112, 129; relations with Soviet
Union, 82, 125, 136, 143n21; relations
with PCC, 36, 51, 52, 61, 85, 136, 137;
Soviet press reporting of, 88, 89,
108–109, 109, 110, 110–111. *See also*
Marinello; "Sergeants Revolt"
Bay of Pigs, 111, 132, 133
Beria, Leventi, 58–59, 107
Bolshevik Revolution. *See* Russian
Revolution
Boughton, George, 21, 61, 110
Brest-Litvosk, 9, 10

Browder, Earl, 55; "Browderism", 55;
effect of "Browderism" on PSP, 57, 58,
60, 68, 107, 113, 124, 127. *See also*
Duclos; Roca; Rodríguez
Bulganin, Nikolai, 59, 93

campaign of rectification of errors, 140
Caribbean Bureau, 30, 41, 42, 43, 45,
72n62. *See also* CPUSA
Castro, Fidel, 121, 133, 138; and Soviet
Union, 20, 62, 112; Soviet press
reporting of, 109, 110, 114, 129; post
1959 relationship with Moscow, 61, 63,
131, 132, 134, 138, 139–140. *See also* ;
Cuban foreign policy; *glasnost*;
Gorbachev; *Fidel personalismo*; "new
thinking; " Russia, *perestroika*; Soviet
Union; 26th July Movement; United
States;
Castro, Raúl, 112, 134; visits to Moscow,
66, 141–142
China, 50, 141
civilizationists, 4–5, 100, 128, 130;
inception of, 11, 25n51. *See also* ;
Cuba; Gould-Davies; Kennan; realism;
Marshall Plan; Soviet Union; United
States
colonialism, 13, 14, 50
Comintern: "third period", 40, 46, 68, 122,
123; "popular front" period, 8, 32, 46,
47, 48, 73n98, 74n126, 75n153, 89;

145

"success" of Cuban party, 50, 51–52, 58, 68, 103, 127, 130, 135; PCC membership of Central Bureau, 31, 36, 47, 52, 122. *See also* August 1933 coup; Batista; Dimitrov; "Browderism; " "dual track diplomacy; " Caribbean Bureau; CPUSA; Marinello

communism, 16, 18, 33, 54, 56, 61

Communist International. *See* Comintern

Communist Party of Mexico (CPM), 33, 51. *See also* Flores Magón; congresses of, 11, 108; Roca

Communist Party of the United States (CPUSA), 23, 34, 42; relationship with PCC, 50, 51, 55, 68, 72n62, 73n104. *See also* August 1933 coup; "Browderism; " "Caribbean Bureau; " Comintern

Concheso, Aurelio, 78, 118n114; meeting with Stalin, 79, 80–81, 91, 125, 129

constructivism, 4, 38. *See also* statists; Tsygankov

Council for Mutual Economic Assistance (CMEA), 140

Cuba. *See also* August 1933 coup; Batista; Caribbean Bureau; Fidel Castro; Raúl Castro; Cold War; Comintern; CPUSA; Cuban Revolution; dependency; labor radicalism; PCC; Platt Amendment; PSP; reciprocity; Soviet foreign policy; sugar; United States

Cuban Constitution of 1940, 14, 53

Cuban exile community, 133

"Cuban lobby", 131, 141. *See also* August 1991 coup

Cuban Missile Crisis, 138, 139

Cuban National Antifascist League, 65, 78, 83; influence of Russian Revolution, 62–63, 125; relations with July 26 Movement, 20, 61, 135; membership and presidential elections, 54, 56, 58, 74n129, 123; influence on Cuban political system, 57–58, 68, 84, 85–86, 112, 124

cultural links, 117n69; Russian performers in Cuba, 96, 107, 127; Russia ballet school in Havana, 96. *See also* Alonso;

Institute of Cuban-Soviet Cultural Exchange; VOKS

Czechoslovakia, 92, 139

dependency, 2, 4; Cuban economic dependence on United States, 22, 39, 58, 92, 94; effect on Soviet interest in Cuba, 45, 67, 107, 113, 122, 129, 130. *See also* labor radicalism; Wall Street Crash

Dimitroff, George, 47

Duclos, Jacques, 55, 56. *See also* "Browderism"

El Trabajado Latinoamericano, 31, 59

Engels, Frederick, 62, 63; interest in Cuba, 69n3

Escalante, Aníbal, 139

Estrada Palma, Thomas, 13, 77, 96

Fidel personalismo, 2

Flores Magón, Enrique, 33, 35, 36

Fursenko, Aleksandr, 20–21, 61. *See also* "geographical fatalism"; academic perception of Soviet foreign policy, 39, 45, 57, 60, 104, 106, 114, 130, 142; Andrew; Fursenko; Miller; Mitrokhin; Naftali; Pavlov; ; Castro; *glasnost*; "new thinking; " *perestroika*

Gould-Davies, Nigel, 11, 100, 104. *See also* Nye; soft power

Grau San Martín, Ramón, 14, 58, 83, 85–86, 89, 115n29

Great Man Theory, 2, 59. *See also Fidel personalismo*

Gris Cinema, 98

Gromyko, Andrei, 83, 125; visit to Cuba, 82–83, 88, 102, 125, 136

Guillen, Nicolas, 65, 99, 105, 127

imperialism, 6, 35, 47, 49, 50, 66, 69n2, 138

Institute of Cuban-Soviet Cultural Exchange, 56, 96, 127, 128, 142; Cuban activities in Soviet Union, 104, 105, 106, 128

internationalism, 62, 66

July 26 Movement, 20, 62. *See also* unity pact
Junta Cubana de Renovación, 33

Kaganovich, Lazar, 58–59
Kalinin, Mikhail, 79, 83, 125–126
Kelly, Robert, 17, 44
Kennan, George, 18; "long telegram", 18, 56, 87, 100, 101. *See also* Cold War; communism; socialism; Soviet Union; U.S. foreign policy
KGB, 107, 111–112, 114, 128; secret speech, 12, 108; post-1959 relations with Cuba, 132, 133, 134, 138
Konstatinaich, E., 63, 66, 67, 137
Korean War, 18, 58, 60, 75n158

Labor radicalism, 45, 130; "hot bed" of, 40, 67, 86, 101, 113, 122, 129
Larin, Eugenio, 26n61
Litvinov, Maxim, 10, 82, 125; visit to Cuba, 65, 78, 82, 91, 116n48, 125
League of Nations,, 1, 10, 48, 50
Lenin, Vladimir, 7, 10, 64, 66, 99; interest in Latin America, 6; writings on Cuba, 6, 69n3; influence on Cuban Revolution, 62–63, 66. *See also* Brest-Litovsk; Comintern; Grigor Suny; realism; Russia
liberalism, 1, 2
Light, Margot, 6, 11, 30, 80, 92

Machado, Gerardo, 34, 36, 40–41, 42, 43, 44
Malenkov, Georgy, 58–59
Malik, Yakov, 85
Mantici, Enrique González, 98, 116n44; visit to Soviet Union, 105–106, 128, 129
Manuilsky, Dmitir, 46, 47
Marinello, Juan, 51, 54, 61, 99; minister in Batista's cabinet, 8–9, 53, 86, 123; visit to Soviet Union, 59, 62. *See also* Rodríguez
Marshal Plan, 18, 55, 56, 87, 128. *See also* communism; Kennan; socialism; U.S. foreign policy
Marti, José, 33, 62, 131
Marx, Karl, 62, 63; writings on Cuba 2n3

Marxist-Leninism, 2, 22, 55, 63, 74n126, 132, 133–134
Matthews, Herbert, 110, 111, 129. *See also* Castro; *New York Times*
Mearsheimer, John, 1, 56, 87, 101, 104, 133. *See also* realism
Medvedev, Dmitrii, 141
Melentiev, N., 63, 66, 67, 137
Mella, Julio Antonio, 33, 34, 35, 35–36, 45, 71n38
Mendieta, Carlos, 14
Mexico, 21, 31, 93, 94, 110, 112; relations with Soviet Union, 6, 10, 77, 107; Comintern and Mexico, 30, 70n5; Trotsky, 20, 81. *See also* CPM
Mikoyan, Anastas, 58–59, 107, 112; post-1959 relations with Cuba, 131, 138, 139, 143n13
Miller, Nicola, 20, 92. *See also* "geographical fatalism"
Mitokhin, Vasili, 20, 92, 121. *See also* "geographical fatalism"
Mitskevich, Eugenio, 103. *See also* VOKS
Molotov, Vyacheslav, 77, 83, 124; pre-April 1942 interest/correspondence with Cuba, 49–50, 51, 123, 127; post-April 1942 interest/correspondence with Cuba, 58–59, 84, 106, 107, 129. *See also* Concheso; Gromyko; Stalin; Soviet foreign policy
Monocal, Mario, 13
Morgentheau,Hans, 1
Monroe Doctrine, 20

national liberation movements, 12, 50, 135
National Confederation of Cuba (CNOC), 38, 43
Naftali, Timothy, 20–21, 61
Nazism, 8, 10, 46, 65, 79, 80, 91, 125
Nazi-Soviet Pact, 10–11, 49–50, 52, 74n117
neo-Realism, 3, 4, 22, 113, 130. *See also* realism; Waltz
New Economic Policy (NEP), 7, 95
New York Times , 110; cited in Soviet press, 110–111, 129. *See also* Matthews
"new thinking", 141
Non-aligned Movement, 140

North Atlantic Treaty Organisation
(NATO), 20
November Revolution. *See* Russian
Revolution
Núñez Jiménez, Antonio, 63, 103, 116n44,
119n118, 127, 134
Nye, Joseph 1n51: soft power, 3, 100. *See
also* Gould-Davies

Operation Barbarozza, 11, 52, 82, 89, 91,
126. *See also* Nazism
Ordoqui, Joaquin, 36, 51, 66
Organization for Latin American Solidarity
(OLAS), 138
Ortiz, Fernanado, 96–97, 102, 103, 127
*Outline History of the Communist
International* , 136

Pavlov, Yuri, 20, 92, 117n69. *See also*
"geographical fatalism"
"peaceful coexistence", 9, 10, 11, 48. *See
also* Light
Perestroika, 141
Pérez-Stable, Marifeli, 57
Platt Amendment, 13, 14, 15, 50. *See also*
dependency; reciprocity; United States
pragmatism: prevalence within Cuban
elite, 134, 140
Prio Socarras, Carlos, 58, 84, 85–86, 88,
89, 124

Rapallo Treaty, 10
realism, 1–2, 16, 22, 82, 95, 112–113, 125,
126, 140; prevalence of in Cuban
leadership, 134. *See also* Brest-Litvosk;
Comintern; Grigor Suny; Mearsheimer;
Morgentheau; neo-realism; Soviet
foreign policy; World War II
reciprocity, 13, 14, 26n65, 50. *See also*
dependency; United States
Roca, Blas, 48, 51; visits to Soviet Union,
46, 47, 52, 62, 73n92; speeches/
writings, 47–48, 52, 73n97, 75n158,
109, 137. *See also* "Browderism; "
Comintern; CPUSA; activities within
Institute of Cuban-Soviet Cultural
Exchanges, 75n139, 98, 103; Marinello
Roosevelt, Franklin, 17, 82, 125. *See also*
Tehran

Russia. *See also* Brest-Litovsk; Comintern;
Cuba; Lenin; Russian Revolution;
Soviet Union; Tsar Nicholas II; World
War I; United States
Russian Foreign Policy. *See* Soviet foreign
policy
Russian Revolution,, 11, 67, 96, 138;
impact on international system, 5, 29;
Cuban interest in, 34, 45, 65–66, 69, 83,
83–84, 97, 98, 107, 125, 126; Cuban
press reporting of, 63, 63

influence on Cuban Revolution, 62, 66,
140. *See also* Brest-Litvosk;
Comintern; liberalism; realism;
Operation Barbarroza

Salinas, Marselo, 34, 34, 63
Santovenia, Emeterio, 79, 80, 102
"Sergeants Revolt", 14
Shvernik, N.M., 84
socialism, 9, 11, 121, 140. *See also* Cold
War; Comintern; Kennan; Marshall
Plan; Soviet foreign policy
soft power, 22, 24n12, 101, 128, 130. *See
also* Gould-Davies; Nye
Soviet Union,. *See also* Castro; Cold War;
Comintern; CPSU; Gorbachev;
Kennan; Khrushchev; League of
Nations; Marshall Plan; Operation
Barbarozza; Roosevelt; Russia; Russian
Revolution; Soviet foreign policy;
Stalin; United States; World War 2
Soviet foreign policy: "dual track", 9, 69,
114, 121, 124, 125, 130. *See also*
Comintern; constructivism; "Cuban
lobby; " "geographical fatalism; "
Kennan; Korean War; Molotov; neo-
realism; "new thinking; " "peaceful
coexistence; " realism; statists;
Tsygankov; United States; westernizers
Soviet Society for Cultural Relations with
Foreign Countries (VOKS), 83,
101–102, 103, 107, 113, 127; Cuban
cultural activity in Soviet Union, 104,
105, 106, 128. *See also* Gould-Davies;
Institute of Cuban-Soviet Cultural
Exchange; Mitskevich; Nye; soft
power; westernists; Zaikan

"sphere of influence", 87, 132

Stalin, Joseph, 58–59, 61, 64, 65, 89, 107, 129; meeting with Concheso, 79, 80–81, 91, 125, 129; interest in Latin America, 30, 31, 69n3, 115n14. *See also* Cold War; Comintern; "geographical fatalism; " Great Man Theory; Grigor Suny; Molotov; Nazi-Soviet pact; neo-realism; realism; Roosevelt; Russian Revolution; Soviet foreign policy; Tsygankov; World War II

Statists, 4, 38, 45, 68, 87, 124, 130. *See also* constructivism

Stretlsov, P., 63. *See also* Melentiev

sugar, 41; impact of World War II, 14, 90–92, 95, 126; pre-1959 Soviet interest and purchase of Cuban sugar, 22, 93, 93, 94–95, 108, 113, 127; post-1959 Soviet interest and purchase of Cuban sugar, 131, 132. *See also* dependency; labor radicalism; neo-realism; realism; reciprocity

Tehran, 55. *See also* "Browderism"

Third International. *See* Comintern

tobacco, 94

trade: Soviet trade with Cuba, 78, 91, 93, 94, 108; Soviet trade with Latin America, 31, 62, 90, 92, 93; Post-1959 Soviet trade with Cuba, 131, 132, 138, 139, 141. *See also* neo-realism; "peaceful coexistence; " realism; reciprocity; sugar; United States

Tricontinental Conference, 138

Trotsky, Leon, 6, 20, 29, 69n3, 81

Tsar Nicholas II, 77, 96

Tsygankov, Andrei, 4–5. *See also* civilizationists; statists; westernists

Union of Soviet Socialist Republics (USSR). *See* Soviet Union

United Nations (UN), 20, 53, 93

United States,, 3, 12–15, 15–18, 22, 49, 133; "Truman Doctrine", 18; "dollar diplomacy", 17. *See also* August 1933 coup; Cold War; Cuba; Comintern; CPUSA; dependency; Gorbachev; Kennan; Lenin; Marshall Plan; Platt Amendment; reciprocity; Russia; "Sergeants Revolt; " Soviet Union; Stalin; World War I: World War II

unity pact, 61. *See also* PSP

Uruguay, 10, 31, 77, 81, 90

Vilar, Enrigue, 66, 142

Virgin Land Campaign, 93

Vivo, Aldo, 66, 131, 137, 142

Vivo, Jorge, 36, 66, 137, 142

Wall Street Crash, 14, 17, 40. *See also* dependency

Waltz, Kenneth, 3, 91, 93, 95, 126. *See also* neo-realism

Warsaw Pact, 66, 93, 139, 140

Wilson, Woodrow, 1, 16. *See also* liberalism

Welles, Summer, 14, 43. *See also* "Sergeants Revolt"

westernists, 4

World War I, 29; effect on Cuba, 14, 26n69; See also Brest-Litvosk; dependency; liberalism; Russian Revolution; United States; Wilson

World War II, 27n90, 59, 81, 83; impact on relations between Moscow and Havana, 14, 49, 53, 65–66, 68, 78, 99, 112, 125. *See also* liberalism; Nazi-Soviet Pact; neo-realism; Operation Barbarozza; realism; Soviet Union; sugar; Tehran; United States; Vivo; Vilar

Yuzantong, 31, 90

Zaikan, Dmitri, 102; correspondence with Soviet Union, 83, 107, 115n29, 128–129. *See also* Gromyko

Zimmerman letter, 15

Zinoviev, Grigory, 30

Bibliography

Adibekov, G.M., Shakhnazarova, E.E., & Shirinia, K.K. *Organizatsionnaia struktura Kominterna 1919–1943*. Moscow: ROSSPEN, 1997.

Alder, Emanuel. "Constructivism," Pp. 95–118 in *Handbook of International Relations*, edited by Walter Carlneas, Beth Simmons, & Thomas Risse. Thousand Oaks, Cal: Sage, 2003.

Aleksandropov, A. "Sovetskia-Kuba otnosheniya i 20–40-e godi." Pp.132–146 in *Rossiia-Kuba i Sovetskia-Kuba svjazi XVIII. XX vekov*. Moscow: Nayka, 1975.

Alexander, Robert J. *Communism in Latin America*. New Brunswick: Rutgers University Press, 1957.

Allison, Grahan T. *Essence of Decision. Explaining the Cuban Missile Crisis*, Boston: Little, Brown & Company, 1971.

Andrew Christopher, and Vasili Mitrokhin. *The World Was Going Our Way. The KGB and the Battle for the Third World*. New York: Basic Books, 2005.

Aquilar, Luis, *Marxism in Latin America*. Philadelphia: Temple University Press, 1978.

Aragon, D. "Tres rusos en la Guerra del 95," *Bohemia*, July 10, 1970, 16–17.

Archive of the Commissar for Foreign Affairs, the Russian State Archive for Social and Political History (RSA), Moscow.

Archive of the Communist Party of the United States (CPUSA), Tamiment Library, New York University, New York.

Archive of the Secretary to the President of Cuba, Cuban National Archive (CAN), Havana.

Archive of the Third International (Comintern), the Russian State Archive for Social and Political History (RSA), Moscow.

"Arte Cubano en la URSS," *Cuba y la URSS,* Num 6 (June 1946): 28.

Ashby, Timothy. *The Bear in the Back Yard. Moscow's Caribbean Strategy*. Lexington: Lexington Books, 1987.

Báez, Luis. *Conversaciones con Juan Marinillo*. Havana: Casa Editora Abril, 1995.

Bain, Mervyn J. *Soviet -Cuban Relations 1985 to 1991. Changing Perceptions in Moscow and Havana*. Lanham: Lexington Books, 2007.

—. *Russian-Cuban Relations Since 1992. Continuing Camaraderie in a Post-Soviet World*. Lanham: Lexington Books, 2008.

Barghoorn, Frederick C. *The Soviet Cultural Offensive. The Role of Cultural Diplomacy in Soviet Foreign Policy*. Princeton University Press, Princeton, 1960.

Bartley, Russell H. *Imperial Russia and the Struggle for Latin American Independence 1808–1828*. Austin: The University of Texas, 1978.

Batista, Fulgencio, to Mikhail Kalinin, Havana, 8 November 1942, in G.E. Mamedov and A. Dalmau, *Rossiia-Kuba, 1902–2002, dokumenty i materially*. Moscow, Mezhdunarodnye otnosheniia, 2004, 40.

—, to Mikhail Kalinin, Havana, 7 November 1943, in G.E. Mamedov and A. Dalmau, *Rossiia-Kuba, 1902–2002, dokumenty i materially*. Moscow, Mezhdunarodnye otnosheniia, 2004, 57.

Batlle, Lucillo. *Blas Roca. Continuador de la Obrara de Balino y Mella*. Havana: Editorial de Ciencias Sociales, 2005.

Bekarevich, A.D. and V.A. Borodaev. *Velikii Oktiabr i kubinskaia revoliutsiia*. Moscow, Nauka, 1987.

Benjamin, Jules R. *The United States and the Origins of the Cuban Revolution. An Empire of Liberty in an Age of National Liberation*. Princeton: Princeton University Press, 1990.

Bethell, Leslie & Roxborough, Ian. "Latin America between the Second World War and the Cold War: Some Reflections on the 1945–8 Conjuncture," *Journal of Latin American Studies*, 20 (1988): 167–189.

Blight, James, and Philip Brenner. *Sad and Luminous Days. Cuba's Struggle with the Superpowers after the Cuban Missile Crisis*. Lanham: Rowman & Littlefield Publishers, 2002.

Boughton, George J. "Soviet-Cuban Relations, 1956–1960," *Journal of Interamerican Studies and World Affairs*, Vol 16, No 4 (November 1974): 436–453.

Brown, Chris. *Understanding International Relations*. New York: Palgrave, 2001.

Brownthal, Julius, *History of the International 1914–1943*. Camden, New Jersey: Nelson, 1963.

Brutents, Karen. *Tridtsat let na Staroi ploshchadi*. Moscow: Mezhdunarodnye otnosheniia, 1998.

Burlakin, A. "Cuba Aflame," *International Affairs*, Num 11, 1957, p.112–113.

Byman Daniel L. and Kenneth M, Pollack, "Let Us Now Praise Great Men. Bringing the Statesmen Back In," *International Security*, Vol 25, No. 4 (Spring 2001): 107–146.

Caballero, Manual. *Latin America and the Comintern 1919–1943*. Cambridge: Cambridge University Press, 1986.

Caldwell Laurence T. "Russian Concepts of National Security." Pp.279–342 in *Russian Foreign Policy in the Twenty-first Century and the Shadow of the Past*, edited by Robert Legvold. New York: Columbia University Press, 2007.

Cardoza Aragón, Luis. "La Fiesta de los Trabajadores en Moscu," *Cuba y la URSS*, Num 33 (April 1948): 4.

Carr, Barry. "Mill Occupations and Soviets: The Mobilisation of Sugar Workers in Cuba 1917–1933," *Journal of Latin American Studies*, 28 (1996): 129–158.

—, "Identity, Class, and Nation: Black Immigrant Workers, Cuban Communism, and the Sugar Insurgency, 1925–1934," *Hispanic Historical Review*, 78:1 (1996): 83–116.

—. "From Caribbean backwater to revolutionary opportunity: Cuba's evolving relationship with the Comintern, 1925–34," Pp. 234–251 in *International Communism and the Communist International 1919–43*, edited by Time Rees and Andrew Thorpe, Manchester: Manchester University Press, 1998.

Carr, E.H. *The Twenty Years Crisis 1919–1939: An Introduction to the Study of International Relations*. London: Palgrave, 2001.

Castro, Fidel. *Fidel Castro Speaks*. London: Allen Lane The Penguin Press, 1969.

—. "Centennial Ceremony," Havana Domestic Service in Spanish 0333GMT 23 April 1970, FBIS 19700423.

—. "Address to First Congress of the PCC," 17 December 1975, *Primer Congreso del Partido Comunista de Cuba. Memorias*. Havana: Departamento de Orientación Revolucionaria del Comité Central del Partido Comunista de Cuba, 1976, 13–154.

Castro, Fidel and Ignacio Ramonet. *My Life*. London: Allen Lane, 2007.

CCCP-Cuba. Documents of Friendship and Socialism. Moscow: izdatevl'stvo politicheskoii literatury, 1985.

Central Committee of the Communist Party of the United States (CPUSA) to Third International, 6 November 1930, *The Communist*, Vol X, No 1 (January 1931): 66–73.

Chestoff, L. "Que es el Bolcheviquismo?" *Cuba Contemporánea*, Volume XXIV, October 1920, 196–211.

Ching, Eric. "In Search of the Party: The Communist Party, the Comintern and the Peasant Rebellion of 1932 in El Salvador," *The Americas*, Vol 55, No 2 (Oct. 1998): 204–239.

Ching, Eric and Jussia Pakkasvirta. "Latin American Materials in the Comintern Archive," *Latin American Research Review*, Volume 35, Num 1 (2000): 138 – 149.

Chirkov, Vladislav. "An Uphill Task" *New Times*, 33 (17 August 1987): 16–17.

Claudin, Fernando. *The Communist Movement from Comintern to Cominform*. New York: Monthly Review Press, 1975.

Clissold, S. *Soviet Relations with Latin America 1918–1968*. London: Oxford University Press, 1970.

Collins, Alan. *Contemporary Security Studies*. New York: Oxford University Press, 2007.

Cuban Antifascist League to Stalin, 9 June 1944, Havana, in G.E. Mamedov and A. Dalmau, *Rossiia-Kuba, 1902–2002, dokumenty i materially*. Moscow, Mezhdunarodnye otnosheniia, 2004, 61.

"Cuba in Flames" *New Times*, No 50 (1957): 21–22.

"Cuban Government to Recognize Russia, Zaydin Announces," *Havana Post*, October 11, 1942, 1.

"Cuban Government to Recognize Russia," *Havana Post*, October 11, 1942, 1.

Concheso, A. to Emeterio Santovenia, Moscow, 21 May 1943, in G.E. Mamedov and A. Dalmau, *Rossiia-Kuba, 1902–2002, dokumenty i materially*. Moscow, Mezhdunarodnye otnosheniia, 2004, 46.

—, to Emeterio Santovenia, Moscow, 29 May 1943, in G.E. Mamedov and A. Dalmau, *Rossiia-Kuba, 1902–2002, dokumenty i materially*. Moscow, Mezhdunarodnye otnosheniia, 2004, 52–53.

—, to V.G. Dekanozov, Moscow, 11 December 1943, in G.E. Mamedov and A. Dalmau, *Rossiia-Kuba, 1902–2002, dokumenty i materially*. Moscow, Mezhdunarodnye otnosheniia, 2004, 59–60.

Cruz Capote, Orlando. *The Comintern and Problems of the Cuban Revolution (1925–1935)*. Moscow: Academia de Ciencias Sociales, 1989.

Cuba y la URSS Nos 1–76 (August 1945–February 1952).

Cuba-URSS *Crónica*. Moscow: Progreso, 1990.

Daily Worker August 5, 1953, 1.

Degras, J. *The Communist International 1919–1943 Documents, Volume 2*. London: Frank Cass & Co Ltd, 1971.

Desfosses Helen & Levesque, Jacques. *Socialism in the Third World*. New York: Praeger Publishers, 1978.

Diplomaticheskii slovar ' A-U, Tom 1. Moscow: Izdatelstvo Nauka, 1984.

Document 1, Cuban Record of Conversation, Mikoyan and Cuban Leadership, Havana 4 November 1962 in *Cold War International History Project Bulletin*, Issues 8–9 Winter 1996/1997, Washington DC: Woodrow Wilson International Center for Scholars, Issues 8–9 (Winter 1996–1997), 339–342.

Dubrovina, Liudmila. "Las Publicanes para nina," *Cuba y la URSS*, Num 59 (August 1950): 21–22.

Duclos, Jacques. "On the Dissolution of the Communist Party of the United States," *Political Affairs*, Vol XXIV, Number 7 (July 1945): 656–672.

Dumpierre, Erasmo. "La Revolución de Octubre y su Influencia en Cuba," *Bohemia*, April 21, 1967, 9.

Durov, Valentin. "50 anos de rusos boxeo" *Cuba y la URSS*, Num 35 (August 1948): 49.

El Mundo. October 11, 1942, 1.

El Mundo,. December 21, 1943, 2.

"El Museu V.I. Lenin" *Cuba y la URSS*, Num 75 (January 1952): 25.

"El Pació de Cultura de los Mineros de Karaganda," *Cuba y la URSS*, Num 73 (November 1951): 26–30.

El Ruso Cubano, Boletín Informativo de le Embajada de le Federación de Rusia, No 59 (9 July 2011): 5–6.

"Emisiones de Moscu para La America Latina," *Cuba y la URSS*, Num 21 (April 1947):29.

"En la Sección de Música de la VOKS," *Cuba y la URSS*, Num 11 (November 1951): 51.

"Enseñanza para Ejercer los Derretíos Democracia en la URSS," *Cuba y la URSS*, Num 40 (January 1949): 53.

Erisman, Michael. *Cuba's Foreign Relations in a Post-Soviet World.* Gainseville: University Press of Florida, 2000.

"Exposición de Moscú," *Cuba y la URSS,* Num 20 (March 1947): 16–18.

"Exposiciones Cubana de Arquitectura y Urbanismo en la URSS," *Cuba y la URSS,* Num 4 (April 1946): 28.

Fagg, John Edwin. *Latin America: A General History.* New York: Macmillan, 1977.

Faleroni, A.D. "Soviet Relations in Latin America," Pp.9–21 in *The Soviet Union and Latin America,* edited by J.G. Oswald and A.J. Strover. London: Pall Mall Press, 1970.

Farber, Samuel. "The Cuban Communists in the Early Stages of the Cuban Revolution: Revolutionaries or Reformists." *Latin American Research Review,* Vol 18, No 1 (1983), 59–83.

—. *The Origins of the Cuban Revolution Reconsidered.* Chapel Hill: The University of North Carolina Press, 2006.

"Felicitación de los Intelectuales Soviéticos con motive deal an Nuevo," *Cuba y la URSS,* Num 53 (February 1950): 53.

"Fidel Castro" *New Times,* Volume 34 (1958): 31–32.

Florinsky, Michael T. "Soviet Foreign Policy. The Paradox of Soviet Foreign Relations." *The Slavonic and East European Review,* Volume 12, Number 36 (April 1934): 531–552.

Fondo Especial, Cuban National Archive (CNA), Havana.

"For Expansion of Cooperation between USSR and Latin American Countries," *Pravda,* January 22, 1956, 5.

"Foreign Review," *Vestnik Evropi,* May 1898, Volume 3: 379–390.

Foster, William Z. "The Congress of the Cuban Communist Party," *The Communist,* Vol XVIII (March 1939): 225–231.

Fursenko, Alexandr and Timothy Naftali, *The Secret History of the Cuban Missile Crisis. "One Hell of a Gamble."* London: John Murray, 1997.

Gamble, Andrew. *Timewalkers: The Prehistory of Global Colonisation.* Cambridge, Mass: Harvard University Press, 1999.

Garcia, Angel and Piotr Mironchuk. *Esbozo Historica de las Relaciones entre Cuba-Rusia y Cuba-URSS.* Havana: Academia de Ciencias de Cuba, 1976.

—. *Raices de las relaciones Cubano Sovieticas,* Havana, Editorial de Ciencias Sociales, 1988.

Goldenberg, Boris. "The Rise and Fall of a Party: The Cuban CP (1925–59)."

Gonzalez, Raúl to Vyacheslav Molotov, Havana, 27 August 1948, in G.E. Mamedov, and A. Dalmau, *Rossiia-Kuba, 1902–2002, dokumenty i materially.* Moscow, Mezhdunarodnye otnosheniia, 2004,75.

González, Rafael, to Soviet Embassy in Havana, Havana, 27 March 1947 in G.E. Mamedov and A. Dalmau, *Rossiia-Kuba, 1902–2002, dokumenty i materially.* Moscow, Mezhdunarodnye otnosheniia 2004, 69–70.

Gott, Richard. *Cuba. A New History.* New Haven: Yale University Press, 2004.

Gould-Davies, Nigel. "The Logic of Soviet Cultural Diplomacy," *Diplomatic History,* Vol 27, No. 2 (April 2003):193–214.

Grau, Ramón, to Mikhail Kalinin, Havana, 7 November 1944, in G.E. Mamedov and A. Dalmau, *Rossiia-Kuba, 1902–2002, dokumenty i materially.* Moscow, Mezhdunarodnye otnosheniia, 2004, 63.

—, to Mikhail Kalinin, Havana, 17 August 1945, in G.E. Mamedov and A. Dalmau, *Rossiia-Kuba, 1902–2002, dokumenty i materially.* Moscow, Mezhdunarodnye otnosheniia, 2004, 66.

Granma International Weekly Review, March 17, 1985, 2.

Grigor Suny, Ronald. "Living in the Hood: Russia, Empire, and Old and New Neighbours," Pp. 35–76 in *Russian Foreign Policy in the Twenty-first Century and the Shadow of the Past,* edited by Robert Legvold. New York: Columbia University Press, 2007.

Grigorian, V. Report prepared for Joseph Stalin 25 November 1950. RSA25/C/2177.

—. Report prepared for Vyacheslav Molotov 25 November 1950. RSA25/C/2163.

Gromyko, Andrei to Vyacheslav Molotov, Havana, 22 December 1943, in G.E. Mamedov and A. Dalmau, *Rossiia-Kuba, 1902–2002, dokumenty i materially.* Moscow, Mezhdunarodnye otnosheniia, 2004, 60.

—. *Pamiatnoe Kniga Pervaya,* Moscow: Politizdat, 1988.

Guevara, Ernesto. "Discurso en el Segundo Seminario Económico de Solidaridad Afroasiática," Pp. 341–354 in *Ernesto Che Guevara escritos y discursos, 7.* Havana: Editorial De Ciencias Sociales.

—. *The Motorcycle Diaries: A Journey Around South America.* London: Fourth Estate, 1995.

Gunder Frank, Andre. *Latin America: Underdevelopment or Revolution: Essays on the Development and Underdevelopment and the Immediate Enemy.* New York: Monthly Review Press, 1969.

Hallas, Duncan. *The Comintern. A History of the Third International.* Chicago: Haymarket Book, 1985.

Haslan, Jonathan, *Russia's Cold War. From the October Revolution to the Fall of the Wall.* New Haven: Yale University Press, 2011.

Havana Post, December 18, 1943, 1.

Herman, Donald. *The Communist Tide in Latin America. A Selected Treatment.* Austin, The University of Texas at Austin, 1973.

Hollis M. and S. Smith. *Explaining and Understanding International Relations.* New York: Oxford University Press, 1990.

"Homenaje a la Cultura Soviética. Selecto Programa Musical." *Cuba y la URSS,* Num 61 (October 1950): 31.

Ignatiev, O, 'A Movement Prompted by Reality,' *Komsomolskaya Pravda,* January 17, 1954, 4.

Jastrebova, V., to the Institute of Cuban-Soviet Cultural Exchange, Havana, 20 June 1946, in G.E. Mamedov, and A. Dalmau, *Rossiia-Kuba, 1902–2002, dokumenty i materially.* Moscow, Mezhdunarodnye otnosheniia, 2004, 68–69.

Kafman, Anatoli. "La amistadad de los Ajedreasitas Rusos y Cubanos," *Cuba y la URSS,* Num 2, September 1945, 5–6.

Kameneva, O.D. "Cultural Raprochment: The USSR Society for Cultural Relations with Foreign Countries." *Pacific Affairs,* Volume 1, Num 5 (October 1928): 6–8.

Karol, K.S. *Guerrillas in Power.* London: Jonathan Cape Ltd, 1971.

Kennan, George. 861.00/2-2246, "The Charge in the Soviet Union (Kennan) to the Secretary of State," http://www.gwu.edu/~nsarchiv/coldwar/documents/episode-1/kennan.htm (accessed 14 April 2012).

Keylor, William R. *The Twentieth Century World and Beyond.* Oxford: Oxford University Press, 2006.

Khrushchev, Nikita. *Khrushchev Remembers.* Boston: Little, Brown and Company, 1970.

Kondrashov, Stanislav. "Language of Gestures in Putin's Diplomacy," *Vremya,* December 22, 2000, 3.

Kremnyov, M. "Cuba in Flames," *International Affairs,* Num 7 (1957): 116.

"La Bandera de Rusa en la cancilleria Cubana," *Bohemia,* October 25, 1942, 31.

"La colaboración cubana-rusa ha cobrado un nuevo dinamismo," 2009, Trabajadores January 30, http://www.trabajadores.cu/la-colaboracion-cubano-rusa (accessed 3 February 2009).

"La Exposicion de Arte Cubano en Moscú," *Cuba y la URSS,* Num 3 (October 1945): 18.

LaFeber, Walter. *The American Age. United States Foreign Policy at Home and Abroad since 1750.* New York: W.W. Norton & Company, 1989.

—. "The U.S. Rise to World Power, 1776–1945" Pp.45–62 in *United States Foreign Policy,* edited by Michael Cox and Doug Stokes, Oxford: Oxford University Press, 2008.

Larin, E.A. *Kuba kontsa XVIII--pervoĭtreti XIX veka.* Moscow, Nauka, 1989.

—. *Politicheskaia istorii Kuba XX Veka.* Moscow: Visshaya shkola, 2007.

"La Mujer en la URSS," *Cuba y la URSS,* Num 39 (December): 53.

"La protección al trabajo de los jóvenes obreros de la URSS," *Cuba y la URSS,* Num 64 (February 1951): 41.

"La URSS y la Cultura," *Cuba y la URSS,* Num 18 (January 1947): 31.

"La URSS, Socialismo y Cultura" *Cuba y la URSS,* Num 56 (May 1950): 53.

Lavrentyev, V. "USSR-Cuban Brotherhood and Cooperation," FBIS LD182341 Moscow Domestic Service in Russian 0615 18 April 1985.

Lazitch, Branko & Drachkovitch, Milorad M. *Lenin and the Comintern. Volume 1.* Stanford University: Hoover Institution Press, 1972.

Ledonne, John P. *The Russian Empire and the World 1700–1917. The Geopolitics of Expansion and Containment.* Oxford: Oxford University Press, 1997.

Lenin, Vladimir. *Polnoe sobranie sochienii Tom 28.* Moscow: Gospolitizdat, 1962.

—. *Polnoe sobranie sochienii Tom 30.* Moscow: Gospolitizdat, 1962.

—. "Theses on the Question of the Immediate Conclusion of a Separate and Annexationist Peace," Pp. 21–24 in *A Documentary History of Communism, Volume 2: Communism and the World,* edited by Robert V. Daniels. Hanover: University Press of New England, 1984.

Leonov, N.S. *Lixoletye.* Moscow: Mezhdunarodnye otnosheniia, 1995.

"Letter of the Central Committee of the CP USA to the Central Committee of the CP of Cuba," 6 November 1930. RSA/495/138 & *The Communist,* Vol X, No 1 (January 1931): 66–73.

Levin, V. "Cuba is Fighting, Cuba Will Win!" *Pravda,* January 3, 1959, 3.

Lewis Gaddis, John. *We Now Know. Rethinking Cold War History.* Oxford: Oxford University Press, 1998.

Librach, Jan. *The Rise of the Soviet Empire.* New York: Praeger, 1964.

Light, Margot. *The Soviet Theory of International Relations.* New York: St. Martin's Press, 1988.

Litviov, Maxim. "Speech to Assembly of League of Nations," in Jane Degras, *The Communist International 1919–1943 Documents, Volume 2.* London: Frank Cass & Co Ltd, 1971, 89–96.

Lowry, M. *Marxism in Latin America from 1909 to the Present. An Anthology.* Atlantic Highlands, NJ: Humanities Press, 1950.

Malik, Yakov, to Alberto Espinosa, Moscow, 8 April 1947, in G.E. Mamedov and A. Dalmau, *Rossiia-Kuba, 1902–2002, dokumenty i materially.* Moscow, Mezhdunarodnye otnosheniia, 2004, 72–73.

Mamedov, G.E. and A. Dalmau. *Rossiia-Kuba, 1902–2002, dokumenty i materially.* Moscow, Mezhdunarodnye otnosheniia, 2004.

Martín, José Luis. "El Embajador Litvinoff en la Habana," *Bohemia,* April 18, 1943, 46–48 & 50.

Martínez, José Agustín, to Vyacheslav Molotov, Havana, 5 October 1942, in G.E. Mamedov and A. Dalmau. *Rossiia-Kuba, 1902–2002, dokumenty i materially.* Moscow, Mezhdunarodnye otnosheniia, 2004, 37.

Marx and Engels Collected Works Vol 140. London: Lawrence and Wishart, 1983.

Marx, Karl "The Part Played by Labour in the transition from Ape to Man" in *Marx and Engels Collected Works Vol 25.* London: Lawrence and Wishart, 1967.

—. "Bolivar and Ponte." Pp. 219–233.in *Marx and Engels Collected Works Vol 18.* London: Lawrence and Wishart, 1982.

—. *The Communist Manifesto.* Harmondsworth: Penguin Books, 1982.

Matthews, Herbert. "Cuban Rebel Is Visited in Hideout," *New York Times,* February 24, 1957, 1.

McCauley, Martin. *Origins of the Cold War, 1941–1949.* Harlow: Pearson Longman, 2008.

McDermott, Kevin. "Stalin and the Comintern during the 'Third Period', 1928–1933." *European History Quarterly,* Volume 25 (1995): 409–429.

McDermott Kevin & Jeremy Agnew. *The Comintern. A History of International Communism from Lenin to Stalin.* Basingstoke: Macmillan Press, 1996.

Mearsheimer, John. *The Tragedy of Great Power Politics.* New York: W.W. Norton & Company, 2010.

Mella, Julio Antonio. "Información para la Prensa Obrea y Revolución." RSA/495/105/1.

—. "La Provocación Imperialista a los Soviets" *El Machete,* CNA, Fondo Especial, 6/63, June 1927.

Melograni, Piero. *Lenin and the Myth of World Revolution. Ideology and Reasons of State, 1917–1920.* Atlantic Highlands, NJ: Humanities Press International, 1989.

Meneses, Yaima Puig. "Intensa y muy útil visita de trabajo." *Juventud Rebelde,* 12 July 2012, www.juventudrebelde.cu (accessed 17 July 2012).

Mesa-Lago, Carmelo. *Cuba in the 1970s, Pragmatism and Institutionalization.* Albuquerque: University of New México Press, 1974.

Mikhailov, M. "Soviet-Argentine Trade Agreement," *Izvestia,* August 15, 1953, 4.

Miller, Nicola. *Soviet Relations with Latin America 1959–1987*. Cambridge: Cambridge University Press, 1989.

Molotov, Vyacheslav to Concheso, Moscow, 31 May 1943, in G.E. Mamedov and A. Dalmau, *Rossiia-Kuba, 1902–2002, dokumenty i materially*. Moscow, Mezhdunarodnye otnosheniia, 2004, 54.

—. to Raúl Gonzalez, 4 October 1948, in G.E. Mamedov and A. Dalmau, *Rossiia-Kuba, 1902–2002, dokumenty i materially*. Moscow, Mezhdunarodnye otnosheniia, 2004, 76.

Montes, Jorge Garcia and Antonio Alonso Ávila. *Historia del Partido Comunista de Cuba*. Miami: Ream Press, 1970.

Morgenthau, Hans. *Politics Among Nations*. New York: Knopf, 1955.

Munck, R. *Revolutionary Trends in Latin America*, Monograph Series, No 17, Centre for Developing Area Studies, McGill University.

Núñez Jiménez, Antonio. "Cuba fue conocida en Rusia desde 1530" *Bohemia*, April 1962, 20–25.

Nye, Jr, Joseph S. *Soft Power. The Means to Success in World Politics*. New York: PublicAffairs, 2004.

Nye, Jr. Joseph S. & Welch, David A. *Understanding Global Conflict and Cooperation. An Introduction to Theory and History*. Boston: Longman, 2011.

"Obras cubanos Expuestas en Moscú," *Cuba y la URSS*, Num 38 (November 1948): 53.

Okuneva, M.A. *The Working Class in the Cuban Revolution*. Moscow: Nauka, 1985.

Olgin, M.J. "X-The Third Period" in Bernard, K. John, *A Documentary History of the CPUSA, Volume III, United and Fight*. Westport, Connecticut: Greenwood Press, 1994.

Paterson, Thomas G., Clifford, J. Gary, & Hagan, Kenneth J. *American Foreign Policy. A History since 1900*. Lexington: DC Heath & Company, 1983.

Pavlov, Yuri. *Soviet-Cuban Alliance 1959–1991*. New Brunswick: Transaction Publishers.

Pena, Lázaro. "Strike Struggle in Cuba," *For a Lasting Peace. For a People's Democracy* March 23, 1956, 6.

Pérez -Stable, Marifeli. *The Cuban Revolution. Origins, Course, and Legacy*. Oxford: Oxford University Press, 1999.

Pérez, Louis A. *Cuba and the United States: Ties of Singular Intimacy*. Athens, Ga: University of Georgia Press, 2003.

Pérez, Louis A. *Cuba Between Reform and Revolution*. New York: Oxford University Press, 2006.

"Pintura Cubano en Moscú," *Cuba y la URSS*, Num 7 (July 1946): 16–17.

Pipes, R. *The Russian Revolution 1899–1919*, London: Fontana Press, 1990.

Plecan, Theodore. "Report" 21 January 1931. RSA495/105/138.

Pogosov, I.U. *Vmeste na vse vremena*. Moscow: Molodaiaa Gvardiia, 1988.

Poppino, Rollie. *International Communism in Latin America. 1917*–1963. London: The Free Press of Glencoe, 1964.

Prio, Carlos, to N.M. Shvernik, Havana, 7 November 1949, in G.E. Mamedov and A. Dalmau, *Rossiia-Kuba, 1902–2002, dokumenty i materially*. Moscow, Mezhdunarodnye otnosheniia, 2004, 77.

—, to N.M. Shvernik, 8 November 1951, Havana, in G.E. Mamedov and A. Dalmau, *Rossiia-Kuba, 1902–2002, dokumenty i materially*. Moscow, Mezhdunarodnye otnosheniia, 2004, 77, 83.

Ravines, Eudocio. *La Gran Estafa*. Santiago de Chile: Editorial del Pacifico, Mexico, 1952.

Rees Tim & Thorpe, Andrew "Introduction" in *International Communism and the Communist International 1919–43*, Pp. 1–11, edited by Tim Rees and Andrew Thorpe. Manchester: Manchester University Press, 1998.

Renard, V. "La Television Sovietica, *Cuba y la URSS*, Num 62 (November 1950): 14–16.

Revolución, December 2, 1961, 1.

Richardson, J.L. "Contending Liberalism: Past and Present," *European Journal of International Relations*, 3:1 (1997): 5–33.

Riddel, John. *To See the Dawn. Baku, 1920: First Congress of the People of the East*. New York: Pathfinder Press, 1993.

Roca, Blas. "Forward to the Cuban Anti-Imperialist People's Front!" *The Communist*, Vol XIV, No 10 (October 1935): 955–967.

—. "Forging the People's Victory in Cuba," *The Communist*, Vol XIX, No 2 (February 1940): 133–140.

—. "People of Cuba Fighting Against War, For Democratic Liberties!" *For a Lasting Peace. For a People's Deomocracy*, May 18, 1950, 3.

—. *Los Fundamentos del Socialismo en Cuba*. Havana: Ediciones Populares, 1961.

—. *The Cuban Revolution. Report to the Eighth National Congress of the Popular Socialist Party of Cuba*. New York: New Century Publishers, 1961.

Rocamora, Serapio. "El Comunismo y sus territorios. España, Rusia y Cuba" *Diario de la Marina*, 10 August 1945, CAN Fondo Especial 6/63.

Rodriguez, O. "Our Present Tasks in Cuba," *The Communist*, Vol X, No 6 (June 1931): 516.

Rodríguez, P. "Evolución del Socialismo Moscovita," *Cuba Contemporánea*, Volume XX, August 1919, 481–499.

Rojelio del Campo. "Fruits of an Antinational Policy," *Pravda*, February 22, 1953, 4.

Rossiiskii, M.A. *Rossiia zarbezh'e na Kuba. Strancy istorii*. Moscow: Veche, 2002.

Roy, M.N. *M.N. Roy's Memoirs*. Bombay: Allied Publishers, 1964.

Rubtsov, G. "In Cuba," *New Times* No 7 (1949): 23–26.

"Russian Revolutionaries For Immediate Peace," *Havana Post*, November 8, 1917, 1.

"Russian truck maker Kamaz considering production in Cuba," 2008, RIA Novosti, 21 November, http.www.rian.ru/Russia/20081121 (accessed 23 November 2008).

"Save the Lives of Vivo and Ordoqui." RSA/495/105/2.

Sabetski, Nikolai. "Alexandr Popov, inventor de la Radion, *Cuba y la URSS*, Num 69 (July 1951): 8–10.

Schulz, D.E. *The Cuban Revolution and the Soviet Union*, Ohio University PhD Thesis, 1977.

"Se Verifico le Clausura de la Exposicion Sobre le Rusia Roja," *El Mundo*, December 21, 1943, 2.

Senn, Alfred E. *Readings in Russian Political and Diplomatic History, Volume II, The Soviet Period*. Homewood, Illinois: The Dorsey Press, 1966.

Shearman, Peter. *The Soviet Union and Cuba*. London: Routledge & Kegan Paul, 1987.

Shulman, Marshall D. *Stalin's Foreign Policy Reappraised*. Boulder: Westview Press, 1985.

Shvernik, N.M, Telegram to Carlos Prio, Havana, 19 May 1949, in G.E. Mamedov, and A. Dalmau, *Rossiia-Kuba, 1902–2002, dokumenty i materially*. Moscow, Mezhdunarodnye otnosheniia, 2004, 77.

"65 Aniversario de la Gran Victoria," *Edicion de la Embajada de la federación de Rusia en Cuba*, Numero 4 (2010): 28.

Sizonenko, A. 'USSR-Latin America: Diplomatic-Technical Aspects of the War Years Relationship,' *America Latina* No 5 (May 2010): 20.

Smith, M.J. "Liberalism and International Reform" in *Traditions of International Ethics*, Pp. 201–224, edited by T. Nardin and D. Mapel. Cambridge: Cambridge University Press, 1992.

Smith, Wayne. *The Closest of Enemies. A Personal and Diplomatic Account of U.S.-Cuban Relations Since 1957*. New York: W.W. Norton & Company, 1987.

Sobolev, A.I. *Outline History of the Communist International*. Moscow: Progress Publishers, 1971.

Spenser, Daniela. *The Impossible Triangle. Mexico, Soviet Russia and the United States in the 1920s*. Durham: Duke University Press, 1999.

Stalin, I.V. *Sochineniia Tom 7*. Moscow: Gospolitizdat, 1947.

—. *Sochineniia Tom 10*. Moscow: Gospolitizdat, 1949.

"Stalin Dead. Soviet Leader Dies Four Days after a Stroke," *Havana Post*, March 6, 1953, 1.

Stern, Ludmila. "The All-Union Society for Cultural Relations with Foreign Countries and French Intellectuals, 1925–29." *Australian Journal of Politics and History*, Volume 45, Number 1 (1999): 99–109.

Stretlsov, P. "Two Months in Cuba in October," *Vestnik Evropi*, May 1898, Volume 3: 129–166.

Sweig, Julia E. *Inside the Cuban Revolution. Fidel Castro and the Urban Underground*. Cambridge, Massachusetts: Harvard University Press, 2002.

Sworakowski, W.S. *World Communism. A Handbook 1918–1968*. Stanford, Ca: Hoover Institution Press, 1973.

Tarasenkov, A. "Maximo Gorki, padre de la literature sovietica," *Cuba y la URSS*, Num 73 (November 1951): 37–39.

Tazhibaiev, Tuelgeun. "La Universidad del Estado de Kazajstan" *Cuba y la URSS*, Num 59 (August 1950): 42–43.

Tennant, Gary. *The Hidden Pearl of the Caribbean. Trotskyism in Cuba*, Revolutionary History, Volume 7, No 3, London: Porcupine Press, 2000.

Thatcher, I.D. *Leon Trotsky and World War One: August 1914–February 1917*. Basingstoke: Macmillan, 2000.

"The People and Dictator" *New Times*, No 15 (1958): 22.

"The Present Situation, Perspectives, and Tasks in Cuba. Resolution of the Second Congress of the Communist Party of Cuba." *The Communist*, XIII, No 9 (September 1934): 876.

"The Russian Orthodox Church" http//www/granma.cu/2008/octubre/mier22 (accessed 4 November 2008).

"The Seventh World Congress of the Communist International and the Tasks of our Party," *The Communist*, Vol XIV, No 12 (December 1935): 1182–1185.

Thomas, Hugh. *Cuba or the Pursuit of Freedom*. London: Eyre & Spottiswoode, 1971.

"Thousands File Past Coffin of Premier Lenine," *Havana Post*, January 24, 1924, 1.

Tikhmenev, V. "Sweeping the Dirt Under the Rug," *New Times*, No 40 (1957): 18.

"Tottering Dictator" *New Times*, Num 10 (1958): 21–22.

Tsygankov, Andrei P. *Russia's Foreign Policy. Change and Continuity in National Identity*. Lanham: Rowman and Littlefield Publishers, 2006.

"Un Músico Cubano Visita La Unión Soviética," *Cuba y la URSS*, Num 75 (January 1952): 4.

"Unity of Action of Cuban Working People," *For a Lasting Peace. For a People's Democracy*, April 17, 1956, 4.

"Valiosa iniciativa: Llamamiento en favour de la amistad cubano-sovietica" *Cuba y la URSS*, Num 76 (February 1952): 35–36.

Vasilchikov, V. "Bloody Atrocities in Cuba," *Pravda*, February 5, 1957, 4.

Vavilov, Sergei. 'Nuestro Aporte a la Ciencia Mundial,' *Cuba y la URSS*, Num 35 (August 1948): 49.

"Visito Gromyko al Ministro de Estado" *El Mundo*, December 21, 1943, 2.

Vlasov, I.A. "J.V. Stalin creado del Estado Socialista Soviética multinacional," *Cuba y la URSS*, Num 52 (January 1950): 8–11.

Vmeste na vse vremena. Moscow: Molodaia gvardiia, 1988.

Vneshniaia torgovlia SSSR statisticheskii sbornik 1918–1966. Moscow: Mezdunarodnye otnosheniia, 1967.

Volskii, V.V. *SSSR i Latinskaia Amerika 1917–1967*. Moscow: Mezhdunarodnye otnosheniia, 1967.

Waltz, Kenneth, *Theory of International Politics*. New York: Random House, 1979.

White, Stephen. *Gorbachev and After*. Cambridge: Cambridge University Press, 1991.

Yaborskaia, N. "Pintura Cubana en Moscú," *Cuba y la URSS*, Num 1 (August 1945): 2.

Yartsev, Yu. "A Soviet View of Cuba," *Literaturnaya Gazeta*, April 8, 1952, 37.

Yeronin, P. "The Big Stick Again!" *International Affairs*, No 9 (1958): 97.

Zaikin, D., Telegram to Vyacheslav Molotov, Havana, 8 November 1943, in G.E. Mamedov and A. Dalmau, *Rossiia-Kuba, 1902–2002, dokumenty i materially*. Moscow, Mezhdunarodnye otnosheniia, 57–58.

—, to A. Ya Vyshinskomu, Havana, 21 October 1944, in G.E. Mamedov and A. Dalmau, *Rossiia-Kuba, 1902–2002, dokumenty i materially*. Moscow, Mezhdunarodnye otnosheniia, 63.

—, to S.A. Lozovskomu, Havana, 23 February 1945, in G.E. Mamedov and A. Dalmau, *Rossiia-Kuba, 1902–2002, dokumenty i materially*. Moscow, Mezhdunarodnye otnosheniia, 64.

—, to KGB, Havana, 8 November 1945, in G.E. Mamedov and A. Dalmau, *Rossiia-Kuba, 1902–2002, dokumenty i materially*. Moscow, Mezhdunarodnye otnosheniia, 67.

Zamora, Juan C. "El Bolcheviquismo," *Cuba Contemporánea*, May 1919, 35–81.